Lifestyle Media and the Formation of the Self

Also by Jayne Raisborough

RISK, IDENTITY AND THE EVERYDAY (*co-edited*)

Lifestyle Media and the Formation of the Self

Jayne Raisborough
University of Brighton, Brighton, UK

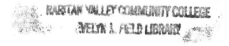

palgrave
macmillan

First published 2011 by
PALGRAVE MACMILLAN

Palgrave Macmillan in the UK is an imprint of Macmillan Publishers Limited, registered in England, company number 785998, of Houndmills, Basingstoke, Hampshire RG21 6XS.

Palgrave Macmillan in the US is a division of St Martin's Press LLC, 175 Fifth Avenue, New York, NY 10010.

Palgrave Macmillan is the global academic imprint of the above companies and has companies and representatives throughout the world.

Palgrave® and Macmillan® are registered trademarks in the United States, the United Kingdom, Europe and other countries.

ISBN 978–0–230–24295–1 hardback

This book is printed on paper suitable for recycling and made from fully managed and sustained forest sources. Logging, pulping and manufacturing processes are expected to conform to the environmental regulations of the country of origin.

A catalogue record for this book is available from the British Library.

A catalog record for this book is available from the Library of Congress.

10   9   8   7   6   5   4   3   2   1
20   19   18   17   16   15   14   13   12   11

Printed and bound in Great Britain by
CPI Antony Rowe, Chippenham and Eastbourne

For Brenda & Tony Kick and Alexander Forshaw

Contents

Acknowledgements

Thanks are extended to the School of Applied Social Science at the University of Brighton for the most excellent of colleagues and for research leave and general support (Dawn Stephen, Mark Bhatti and the sociology team especially). Extra thanks to Matt Adams, Hannah Frith and Orly Klein for all I have learnt from our close working in the *Consuming Identities Research Forum* based there. Thanks are also directed to Peter Coyne – a wizard of information resourcing; to Philippa Grand of Palgrave Macmillan – infectiously enthusiastic from the start; Olivia Middleton for solving the cover-image problem; Katherine Johnson for our discussions of the writing process; Elena Steier for the generous use of her cartoon in Chapter 1; and to past but important inspirations – Rosemary Deem, Rosie Campbell, John Lally, Edward Davies, Julie Scott Jones, Dawn Jones, Dave Merryweather, Sal Watt, Maddy Castro, Emma Rouse and Holly Hill.

Closer to home, thanks to Eastbourne's *Coast* guesthouse; Barbara and Graeme kindly loaned me their much-loved mobile home to work in while my home was having its own makeover. Anne Lesley Dobson kept the chickens fed and home fires burning (literally) – I owe her more than can be expressed. Alexander Thomas Forshaw was born as this book was in its own gestation period, so I would like to dedicate this to him and to his grandparents – Brenda and Anthony Kick – without whom I would not have had the opportunities, encouragement and support to be in a career and life that I love.

All errors, blunders and shortcomings are my own.

Being Scrooge-Like:
An introduction to *Lifestyle Media and the Formation of the Self*

Fourteen-year-old Adam is sick of his mates: they drink, smoke and look forward to a life on benefits. Adam yearns for something different. He has ambition. He wants to do more than just hang around and he nurtures hope for a future career. In the five-part television series *How to Dump your Mates*, psychologist Geoff Beattie is sympathetic, 'friends', he states, 'exert great influence over early personal development, the wrong crowd can hold you back, stop you trying new things and ultimately, prevent you from being yourself'. Over four days Beattie takes Adam through a crash course in 'dumping'. Adam learns to confront his old mates and tries new friends on for size. After a dramatic moment when his separate 'worlds' collide and the two groups of friends surprisingly meet, Adam's final task, and the show's reveal, is to decide which mates to keep and which to dump.

If Adam is having problems with his friends, he is certainly not alone. Difficult friendships are familiar territory for best-selling self-help books: *Toxic Friends/True Friends* (Isaacs, 1999) helps distinguish the 'good' friends from the 'bad' while *Toxic Friends: The Antidote for Women Stuck in Complicated Friendships* (Barash, 2009) gently guides our extrication from poisonous friends. Extrication is only half the story: The latest edition of Dale Carnegie's 1936 global chart-topper *How to Win Friends and Influence People* (2007) reminds adults that the 'right' friends are an important resource for a successful, happy life. Meanwhile, the seemingly recession-proof children's self-help market strikes a preventative blow: *How to be a Friend: A Guide to Making Friends and Keeping Them* (Brown and Brown, 2001) is one of a number of texts instructing school children on how to make the 'right' friendship choices in the first place. With the American Psychological Association recognising the term 'toxic friendships' and with the 'problem' of toxicity featuring in radio and TV talk shows alike, it may be unsurprising that like Adam, we might be tempted to start some strategic dumping. However, before we start, it's worth exploring more closely the happy ending on offer in these examples of lifestyle media – that some dumping will lead to a better life – and a better *you*.

'How can anybody object to a happy ending?' asks cultural critic Gareth Palmer (2004, p. 187). There is, he says, something Scrooge-like in raising such an objection – if Adam and others can 'de-tox' their friendships and are happier for it – shouldn't we leave well alone? Well, no: I agree with Palmer that the happy endings on offer in these TV and self-help books are emblematic of historically specific organisations of society and of the self – as such, they demand closer attention. As Adam's story illustrates, the happy ending concludes a journey of transformation, which is mapped out through a series of emotionally charged choices (just *who* will you dump to get the life you deserve?). This book is interested in that journey, its promised arrival and, specifically, in the active cultural imagination that makes the journey of self-betterment through such choices intelligible. With the risk of being scrooge-like this book explores how the happy ending incorporates a certain *imagining* of a past and present self, as a self in need of change, with a certain imagining of a future, happy self. These imaginings circulate particular knowledge about the self and about citizenship. This book explores what formations of the self are promoted in these circulations and with what consequence. According, this book revolves around three orientating questions: What imaginings of the self are possible in this historic juncture? What selves are possible through these imaginings? What are the consequences to those selves imagined as possible and those imagined as *im*possible recipients of the happy ending? These questions necessarily include an exploration of seduction – just how are we seduced into what may be very specifically defined happy endings of lifestyle media, which begs the further question of how are these carefully crafted endings *happy*?

Lifestyle media

Fans and critics of reality television alike will find much in *How to Dump Your Mates* that is familiar. It's well noted that the pacey evolution of reality television makes the task of defining it difficult (Holmes and Jermyn, 2004): the chase for ratings and advertising revenue force ever-creative refashioning of game shows, documentaries, dramas, chat shows and such like, producing new hybrid formats. Yet, even in this somewhat sprawling genre, it's possible to say that reality TV generally focuses on the ordinary: people negotiating their ordinary lives and facing ordinary problems and decisions (Bonner, 2003). At times, shows may follow the lives of extraordinary people or the coping mechanisms of people in extraordinary circumstances, but what Adam shares with the stars of *Jon and Kate Plus 8* or *Big Brother* is an amplification and melodramatisation of the ways that ordinary life may be done. It's this grip on the ordinary that allows successful reality TV to be seen and *felt* as 'real' and authentic even when the audience are aware of its mediated and edited nature (Murray and Ouellette, 2009). Adam, then, is presented as an ordinary teenager with a familiar problem. The audience may be aware that Adam is 'set up' when his two groups of friends meet – our past viewing experiences of reality TV would lead us to expect some moments of tension. Despite, or because of this, *How to Dump Your Mates* invites us to identify with Adam and to feel the emotional weight of his decision. If the show gets it right, our interest is caught and we're snagged into a skilfully produced moment of suspense were Adam decides just who to dump. If we are hooked – it's good TV.

More specifically, *How to Dump Your Mates* is an example of a subgenre of reality TV that can be described as *lifestyle TV* (Bell and Hollows, 2005; Palmer, 2004). This term speaks to a range of formats that not only present the ordinary for an audience's delight or horror, but whose primary task is with its transformation, betterment and management. It is possible then to tease out lifestyle TV from reality TV shows covering the lives of those who work in the emergency services (*Cops*) or shows serving up dining experiences (*Come Dine with Me*). Although some blurring makes any sharp distinction undesirable,[1] lifestyle TV shows are more likely to explicitly focus on the need, process and result of a journey of transformation. This focus is usually narrated through the device of the makeover. Once restricted to magazine-style daytime television where lucky viewers were rewarded with expert attention in cosmetics and wardrobe choices, the makeover has in recent years both broadened its reach and come to dominate prime-time viewing (Fraser, 2007; Lewis, 2008). The makeover now extends to cars (*Pimp My Ride*); gardens (*Burke's Backyard*); personal finance (*The Bank of Mum and Dad*); homes (*HomeMade*); parenting (*Nanny 911*); appearance (*What Not To Wear*); wedding days (the newly commissioned *Pimp My Bride*); and in Adam's case, a future life. The makeover is, as is now well known, presided over by the ubiquitous expert (Powell and Prasad, 2007). Doctors, psychologists, nutritionalists, life-coaches, designers, stylists, architects, botanists and specialist cleaners are amongst those who flourish in lifestyle TV. They use their specialist knowledge, experience and natural 'know how' to steer participants through the journey of the makeover to the successful point of the 'reveal' – the 'money shot' of lifestyle TV – when the participants like Adam, more often than not, emerge as transformed and empowered, with their problems solved in a show's 30-minute time slot.[2]

The solving of ordinary problems, and the 'making over' of ordinary lives, is the very stuff of lifestyle media (Roy, 2008). In helping us to transform to a better, more efficient, happier self, lifestyle media ties the journey of self-improvement into 'ordinary' aspects of daily life such as redesigning our homes, getting the jobs we want, managing a divorce and rearing our children. This tying of self-improvement into the general unfolding of everyday life may be most apparent in lifestyle TV, but it also resonates through other lifestyle media: self-help literature, popular journalism, the Sunday supplements, magazines, radio and TV talk shows, advertising, agony columns and health promotion literature, to name but a few. This book will draw upon examples primarily from lifestyle TV and then from self-help books and advertising, but this isn't to suggest that the journey of transformation and its happy ending are the sole preserve of lifestyle media. These promises enjoy wider and diverse circulation; from classic fairy tales, to the 'American Dream', to the hopes of an urban regeneration policy that a 'makeover' will happily boost a city's economy. Even Scrooge, despite his initial reluctance and hum-bug sensibility, underwent a grateful transformation when Dickens repatriated him to the family hearth and responsible business community.

Why lifestyle media?

If the story of transformation is not 'new' and is found elsewhere, why focus on lifestyle media? This book is attracted to lifestyle media on several grounds. It is within recent lifestyle media that prevailing idealisations about what we should be, who we should *become* and how we should manage our lives appear to circulate most energetically, seemingly harmlessly and with widespread popularity. By way of example, Blair Singer's recent self-help book *Little Voice Masterly: How To Win The War Between Your Ears In 30 Seconds Or Less And Have An Extraordinary Life* not only topped Amazon's best-seller lists on its launch day in March 2009 but it sold out within hours (Commodity Online, 2009). This rush of sales might explain why the UK self-help book sales net over £50 million per year and why the US market is estimated to be running at $13.9 billion in 2010 (Kline, 2009; Merritt, 2008). At the time of writing there is excited speculation about the success of Rhonda Byrne's already multimillion dollar book and film *The Secret* as it becomes specially adapted for teenagers. *The Secret*, the means of transforming your life through the law of attraction, already has 10 million copies in print and has enjoyed success in 41 countries before it enters the relatively untapped teen market (Sellers, 2009). And the genre is developing; Cathy Alter's (2009) memoir *Up For Renewal* could signal the start of a meta-genre of self-help books explaining just how to select and use self-help books (Merritt, 2008).

If we turn to lifestyle TV, not only does this programming dominate primetime viewing schedules (Skeggs, 2009), it also commands its own channels (for instance; *Home & Garden* and *Style*) and is happily utilised in social networking sites like Bebo (Parker, 2009). While many shows are 'home grown', meaning that they are conceived, produced and screened within their country of origin (China's *JoJo Good Living*, Australia's *Burke's Backyard* and the Dutch show *Perfect!* are prime examples), this shouldn't suggest that shows do not have a wider, global circulation (Waisbord, 2004). The BBC channel *Lifestyle*, airing a range of the UK and the US lifestyle shows, was recently launched on South Korea's SK Broadband platform (Hurrell, 2009), and the airing of Western lifestyle shows in China is regarded as a crucial dimension of the 'consumer revolution' instigated by Deng Xiaping (Xu, 2007). Furthermore, formats are eagerly sought on international markets because of their ability to pull in high audience ratings and, in turn, attract the attention of advertisers (Dixon, 2008; Morganstein, 2008). The success of *The Bachelor*, for example, made a $38.2 million profit for its network: with high viewing figures it could command $231,400 per 30-second advertising slot (Dubrofsky, 2007). It's successes like these that make formats hot property. Deborah Phillips (2005), for example, notes how the BBC's format for *Changing Rooms*, which enjoyed success in the United Kingdom, was sold to over 20 countries. Indeed, the United Kingdom is now a global leader in format exports, generating 53 per cent of all exported format hours in the worldwide market (their closest competitor is the Netherlands who come in at 18 per cent). *What Not To Wear* and *10 Years Younger* are amongst the most popular exports (UK Trade and Investment, 2008). Lest we think that the recession and subsequent credit crunch, which first took hold in 2007, should limit its ability to remain relevant to our cash-strapped lives, lifestyle media ensures its own survival with such self-help titles as *Happiness on $10 a Day: A Recession-Proof Guide* (Wagner, 2009) and programming like *The Home Show* where a house is viewed less as a financial investment (a popular pre-credit crunch theme) and re-positioned as a site of family-based relaxation – as an *emotional* investment.

I am also drawn to lifestyle media because it's here that the journey and happy ending of self-betterment are most obviously reproduced, narrativatised and condensed. The narrative arc of the journey is edited, presented and consumed in neat self-contained bundles of the half-hour makeover show, the 30-second advert, the length of a CD self-help recording or within the confines of a book binding. These necessary processes of distillation allow a scrooge-like eye to better glimpse something of the way that cultural imaginations of the past/present self and the hopeful shaping of the future self can be exercised. At their bluntest, these may be herded into the 'before' and 'after' shots and equivalent rhetorical devices, but can be evident in less straightforward ways as different forms of lifestyle media, lifestyle TV, self-help, advertising and so on continually reinvent their products and presentation to maintain market share and interest.

Despite this changing ground, repeated, yet diverse, representations of certain ways of living and ways of being can be observed. What can also be observed is how these form part of an ethos of transformation and re-creation that permeates most, if not all, aspects of our daily life and social organisation. Meredith Jones (2008) refers to this as 'makeover culture', whereby transformation and change become central organising principles; no longer confined to inspirational stories, or moralising fantasies, transformation is now a cultural *imperative*. It is what this transformation entails, what it expects and what is produced in relation to the self that concerns this book. It may seem overly simplistic to talk about 'winners' and 'losers' in a makeover culture, yet social divisions are being carefully redrawn in ways that trace the lines of social class, gender and race. Thinking about winners and losers can provide a useful nudge towards the cultural work performed in and through lifestyle media that this book aims to tease out.

The 'Contextualisation Project'

It is through a consideration of makeover culture that I hope to make a modest contribution to what can be called a contextualisation project currently in evidence across the social sciences, but is perhaps more energetically pursued in Western critical sociology. The contextualisation project refers to critical debates and the deployment of empirical research that focuses on the various, intersecting ways in which individuals are embodied and embedded within their social, cultural and historical contexts (discussed in Chapter 1). It is the means by which the conceptual merit of 'gender', 'class', 'race', 'sexuality' and 'disability', amongst others, are being fought for, and through this fighting, being re-invigorated as more meaningful, politically sensitive tools of social analysis. That such a project is necessary is explained by a growing tendency for some social theory, albeit with different emphasis and intention, to *de*-contextualise the self. That is to say, there is tendency to move from an observation that vast processes of economic, political and social change have loosened the self from strictures of tradition, obligation and duty, to make celebratory claims for the self's ability to transform itself, and in so doing, presumably *design out* the very aspects that are once associated with material and symbolic inequalities. While there is something exciting in the talk of an empowered and reflexive agency conjured in these accounts, they sail close to relegating concepts such as 'class' to mere descriptive variables not as ways of exposing and opposing the grounds upon which social privilege and injustice can be repeatedly and *heavily* etched on people's everyday experiences (Skeggs, 2004). This book is part of a project that re-asserts that class and other social divisions still *matter* and it does so by exploring how they are swept up and into the promise and invitation of transformation presented in lifestyle media.

One of the features of contemporary cultural politics is its hetero-geneity. Media texts, like other texts, are polysemic – they can be read and engaged with in a number of ways, some of which may be critical and resistant (Negra, 2009). There are, as Jones (2008, p. 20) argues, 'inconsistencies, denials and contradictions' that are part and parcel of the grip of makeover culture, as there are in the contested space of the mass media (Silverstone, 2007). However, rather than destabilise the imperative to transform, contradictions *can* work to embolden and fortify it by incorporating its opposition and tensions. Even heated debates questioning whether cosmetic surgery, the ultimate makeover, has gone 'too far' serve to further publicise surgery and transformation. TV shows like *Face Lifts from Hell* do, as the title suggests, graphically illustrate all that can go wrong. But instead of opening up critical space to discuss the cultural role and function of surgery, the 'problem' is deftly re-packaged into questions of what is 'enough' surgery or onto the practices of unscrupulous surgeons: surgery and the ethos of the makeover remain unscathed. Further, the prevailing ethos of transformation tends to incorporate its distracters through the sheer variety of its options (cosmetic surgery too drastic? Try *Botox* or the self-applied L'Oreal *Revitalift* to firm up); by promoting the voluntary and self-interested nature of engagement (you don't *have* to make more of yourself, but you'd be better for it) and through the suggestion that a makeover culture is largely consumer led – whereby the market of expertise and technologies of change mushroom around consumer desire (Doesn't L'Oreal engage in research effort and innovations just 'because *you're* worth it'?). This latter point suggests that if we don't like makeover culture we must remember that not only did we ask for it but that we continue to drive it through our consumer choices.

My discussion is based on what is called a 'preferred reading' (Dworkin and Wachs, 2004). This means that I'll be charting certain consistencies and continuities arising from convergences of societal values, beliefs and economic pressures which run across media texts despite their fragmented and polysemic nature (Silverstone, 2007). Imogen Tyler (2008), for example, is among a growing group of sociologists who devote their attention to a pernicious percussion of repeated class representations thumping through comedy shows, lifestyle media, news reportage and so on. While there is space and hope for contestation, this book is concerned about the consistencies and repetitions because they help create a bundle of resources which can inform commonsense cultural literacy about the self and about various Others (Mitchell, 2005; Negra, 2009). This is how social psychologists Hélène Joffe and Christian Staerklé express it:

> Mass media...play a major role in constructing common sense concerning outgroups by disseminating the representations on which lay people draw when forming representations of social problems such as criminality, poverty, deviance and illness. These phenomena tend to be constructed in terms of responsibility and blame and associated with social groups...They raise questions concerning who is dangerous and threatening, and who should be avoided.
>
> (2007, pp. 402–403)

This book discusses how notions of responsibility, blame and danger are enfolded into the imperative to transform the self. But, this book isn't 'about' lifestyle media 'bashing' – lifestyle media presents too much of a wide and moving target to make this a possible task, even if it was desired. While Angela McRobbie (2004) rightfully charts the cruelty in some lifestyle TV, we can't ignore that many people find comfort, strength, inspiration and even what they may describe as empowerment in lifestyle media (Gray, 2003; Sender and Sullivan, 2008). As Meredith Jones notes, cosmetic 'fixes' on makeover shows can help people otherwise 'left behind by the brutal US health system' (2008, p. 51). Similarly, media scholars Laurie Ouellette and James Hay have noted how, in a time of declining and failing public welfare provision, that 'hundreds of thousands of people now apply directly to reality TV programmes for housing, affordable health-care and other forms of assistance' (2008, p. 5). We might add that for those with eating disorders, for example, self-help may provide refuge from, and resistance to, mounting medicalisation. Furthermore, TV shows showcasing 'embarrassing illnesses' may well provide comfort and practical assistance to the concerned. So, while the notion of empowerment demands some unpacking, it's hard to dismiss the tangible 'feel-good' factor when, for example, a participant emerges from her (it is mostly women) journey of transformation to experience her happy ending in a makeover show's final 'reveal' – isn't that one of the reasons we so enjoy the makeover show?

This book is reluctant then, to approach lifestyle media *solely* in terms of its overt reproduction of class antagonism, racialised ridicule or homophobia. These do find overtly strong and offensive expression but they also work their way through irony and humour (Raisborough and Adams, 2008). We might also want to consider what cultural work is performed when self-help titles seem to address us as 'unmarked' individuals, as the neutral and universal 'you' in *Weekend Life Coach: How to get the life you want in 48 hours* (Field, 2004) or when lifestyle experts and participants are increasingly drawn from wider demographics. Gay hosts and contestants, for example, enjoy greater visibility on lifestyle TV often without comment nor are they recruited just to provide the drama of clash and conflict. Papacharissi and Fernback (2008, p. 349) note in their discussion of the US makeover show *Queer Eye for the Straight Guy* that some lifestyle TV shows are departing from the once standard narrative of 'trash-talking'. They, like Peter Lunt and Tanya Lewis (2008) and more recently Hannah Frith et al. (2010), are sensitive to the complexity at work in stories of self-transformation that manifest as benign, positive and empowering. Accordingly, this book explores how social divisions both shape and are shaped in the story of the journey of transformation and are invoked in its happy ending, even as they operate in more 'neutral' and benign calls to self-betterment. In particular, this book argues in its first chapter that something happens when selves are cast as 'ordinary' and 'normal' (and as such, 'unmarked'). I am alerted to the 'ordinary' as a site for cultural work and cultural production by the critical analysis of gay representation in lifestyle TV and wider media. Gorman-Murray's (2006, p. 233) analysis of the ways gay men are increasingly presented as 'ordinary' concludes that ordinariness masks active processes which regulate and sanitise homosexuality, adding weight to Mitchell's

(2005) argument that we could be witnessing the emergence of a new homophobia. This book will explore what else is happening within what is a specifically shaped 'ordinary' in lifestyle media.

Neoliberal contexts

For many critical commentators the specific imagining of the self as requiring transformation cannot be divorced from a prevailing social, political and economic rationality generally referred to as neoliberalism. I want to provide a brief outline and explanation of neoliberalism now to support further discussion in subsequent chapters.

A liberal school of economics is based on two fundamental beliefs. The first is that the natural laws and rhythms of a free market can spur competition, efficiently distribute and utilise resources, secure social justice and produce economic growth. Hence, processes of deregulation and decentralisation are favoured strategies. These remove or reduce state or external control of the market. The second is the assumption of people's self-interest – 'that human beings will always favour themselves' (McGregor, 2001, p. 83) – a belief which underpins an imaging of the self as a self-propelled *entrepreneur* of free-market conditions. Neo (as in 'new') liberalism generally refers to a form of liberalism aggressively ushered into Western democracies, particularly those of Britain and the United States under the Thatcher/Major and Regan/Bush Senior's administrations (Peck and Tichell, 2002), and which still thrives under more socialist democratic leadership (Clarke and Newman, 2007). The 1980s in particular were characterised by a spread of market rationality into social organisation and by an uncompromising individualism. Specifically, unstinting privatisation, extensive policies of deregulation and cuts in public spending devolved the responsibility of welfare from the state to the individual, helped fuel a fierce individualism that heaped rewards on those who could ride the markets *and* served to denigrate dependency, need and care. It's interesting to note that lifestyle TV owes its current popularity to the processes of neoliberal deregulation – the explosion of channels and production companies have privileged the relatively cheap-to-produce formats of lifestyle TV (Ouellette and Hay, 2008) and a commodification of the ordinary; ordinary lives, stories and problems are converted into commodities to attract audience and advertisers' attention (Illouz and Wilf, 2008).

Neoliberalism is not an even process, it is marked by inconsistencies and conflicts (He and Wu, 2009), yet the overarching result is the construction of an ideal kind of citizen as one able to withstand the tidal forces of the market-economy through flexibility and enterprise. The neoliberal economy, more so in times of recession, demands fit, flexible bodies with transient skills who are sufficiently mobile to meet the demand of business (McRobbie, 2004) and its citizenry must be ready and willing to fit any place afforded. Sociologist Zgymunt Bauman despairingly describes this ideal worker as a 'Jack of all trades' type encouraged by employers who prefer 'free-floating, unattached, flexible, "generalist" and ultimately disposable employees' (2007, p. 9). However, companies with a vested interest in 'flexible solutions' for government and business such as flexibility.co.uk and *Swiftwork* frame flexibility as an efficient and environmentally aware alternative to traditional working practices. As workers labour at home, when needed, absenteeism is reduced; commuting and commuting time is cut; companies save money on property and maintenance costs; and workers can realise a better work–life balance. The UK Office of Government Commerce's paper *Working Beyond Walls* goes further; it maps out its vision for a Civil Service of 2020 as virtual and transient, with individuals momentarily joined for specific tasks via 'wireless connectivity' and 'real-time interactive frameworks' (Hardy et al., 2008).

How flexibility relates to stories of transformation may already be clear. A literal transforming landscaping has occurred; home makeover shows have designed desirable 'must have' studies and 'work zones' in our newly transformed homes and gardens. The physical landscape of office life has also been made over. Walls have been hardest hit – regarded as physical and metaphorical obstacles to the neoliberal project, they have been demolished:

> More than seven miles of internal walls were removed as part of the Treasury redevelopment project. This physical change was symbolic of much deeper cultural, business and technology transformation within the Treasury, where numerous time-bound organisational barriers were removed to support the more agile and dynamic organisation that is evolving today.
>
> Paul Pegler, Her Majesty's Treasury
> (cited in Allen et al., 2004, p. 2)

However, it's the self that requires some reconfiguration to work and live in these new 'agile and dynamic' spaces. Neoliberalism, as already said, depends on a heightened individualism and one could suspect that discourses of change within lifestyle media help to 'push' the individualised self towards practices of flexibility and adaptability. Yet, philosopher Axel Honneth (2004) warns against seeing self-transformation as a tool strategically developed by a neoliberal progressive agenda. Rather than the result of a 'deliberate strategy', self-transformation and self-realisation have a longer and quite diverse history which has been gradually appropriated or 'transmuted' to become an ideology of neoliberalism. Through this appropriation, self-work becomes the result and justification of deregulation *and* it takes up a very different shape in its transmutation: the ideals of self-realisation are, Honneth argues, 'inverted into compulsions and expectations' (p. 474) that force individuals onto lives that are intelligible only in terms of enterprise, strategy and sound choice-making. Furthermore, the ability to transform and to demonstrate flexibility is quickly spun into definitions of ideal and *moral* personhood. Despite the recent economic crisis, caused by unfretted free markets, greed and exploitation, neoliberalism has taken hold as 'a commonsense of our times' (Peck and Tichell, 2002, p. 381), and one that seems to have survived the recent global 'slow down'.

It's important to stress, as do John Clarke and Janet Newman (2007), that neoliberalism recasts its citizens as *consumers*. They cite David Marquand (2004, p. 118) who has said of New Labour that 'Ministerial rhetoric is saturated with the language of consumerism. The public services are to be "consumer focused"; schools and colleges are to ensure that "what is on offer" responds to the needs of consumer.' The 'language of consumerism' purports to place the control of the markets (and newly marketised services) within the internal mechanism of consumer choice. In a form of demand-led capitalism, consumer choices are imagined as being able to drive out faulty or unfair companies, products and service-providers from the market and force others to adapt to consumer needs (Fraj and Martinez, 2007). This *consumer sovereignty* necessarily rests on a self imagined as rational, calculating and importantly as market-literate (able to read and understand consumer capitalism). It also rests on a trust in the self-correcting dynamics of the market itself. One upshot of this is the increasing tendency for social or individual problems and their solutions to become firmly positioned in the market. Ethical consumption is one example of how 'good' consumer choices are presented as the solution to the problem of the human, ecological and environmental cost of consumption (Adams and Raisborough, 2010). Ethical consumption currently enjoys increased dedicated attention from lifestyle TV shows (Lewis, 2008), a bevy of 'how to be greener' self-help books and has been harnessed by advertising extolling the 'green' (ecological) and 'red' (social) status of its products (Renault's 2010 UK ad for its electric cars combines both with its slogan 'cars for all'). All in all, neoliberalism places great store on the power and exercise of consumer choice. Not only are individuals obliged to make the right choices from a number of choices extended by policies of deregulation and privatisation, but they are increasingly encouraged to express themselves and exercise their agency through those choices. How lifestyle media presents, frames and entices us into the market is discussed in Chapter 2.

However, the so-called rolling back of the state characterising neoliberalism shouldn't suggest that state power, government and social control no longer exist or that they are fatally wounded. Instead neoliberalism represents new forms of regulation, governance and control even in acts of displacement and decentralisation; it demands and forges new relationships between the self, capitalism and the state. James Hay (2000, p. 54) claims that neoliberalism 'relies on new kinds of citizen-subjects' which we briefly discussed above, *and* 'new techniques for governing them'. It is the role of lifestyle media to this project of governance that interests this book.

Governance

Much work on lifestyle media in its neoliberal context has lent heavily upon the formulations of the French philosopher and historian Michel Foucault, particularly his later work on governmentality, so I will briefly sketch it here. Foucault's later work on power revolved around his resurrection of an earlier use of the term 'government', which even into the eighteenth century referred to religious, medical or philosophical materials aimed to direct and guide household management, family life, the rearing of children and so on (Lemke, 2000). Reviving these earlier meanings allowed Foucault to define 'governmentality' as the 'conduct of conduct' – the ways that individuals and groups are governed through guidance, prompts, instruction, incentives and support: governance can be broadly understood as 'techniques and procedures for directing human behaviour' (Foucault, 1977, p. 81). It combines two related aspects. The first is the way that a modern rationality of 'management' (of things and of self) takes hold of social organisation and grips the social imagination as the most efficient means to realise and maximise the best interests of the population (well-being and security, for example). Secondly, it involves 'techniques of self' through which individuals are recruited into, and enact, specific bodily disciplines of self-management and self-improvement in pursuit of those best interests (Moss, 1998). Bluntly put, the power relations that constitute governmentality produce the means of 'acting on ourselves, so that the police, the guards and the doctors do not have to' (Cruikshank, 1993, p. 327). As such it is government in a terrain marked by the retreat of the state – it is government at a distance.

Governance relies on Foucault's emphasis on the *productive* relations of power. In this emphasis, Foucault attempts to prise (not always successfully) some distance from models that conceive power as possessed by a ruling body (such as the state) and used to impose social control. Instead of understanding power as working solely through one source and exercised through repression or prohibition, Foucault envisaged a more complex model of power:

> We must cease at once and for all to describe the effects of power in negative terms: it 'excludes', it 'represses', it 'censors', it 'abstracts', it 'masks', it 'conceals'. In fact power produces; it produces reality, it produces domains of objects and the rituals of truth.
>
> (Foucault, 1977, p. 194)

As productive, power enables agency, it produces 'a reality' of social identities, social orders, opportunities, choices *and* a rationality that makes these legitimate and 'commonsense' ways of being. It does so through what Foucault imagines as a *microphysics* of power, where power is exercised through multiple, infinite points (no core centre), and through a multitude of social relations and everyday practices. This multi-modal power produces and works through subjects who are 'free' to be governed through their choice-making. Here Foucault engages in some characteristic acts of redefinition; 'freedom' is rede-fined from an escape from systems of oppression, to refer to the ability of a subject to face and realise an option from a range of pos-sibilities and choices: 'Power is exercised only over free subjects, and only insofar as they are free. By this we mean, individuals or col-lective subjects who are faced with a field of possibilities in which several ways of behaving, several reactions are realised' (Foucault, 1982, p. 789).

Similarly, power is redefined. Traditional understandings of 'power' as repressive are understood by Foucault as 'domination' or as rela-tions of violence (the exercise of which forecloses the 'field of possibilities'). This leaves the term 'power' to refer to the productive and generative modes of everyday relations and practices. Whereas violence depends on passive subjects, relations of power are impos-sible without the subject's actions and agency – hence, power is exercised '*only* over free subjects'. Foucault is adamant then that governance is not about *forcing* individuals 'to do what that gover-nor wants' (Foucault, 1993, p. 203), rather, governance speaks to the *cultivation of the self* which is encouraged and fostered by various gov-ernmental agencies, working unevenly in what Derek Hook describes as an 'unorchestrated synchronicity' (2003, p. 621). Relationships of (productive) power depend on what Foucault calls 'strategic games between liberties' (1988, p. 19). These games play on and through freedom, working to align and orchestrate individuals, through their techniques of self, to neoliberal agendas of various, diverse agencies. The point for Foucault is not whether this orchestration and align-ment is 'good' or 'bad', a serious failing for those who seek a more normative theorisation, but rather to question just how freedom is *shaped*.

What of resistance? Foucault's ambition was to destabilise the nat-ural, taken-for-granted forms of modern power by demonstrating that it operates through particular ways of thinking (rationality) and specific ways of acting (technologies). The political project for Foucault is a constant act of refusal to *be* a self that can be addressed through specifically shaped conduct. In short, to reject ways of being that constitute neoliberal individualism and to 'promote new forms of subjectivity through the refusal of this kind of individuality' (Foucault, 1982, p. 211). The point for Foucault is that we are each freer than we think.

Governance and the pedagogic function of Lifestyle Media

Coming at the end of his life, it's unsurprising that Foucault's thinking on governance is uneven and undeveloped (Moss, 1998). Mitchell Dean, for example, finds that Foucault's governance is a 'mixed substance and one that only works when alloyed with others' (1999, p. 7). Cultural and Media scholars would agree and have, in the main, yoked Foucault's thinking to a generally more Marxist-infused criticism to excavate the cultural politics underpinning neoliberalism. The resultant emphasis is a prevailing focus on social control and the shaping of self. The cultural critic Toby Miller argues that governance 'seeks to manage subjectivity through culture' (2007, p. 2), and he invites attention to the role of lifestyle media in orchestrating conduct and its relationship to a project of governing at a distance. Lifestyle media provides a suitable site: its focus on the minutiae of the 'everyday' and its dramatisation of self-regulation have led many to conclude that lifestyle media is a most visible attempt at shaping an ideal citizenry (Lewis, 2008; Palmer, 2004; Phillips, 2005). The political nature of lifestyle media in this regard cannot be underestimated; Laurie Ouellette and James Hay (2008) argue that lifestyle TV 'circulates informal "guidelines for living" that we are all (at times) called upon to learn from and follow' (p. 2). They ask just how *useful* is lifestyle TV to a rationality of government that operates through the self-management of its citizens. They conclude that TV, as a promoter and shaper of self-actualisation, operates as a 'form of citizen training' (p. 15). Jack Bratich (2006, p. 67) concurs, seeing lifestyle media as 'instructional devices that encourage self-responsibility, self-entrepreneurialism, and self improvement as a neoliberal form of governance'. Ouellette (2009) expands this point to demand that lifestyle TV be seen as a specific *technology* of neoliberal governance. In short, once we add the argument that lifestyle media sutures practices of transformation to expert-mediated choices in consumer culture (Heller, 2007; Xu, 2007), it's possible to conclude that it is the *pedagogic function* of lifestyle media that has captured the attention of many scholars. Lifestyle media offers us instructive templates for how we ought to act, behave, to *be* and how to express tasteful choice through knowledge of consumer markets. The lessons here are often taught through narratives of disgust, humiliation, mockery or pity – indeed, these make up the 'entertainment' of lifestyle TV and it's the promise of an escape from a life of humiliation that helps sell self-help texts.

Additionally, we are taught a level of acceptance and gratitude for the current neoliberal rationality *itself*. Media studies scholar Kathryn Fraser (2007) is among those who note how neoliberal ideas are constantly narrated and dramatised in lifestyle media. By consistently presenting problems as those 'of living' and locating them within the intimate lives of ordinary people, we are all 'taught' that problems and solutions are personal and individual responsibilities. What is apparent here is a deft deflection from the possibility that personal ills could be consequences of societal organisation or structural injustices: the result is a reinforcement of individualised responsibility – an action which Heidi Rimke (2000) has critically charted within self-help literature. Fraser adds that the deflection also serves an increasing level of *democratisation* evident in lifestyle media – self-transformation is opened to *everyone* once structural issues and structural relations of class and so on have been conjured away. This scholarship critically charts the forms and expressions of moral instruction and successfully maps out the specific contours of governance working through the mediascape. This adds academic weight to a study of cultural forms that are still dismissed as trivial or ridiculed for their role in a perceived general 'dumbing down' of society. Foucault then lends credibility and political urgency to researchers who regard lifestyle media, reality TV and the like, as fertile sites to question just how the self is *made,* to consider *what* self is possible through its own refashioning and to generally seek to make *visible* the diverse workings of governance through culture.

Yet there are enduring criticisms lodged at Foucault's governance, whose consideration could bolster the analytics of lifestyle media. Matthew Adams (2007), for example, finds too little in governance to explain why we may be motivated or indeed desire one form of regulatory 'conduct' over another, and too little to question what sorts of investments or intentions a self nurtures in the relations of 'conduct of conduct'. Adams is not alone; the sociologist Anthony Elliott argues that 'psychic dispositions, emotional desires' and personal biographies are, to be blunt, written out by Foucault (2001, p. 94). McNay (1994) adds the related criticism that despite an insistence on everyday relations of power, Foucault's stress on bodily discipline foregrounds the self's relation with *itself* not with others –

the intersubjective dimensions of selfhood can thus fade from critical view. In short, across Foucault's work 'complexity and heterogeneity of psychic life, intersubjectivity and social structure' suffer too much reduction (Adams, 2007, p. 103) and governance can't quite shake off the 'hollowed out, atomised self' that shadows Foucault's analysis (p. 130).

Recognition as alloy

This book attempts to work from these to argue that the obligation to transform conjures up and speaks to a presumed (normative) desire to belong and to be *somebody* in a makeover culture. More specifically, it argues that lifestyle media, as a bundle of diverse cultural labours, sells the promise and solves the problems of being that somebody. This book turns towards the politics of recognition to make its claims. Recognition offers a useful alloy because there are necessary dialogical, intersubjective relations at play; 'recognition from others is... essential to the development of a sense of self', argues Nancy Fraser (2000, p. 109). And it is this, and the belonging and promised security that comes from being recognised as a 'worthy somebody' that may very well account for our seduction into practices of transformation and our desire to be transformed.

By way of explanation, a politics of recognition speaks to structural inequalities (such as economic injustice) *and* to cultural inequalities. Cultural inequalities can stem from cultural domination such as, for example, being subject 'to alien forms of judgement' (Wright and Madrid, 2007, p. 258) and/or the threat or possibility of *non*-recognition or *mis*recognition, such as being rendered invisible – *being looked through* or being subject to denigrating stereotypes. The harm that falls from distorted/non-recognition, as Hegel's thesis of the dialogical self indicates, is experienced as a bitter blow to one's very sense of self. It is worth here reciting Nancy Fraser's explanation that the harm of misrecognition is:

> Not simply to be thought ill of, looked down upon, or devalued in other's conscious attitudes or mental beliefs. It is rather to be denied the status of a full partner in social interaction and prevented from participating as a peer in social life – not as a consequence of distributive inequality (such as failing to receive one's

fair share of resources), but rather as a consequence of institutionalised patterns of interpretation and evaluation that constitute one
as comparatively unworthy of respect and esteem.

(Fraser, 1995, p. 280)

Recognition in these terms allows this book to consider if 'institutionalised patterns of interpretation and evaluation' can speak to
the ways prevailing notions of class, gender, sexuality, *inter alia* are
being swept up into cultural imaginations of a responsible self and its
associated values of 'worth' 'respect' and 'esteem'. The L'Oreal advertising tag line 'because I'm worth it' is, for example, a celebratory
declaration of a happy ending as well as a justification for the journey of transformation itself. But, we may now ask questions of how
that 'worth' is defined and recognised.

Judith Butler has recently called for social scientists to pay more
attention to the terms by which we are recognised as *viable* human
beings. By arguing that who we are and can be is 'fundamentally
dependent on . . . social norms' (2004, p. 2), she forcefully concludes
that these norms can 'do' *and* also 'undo' one's personhood. What
is important here is the association between norms and violence to
the self – that is to say, that the designing of the self, or at least the
design of culturally intelligible self, involves a squeezing, in Butler's
words an 'undoing' of the self to 'fit' with prevailing imaginations
of worthy, viable personhood. Butler helps cast a critical light on
the journey of self-betterment and transformation – What undoings
are necessary? What normative registers are the self encouraged to
squeeze into to be *recognised* as worthy and as having worth? What's
further, Butler's argument also suggests that the risk of being *unviable*
may be a key motivation, an incitement, for our own involvement
and interest in the journey of transformation – the risk of not-being
spurs us to action. This offers much to the proposed contextualisation
project for it gives some indication of the ways desires and agency can
be worked upon and worked up in the promise of the happy ending.

The book

This book is divided into three parts. Part I starts by placing lifestyle
media in its wider context. Taking the Fat Face advert tag line 'just living is not enough', Chapter 1 explains how various, uneven processes

of social change have jostled the self from pre-given identities and life-trajectories onto a life of self-authorship. For some sociologists this has resulted in looser, more fluid relations between the self and society, enabling greater personal reflexive agency, personal expression and choice. Charting the sociological debates around the self and its 'new' relationship to society, this chapter draws on the work of Beverly Skeggs (2004) to claim that the resources for self-authorship and self-transformation are not equally available to all. Chapter 2 opens by observing the importance of 'becoming' in lifestyle media. Self-help books urge us to be better in all we do and encourage us all to engage in ceaseless acts of improvement. This ceaselessness is captured by Meredith Jones's (2008) concept of the 'makeover culture', which this chapter argues provides the imagination and resources for the self's labours of 'becoming something better' in consumer capitalism. More importantly, this chapter argues that the makeover culture provides an interpretive framework that recognises and rewards certain labours of being and becoming and serves to denigrate others.

Part II furthers this theme by focusing on the construction and representation of normal/pathological selves in lifestyle TV shows. More specifically, Chapter 3 explores how 'insides' (bodily organs and the inner self) are mediated through specific frames of health and personal responsibility to firstly help us all picture an abject life and the 'type' of person who lives it, and secondly to celebrate the transformation of that life into that of a recognisable neoliberal citizen. Chapter 4 takes Judith Butler's (2009) observation that to be framed also means to be 'set up' as a guilty party. It argues that some bodies are 'set up' as abject when self-control and responsibility become benchmarks of normative, respectable selfhood. In particular, it focuses on how the fat body is represented in weight-loss TV shows and in wider rhetoric producing the current global 'obesity epidemic'. What's important to both chapters are the ways selfhood is *allocated* in ways authorised and legitimated through frames of health and personal responsibility.

The final part of this book unpicks two standard narrative blocks of lifestyle media; the 'before' and the 'after'. Chapter 5 argues that formations of self don't just occur in the narrative space between the 'before' and 'after' in the journey of transformation, rather, that selves are specifically shaped as they are herded into the 'before' through particular performances of suffering and deservingness. This chapter argues that successful performances are those which resonate with prevailing neoliberal values and a 'self-control ethos'. Chapter 6 takes the 'reveal' at its focus, arguing that these momentary and fleeting moments of successful selfhood reveal just who and what counts as a self in this cultural juncture. It militates against any suggestion that the self is a neutral concept to argue that individuals and selfhood are contextualised properties: they are embedded, embroiled and embodied within their social-cultural contexts. What this all means for those exuberant claims for empowered, individual, choice-making forms this book's concluding discussion.

Part I
Introducing Lifestyle Citizens

1
When Life is not Enough: Making More of the Self

To start with a clean slate. English Proverb.

The unmarked character of the one very often becomes the condition of articulation of the other.

Judith Butler (Bell, 1999, p. 168)

Introduction

Fat Face, the international outdoor clothes retailer, liberally smatter motivational adages over their merchandise: 'just living is not enough' is stamped on packets of buttons in their summer 2010 range (FatFace.com). Fat Face invites us to add value to our ordinary lives – suitably clothed of course. What interests me at the start of a chapter charged with the task of introducing the self in relation to lifestyle media is the use of 'just' in the context of living. Colloquially 'just' can mean 'barely', 'simply' and 'no more than'. To be 'barely living' suggests passivity, a rudderless life that rolls up and over us, a life scarcely noticeable. Taking another meaning of 'just', *simply* living seems to target a familiar excuse – if we felt that there was 'enough' to do simply coping with tempo of, say, employment and the irregular rhythms of domestic life and excuse ourselves from Fat Face's invitation, we are advised that we risk being 'no more than' those modulations. If any uncertainty remains, we are cautioned that a life without added value 'is not enough'. This packet of buttons then suggests that *just living* is a mark of failure and missed opportunities. What is striking is that ordinary life can be imagined – can be *intelligible* – as such. How the ordinary is imagined in this way is explored in this chapter.

Perhaps it's a fair comment to observe that I am only talking about a packet of buttons – surely they are likely to be thrown unheeded into the back of a drawer? Maybe – yet, the notion that 'just living is not enough' pulsates with varying intensity and in various manifestations throughout all of lifestyle media. It is not too crude to suggest that if life was 'enough' then there would be no need to embark on a journey of self-transformation. The suggestion of lack and the out-manoeuvring of familiar excuses efficiently scaffold the increasingly normalised emphasis on change and self-betterment circulating in what Meredith Jones (2008) describes as a makeover culture, a discussion of which follows in the next chapter. There is also something interesting about these being 'only' buttons; as everyday items that can be easily cast aside, they indicate something about the casual way that calls to self-betterment reach into the darkest, forgotten recesses of our private life. Further, as the buttons were acquired through the act of consumption, their injunctions are directed to us as consumers. As this book goes on to explore, lifestyle media works to reconfigure the contours of our everyday lives as we transform to better selves through carefully guided consumer choices. However, this chapter's main concern is to tackle suggestions that the self, its efforts to be 'enough' and the choices it is offered and makes are somehow neutral, that is, that they are untouched by context-specific power relations. Describing this suggestion of neutrality as the effect of a theoretical illusion, this chapter starts work on the contextualisation project. This project was described in the introduction as the argument that class, gender, race and other lines of social division still *matter* and that, further, they play out in purportedly 'neutral' fields. This chapter starts, however, by introducing the self as a substance deemed in need of self-work and improvement.

Unsettling the ordinary life

Fat Face suggest that ordinary life can be 'just living' or the grounds for a different, more engaged life and for a better, more engaged you. How ordinary life can be imagined as such directly relates to historic processes of social, economic and political change which constitute what is variously referred to as second or late modernity.

I want to briefly sketch these out before considering what they mean for the 'ordinary'.[1] There are three main bundles of social change processes. Firstly, detraditionalisation speaks to the weakening of traditional bonds of community, family and role. It describes a loosening of authority, which enables the questioning of certain values and beliefs such as, for example, the 'natural' link between sexuality and reproduction. Of course, there are new opportunities generated in the weakening of traditions, such as the widening of sexual expression, but there is also a cost. Frank Furedi (2004, p. 86) is among those who recognise that tradition provided the self with 'a model of action' – a way of living a life – and 'readily understandable identities' – ways of being in that life, and he worries that processes of detraditionalisation erode these anchor points, casting the self adrift in search of its own meaning and identity. For Furedi the result is social isolation and increased anxiety.

The second set of processes is deindustrialisation. This generally refers to the decline of industrial organisation and practices.[2] The sociologist Ulrich Beck states, 'people are being cut loose from the ways of life of an industrial society, just as at the entry to the industrial epoch they where (and still are being) cut loose from the self-evident feudal and status-based understandings, ways of life, societal forms' (1996, p. 94). The 'cutting loose' is a response to a perceived series of shifts from economies of production (the manufacture of goods) to consumption (the circulation of knowledge and symbols). Through these shifts the labour market becomes crowded with 'cultural intermediaries' working in marketing, fashion, design and media, and 'consultants' ready to help others work on their impression management, diet and motivation (Binkley, 2004; Gray, 2003). The explosion of this 'service' sector has been accompanied by a trend in the wider labour market for 'flexible working', short-term agency work, 'zero-hour' contracts (so called because work hours are not guaranteed) and a privileging of 'transferable skills' over studied craftsmanship. The fragmented nature of employment may provide space for opportunity and enterprise, but it has become increasingly difficult to define the self solely in terms of employment (what one *does*) and also beckons high levels of insecurity and anxiety (Sennett, 2006).

Globalisation is the third process. Like the others, this is a contested term, but generally refers to the ways that technological advances have produced a scattering of culture, information, capital and people around the globe on an unprecedented scale and pace (Massey and Jess, 1995). Not only do increasing migration flows and news coverage 'expose' us 'to a wider set of meanings for the construction of identity' (Callero, 2003, p. 123) but as a condition of *connectivity*, globalisation refers to increased and increasingly complex 'interconnections and interdependencies' between the 'far' and 'near' so that both are altered (Tomlinson, 1999, p. 2). In consequence, meanings of culture, place and belonging start to destabilise. Tomlinson concludes that globalisation 'fundamentally transforms the relationship between the places we inhabit and our cultural practices, experiences and identities' (1999, p. 106). Although these processes have been simply put, many social scientists observe how processes of social change have corroded the cardinal points of self-meaning and identity. The overall image is one of fragmentation and instability. I want to pursue this image to see if it offers any explanation for ordinary life being imagined as both a potential site of failure ('just' living) and a site of transformation.

The jostled self

It's been forcefully argued that these fragmenting processes effectively *jostle* the self out of once set and prescribed trajectories. As 'pre-given' roles dissolve, more is demanded of the individual; roles, expectations, duties and narratives associated with social class, gender and so on start to melt becoming 'fluid and flexible', no longer dictating our lives (Beck and Wilms, 2004). The consequence is that the self is forced to map out and navigate its own definition and place in the world; as Beck and Beck-Gernsheim (1995, p. 6) have it, individuals are now compelled to 'build up a life of their own'. The sociologist Anthony Giddens has been at the fore in tackling theoretical considerations of what these changes might mean for the self. For him, 'building up a life' demands a construction of a coherent self-narrative. This provides a sense of cohesion by placing the self within the unfolding of time, that is to say, with a meaningful past and directed future. By constructing this narrative the self becomes the author and subject of its own biography. The challenge is to construct this narrative from the shards of a fragmented social and political terrain. For Giddens this lifelong challenge demands *and gets* the application of a heightened reflexivity. By this, Giddens means that the self, through a self-conscious awareness of itself, can reflect and monitor its preferences, activities and behaviours, and even critically consider the process of reflection itself (Giddens, 1991). For him, the self now jostled from its traditional identity markers has little choice but to become 'a reflexive project' (1991, p. 32) involving 'the strategic adoption of lifestyle options' related to a planned 'trajectory' of a meaningful biographical narrative (1991, pp. 243–244). He concludes that in late modernity 'we are not what we are, but what we make of ourselves' (1991, p. 68). Ordinary life, the work of *being*, is then recast as a site of intense labour required to keep a 'particular narrative going' in sorting choices and decisions out into an 'ongoing "story" about the self' (Giddens, 1991, p. 54).

It is important to note that while Giddens is aware that social changes inflict great upheaval and loss, his prognosis is nonetheless upbeat. His argument is that reflexivity within the context of looser and freer social arrangements can enable emancipatory practices and relations. A reflective self can, for example, seek relationships it wants and reject those which can become, if we may borrow an expression directly from self-help books, *toxic*. He understands this as a dialectic of control and loss; as traditions bend, duty no longer forces us into relationships or prescribed roles within them. Instead we can reflexively assess and create the relationships which best suit the self we imagine ourselves to be. A loss of prescription combined with an expansion of strategic control fans Giddens' hope that more *democratic* and more meaningful relationships are within our grasp. On this level, there is much hope for those who have argued that conventional gender relations require romantic love only as an ideological ploy to bring subordinate gender groups into the willing servitude of dominant gender groups (Jeffreys, 1990). So, while theorists like Zygmunt Bauman (2007) may have fears for the demise of commitment in the face of 'pick and mix' relationships, for Giddens there is a promise of a 'pure' relationship unsullied by prescription or the inheritance of unequal roles.

Reflexive agency and strategic choice-making are not just played out in the context of intimate relationships – increasingly consumer culture predominates as a site of the self's reflexive labour (Smith Maguire and Stanway, 2008). The history of consumer culture observes how the self has been gradually orientated to seek

itself status and distinction from other selves through its engagement with consumer culture as opposed to (solely) employment or
role. From the mid- to late nineteenth century the application of
scientific management, Taylorism, to industrial production boosted
not only the amount of goods produced but reduced the timescale
of their production. In addition, advances in marketing technologies, primarily psychology-influenced and aided by the widespread
popularity of the television, dispelled the guilt once associated with
unnecessary consumption by stressing that exercises of indulgence
and immediate gratification were both 'deserved' and required by
a 'well rounded' self. Laermans' (1993) analysis of the rise of the
department store demonstrates how the visual presentation – the
spectacle – of goods served to ignite consumer desire and insti-
gate degrees of emotional attachment as consumers, immersed in the
spectacle, browsed, strolled and importantly *imagined* the symbolic
power of new products in their lives. Further, the reduction of paid
work hours, the expansion of leisure time and the growth of leisure
industries combined with a relative post-Second World War prosper-
ity allowed more people, more time and better purchasing power
to make browsing, imagining and consuming possible (Paterson,
2006).

In sum, processes of change have led to newly configured relations between the self and consumption which primarily rest on the
recasting of a product's value in terms of its symbolic efficacy – that
to say its ability to circulate within the symbolic domain, investing
and being invested with meanings and emotional attachments to the
degree that even the most mundane of purchases can, and do, say
something about the self. When George Clark, the celebrity architect
of C4's makeover programme *The Home Show,* asks each week 'what
does your shower/sink/toilet/sofa say about you', he is directly refer-
encing the *textuality* of material goods and their importance not just
as 'props' in the story of self, which can be touched, used and read
from and into, but as narrative devices that shape and give future
form to the narrative arc: your shower/sink/toilet/sofa may well say
something about you now, but they also speak volumes about where
you imagine you are going. Consumer culture then becomes the
main site where the self staves off any existential doubt or ontological insecurity, both recognised by Giddens as likely accompaniments

to the pressure of self-construction. It is in consumer culture that we seek meaning, resource the 'ongoing story' and find the means to express and display individuality (Belk et al., 2007; Gartman, 2004).

Jostled self seeks lifestyle for meaningful relationship

What is especially interesting for the purposes of this book is Giddens' argument that the jostled self is drawn to 'lifestyle options', which are not exclusive to, but tend to be constantly paraded in, consumer culture (Giddens, 1991) and particularly within lifestyle media (Gauntlett, 2008; Xu, 2007). As Mike Featherstone (1991, p. 86) explains,

> Rather than unreflexively adopting a lifestyle, through tradition or habit, the new heroes of consumer culture make lifestyle a life project and display their individuality and sense of style in the particularity of the assemblage of goods, clothes, practices, experiences, appearance and bodily dispositions they design together into a lifestyle

Primarily a marketing term 'lifestyle' addresses shared preferences and tastes across otherwise disparate individuals (Maycroft, 2004). Once social class, for example, may have provided sufficient targeting material for advertisers and retailers, allowing them to pitch their goods at presumed class-based collective interests and income. Now, lifestyle allows close niche marketing and 'narrowcasting' by addressing clusters of *individual* tastes as they appear scattered across the 'old' divisions. For some, this is a further indication of the redundancy of collective categorisations like social class and further testimony of the rise of individualism and individuality (Beck and Wilms, 2004). Defined as bundles of preferences, practices and outlooks, that aren't constrained in their scope by 'old' traditional collective tastes, media-paraded lifestyle options offer flexible mooring points for the display of individuality. Lifestyles can be incorporated into a narrative of self-identity and customised through reflexive engagement.

David Gauntlett (2008, p. 112), following on from Giddens, imagines a lifestyle as a 'rather orderly container for identity' coming as it does with a set of expectations. These are neatly evidenced in the following online advertisement targeting a recently celebrity-endorsed lifestyle, the yummy mummy:

> You've decided to listen to our *Yummy Mummy Makeover Teleseminar Series*, and you're undoubtedly excited about getting your own personal makeover. You're going to learn the secrets to:
>
> - Getting back your pre-baby body
> - Developing your own personal style
> - Enjoying a happier, more rewarding relationship
> - Reaching all your personal goals
> - Letting your radiance shine through (http://yummymummy makeover.com/)

I want to draw out three related points from this ad to argue that ordinary lives and ordinary selves are sites of labour and appraisal. The first is the way the advert *defines* the yummy mummy through its list of characteristics (fit, individual, happy, in control and looking good). These characteristics serve to make the lifestyle recognisable, not only to the jostled self but to others. Secondly, if we accept Gauntlett's description of lifestyle as a 'container', we don't simply step into it. *Being* a yummy mummy involves a lot of *doing*. Being recognised as a yummy mummy demands a degree of conspicuous consumption, a certain organisation of time, fashionable clothes and hairstyling, the privileging of leisure time and most importantly the rapid regain of the pre-pregnancy body: the lifestyle becomes a site of ongoing transformations and of self-labour. This brings us to the third point, the 'doing' becomes a portal through which the self comes into contact with experts and their mediatised expertise in time management, nutrition, exercise regimes, goal-realisation and impression management. A battery of expert help mushrooms around lifestyles because as Jennifer Smith Maguire (2008, p. 212) explains, the process of self-construction 'is fraught with risk, insecurity and uncertainty' – we could be getting it wrong: experts direct our aspirations and motivate us to realise them by offering 'guidelines and reassurance (as well as goods and services) to individuals in search of better selves'. Self-help titles such as Susan Callahan et al.'s (2008) *Mothers Need Time Outs Too: It's Good To Be A Little Selfish – It Actually Makes You A Better Mother* and the newly launched *Yummy*

Mummy TV – 'for the woman in every mother' are clear examples of reassurance that the labours and energies spent on the self are vital not only to avoid being subsumed by the roles and duties of motherhood, but to perform those rules and duties *better*. More specifically, as the next chapter explores further, such work carefully ties the doing of lifestyles like the yummy mummy to practices of consumption. For here, it is enough to say that experts and their expertise are a further purchasable resource for the self. Consumer culture then not only offers a lifestyle option but guides further consumer choices to help us to fully live it.

Giddens, concerned about the effects of commodification at play here, worries that a 'standardisation' would simply replace the 'old' traditions that lifestyles could supplant – in which case the strictures of the yummy mummy would simply replace the traditions and role of 'good mother'. But again, it's a flexing of reflexivity, a strategical take-up and deployment of lifestyle that Giddens envisages, so that it's possible to see lifestyles as sites of creativity and unpredictability. As lifestyles are assimilated into ongoing life narratives they are necessarily adapted in accordance with the coherence impulse at the heart of the self-story. Individual agency for the jostled self is thus given increasing scope and responsibility as it is imagined as an 'author' using consumer culture as a resource. That said, the doing involved in lifestyles strongly suggests their performative demands and the need for these to be coherent enough to be recognised, valued and desired (Featherstone, 1991). These may limit the range of creativity that one can enjoy within the lifestyle yummy mummy – its definitional parameters will only stretch so far before it comes unrecognisable or indeed, something else. In sum, however, there is, as Micki McGee (2005) acknowledges, something understandable about the self seeking refuge from the upheavals of vast change by finding meaning in lifestyle options and expert-led guidance. She is unsurprised that times of economic and ontological insecurity bear witness to vast increases in self-help titles and a greater popularity of self-improvement mantras pulsating throughout lifestyle TV and other media.

What we can draw from this section is that the self is forced on a journey of self-creation. Through Giddens we can imagine this self as reflexively armed, busied on an internal project and in reflexively inflected, strategic engagements with others (experts, partners) and the social world. Yet, lifestyle choices made 'freely' are nonetheless governed by a continuity demanded by the biographical trajectory and hedged by the anxiety of getting it wrong. The defining and guidance of how 'yummy mummy' could or should be done suggests something about the ways lifestyles are spun from a nexus of expertise, consumerism, desire and identification to offer some security to a jostled self in its search for meaning and identity. However, it is the *ongoing* nature of acquiring security, the stress on *being* as a matter of *improvement* (thinner, healthier, better organised) that returns us to the question which started this section. The Fat Face buttons have it right: just living *isn't* enough. For Giddens, Beck and others, living is a site of choice-making, endless labour, design and creativity. Sociologist Micki McGee (2005, pp. 15–16) sees the self as 'a site of effort and exertion, of evaluation and management, of invention and reinvention' – even the most ordinary of lives is a series of achievements. And while Giddens nurses hopes for better, democratic relations as a result, once the self is a site of labour, of choice and agency, it is increasingly intelligible to then assess whether that labour is good enough and to ask whether the choices were the right ones made: once life is about 'doing' it is a small step to ask if one is doing enough. In this regard 'making something of one's self' speaks not only to self-construction (just being) but to a project of betterment (being better).

It is tempting here to liken lifestyle media to a cat-walk of expert-guided lifestyle options perused by a meaning-hungry and strategic self. However, this slides us past some of the assumptions of the self that are already starting to circulate in these pages: just who are the selves that Giddens and others imagine as builders of their own lives and authors of their own narratives? Who can be these selves? These questions indicate that there is more that can be said about the self – that while we can accept that the self may be now more a site of labour and of choice than ever before, there is, rightfully, some suspicion of the ways ordinary life and the ordinary self might be specifically imagined as reflexive self-designers.

The jostled self and the fallacy of the blank slate

The Fat face buttons suggest that the choice to 'just live' or not is an individual one. Nike's popular strap-line *Just Do It* is very similar in this respect – you can just *decide* to change your life: there is a 'get going' mentality here, a rally call to action that privileges individual choice and agency over all else. What both ads share with the self-authored, jostled self as it is presented so far is its overwhelming neutrality. I want to discuss this neutrality through Plumridge and Thomson's notion of a blank slate explained in the following quote:

> Giddens' understanding of the making of self-identity as a constant imperative presumes an equal starting place in which choice and reflexivity are fully formed and in the possession of the individual. Empirical work, and particularly longitudinal empirical work, makes it clear that there are *no blank slates* from which to theorize – individuals, including children, are always *already situated and in relationship.*
>
> (Plumridge and Thomson, 2003, p. 221, added emphasis)

The self as a 'blank slate' presumes a self that is unmarked by inscriptions of class, gender, ethnicity and other social divisions, suggesting that we can all be the selves Giddens imagines – we can all 'just do it' – there are no class barriers or race inequalities to overcome or to block our progress. Yet, this presumption sociologist Beverly Skeggs (2004) and other critical voices would argue is the result of a theoretical sleight of hand. It is an illusion that magics the self away from the contexts in which it is defined and from which it garners the knowledge, ways of interpretation and understandings, and resources to know itself and to be itself – contexts which, Skeggs argues, are both inscribed and are inscribers of class, gender and other points of social inequality – a point I want to return to below. For social theorists Lisa Adkins (2000) and Lois McNay (2000) the 'trick' of the self as a blank slate demands a deliberate exaggeration of the effects of detraditionalisation. McNay questions whether the self has been so effectively dislodged from old roles and traditions as Giddens and Beck presume. Meanwhile, Adkins charts the ways a *retraditionalisation* shapes a different 'individuality' for men and women. In her analysis of work and management, she critically notes how men can be rewarded by harnessing 'new' 'feminized' modes of management in the workplace. However, as these 'new' management strategies are also coded as 'essentialised' natural qualities of women, women are not rewarded or indeed might only attract negative attention if they depart from them. The grounds of doing a self are then still characterised by engendered power relations. For these theorists, gender relations and identities persist and *thrive* in such ways that cannot be simply shrugged off through the flexing of reflexivity.

For other critics, such as Ian Burkitt, the 'trick' dismisses the relational, dialogical dimensions of selfhood, whereby the ways we see and know our selves 'can never be disconnected from the ways others see us' (2008, p. 171). Burkitt's argument gestures towards the emotional investment and return, pleasure and security gained from being a socially recognised and socially *approved* self (Butler, 1997). Carol Harrington (2002, p. 110), drawing on Butler, explains that pleasure comes from 'living out' a recognised identity – 'it is the pleasure of being somebody and of escaping not-being'. For Butler it is also about escaping the punishments that are corralled in support of authoritatively recognised identities, helping to make particular lifestyle choices intelligible and *right* (1990). The dialogical nature of selfhood necessarily situates the self 'in relationship' as Plumridge and Thomson argue above, but Burkitt helps to situate the self more specifically within relations of recognition – to be seen, recognised and approved (or not) brings into play a host of culturally specific norms and values against which the self is evaluated. This point considerably dilutes the potency of atomised individualism suggested by the 'blank slate'. As the self is so situated, some questions can be raised of the voluntarism presumed in arguments that lifestyles are taken up by the neutral exercise of choice. As Alice Jones (1993, p. 162) puts it, many of our self-design choices are those 'between being "OK" or "normal" or "weird" – between being on the margins or in the centre'.

Yummies and slummies

It's useful here to return to the yummy mummy advert discussed earlier to consider Jones' point further. Although it is unspoken, the ad cleverly hoists a definitional membrane between the yummy mummy (fit, healthy, relaxed) and her binary opposite and threatening shadow – the *slummy* mummy (unfit, unhealthy, stressed). The relationality between the yummy and the slummy reverberates through other media such as newspaper accounts praising Sarah Michelle Gellar's, star of *Buffy the Vampire Slayer*, return to her pre-pregnancy body and lifestyle within a month of the birth of her daughter; 'with high heels and groomed hair, Gellar, 32, looked nothing like your typical stressed-out new parent' (*Daily Mail*. October, 2009). The *Daily Mail's* celebration, accompanied by before- and after-pregnancy shoots of Geller,[3] reinforces an idea that a specific *doing* is required to avoid a specific threat (of being 'the stressed-out' parent). Geller could be a poster girl for the many lifestyle magazines aimed at pregnant women. Shari Dworkin and Faye Wachs' textual analysis of these notes how 'featured article titles' include 'Secrets to Bouncing Back', 'Getting your Body Back', 'Bouncing Back after Baby', and 'Bounce Back Better than Ever' (2004, p. 616). It would seem from *The Sunday Express* (November 2009) interview with TV presenter, fashion stylist and author Nicky Hambleton-Jones that a plan to 'bounce back' can't start early enough. In an equally celebratory account, Hambleton-Jones discusses her two-year pre-conception regime of weight training and Pilates. Her (reported) intention was to develop a 'core fitness' which would not only restore her to her pre-pregnancy body quickly after the birth, but to also keep the present pregnancy 'bump' itself 'neat' and 'contained'. With her 'enviously neat bump', Hambleton- Jones hopes to inspire other mums and ends the interview saying 'you don't have to become a slummy mummy just because you've got a baby'.

The repeated characteristics (and labours) of the yummy and the invocation of a shadow lifestyle strengthen and support the need for expert intervention so that the self can navigate *within* the yummy and *away* from the slummy – a navigation between the 'centre' and the 'margins' as Alice Jones would have it. The navigational work, the *feeling one's way,* and the increasingly normalised notion that mothers should be steering this path are clearly expressed in the many self-help books, TV shows, websites and blogs for 'ordinary' moms concerned about school-gate couture (getting it right seems to have a positive effect on a child's rate of playdate invitations); the success of one's relationships and the all-important hold on independence and a 'sense of self' (for example superkawaiimama.com and sofeminine.co.uk). Thinking about the self 'as in relationship' then, strongly suggests that the self negotiates a sense of belonging, recognition and *itself,* within a context of expertise, social norms and values which define the 'normal' and 'OK'. The pleasure in getting it right derives from the benefits gained for the 'woman in every mother', her sexual relationships and the social success of her children – in short the rewards which fall from inhabiting a recognisable position to prevailing norms and moral frameworks. These points encourage us to heap suspicion upon the assumptions of the 'blank slate' and serve to overcome its trick of decontextualisation by regarding the self as always situated. They also open up space to consider more carefully the appraising frameworks of culturally specific norms and values through which the self negotiates recognition and the subsequent pleasures of being. This is something that is explored further in the next chapter.

The abundance of self-help 'top-tips' helping mothers convert from the slummy to the yummy would suggest an inclusivity. Any mummy can be yummy, it's simply a matter of organisation and practicalities – 'your stilettos aren't exactly practical now...but trainers just aren't glam! Opt for some sparkly ballet pumps instead – they're both practical and stylish' urges the TV morning magazine show GMTV (http://www.gm.tv/lifestyle/families-and-parenting/34538-yummy-v-slummy.html). It would be reasonable to suggest that the levels of consumerism necessary for the yummy mummy lifestyle would exclude many, regardless of the money-saving tips GMTV offer (doing your own manicures when the children are in bed is one such tip). However, thinking about the self as situated forces closer attention to the possible ways in which class and other points of social division are enfolded into lifestyles, despite or because of their blank slate presumptions. Motherhood presents an interesting example because feminist analysis of the institution and cultural representations of motherhood have long noted that while the desire to be a mother continues as a central feature of hegemonic femininity (Dworkin and Wachs, 2004), some women, or rather some 'types' of women, are repeatedly constructed and represented as unsuitable, bad and even 'dangerous' mothers (Cassiman, 2008; Daniels, 1997; Lloyd, 1995). In this case, it's possible to see how certain identities, lifestyles and subjectivities are unavailable for some women.

For Beverly Skeggs (2004) and fellow sociologists, Steph Lawler (2005) and Imogen Tyler (2008), images of maternal villains are heavily classed and enjoy a repeated circulation across a range of media. Comedy shows *(Little Britain)*, Lifestyle TV (*What Not To Wear, You Are What You Eat, Honey We're Killing The Kids*), as well as 'satirical' websites (urbandictionary.com, chavscum.com), comic strips, talkshows, news reportage and graphic novels that construct the white, working-class mother as a distinct social type – an 'abject person with a mismanaged life' (McRobbie, 2004, p. 102). Although class is rarely spoken as such, it is successfully coded along three overlapping lines, which sociologist Andrew Sayer (2005) identifies as those of the aesthetic (appearance, bearing and taste), the performative (behaviour, such as poor parenting) and the moral (attitudes and will, for example 'choosing' a life of welfare dependency). It is along these lines that historical and contemporary anxieties over reproduction, poor parenting, 'welfare mums', excessive consumption, tastelessness (bling!), teenage pregnancy, foetal harm and wider concerns about the degeneracy of the working class more generally are effectively swept into over-determined, crass caricatures of overly emotional, ignorant, aggressive, white, working-class mothers (Tyler, 2008). Through these representations, the working-class mum is constructed as a risk not only to her children but to the moral ordering of society itself.

Why this over-determination? It would be a mistake to regard this as a matter of middle-class people 'looking down' on working-class people (Lawler, 2005). It is more instructive to see the coding of the working-class mum as 'slummy' as part of a wider process of what Imogen Tyler (2008) and others have identified as 'class making'. By this, they refer to processes of 'othering' through which the middle classes defend, reassert and justify their own moral worth by recasting the working class as pathological villains – as *unworthy*. As social psychologists Holt and Griffin argue, 'othering enables the middle classes to focus on aspects of their identities which they wish to hold up as defining their groups' characteristics (e.g. middle class taste, intelligence, refinement), while denying these characteristic to the working class Other' (2005, p. 248). A successful ring-fencing of taste and refined sensibilities as middle-class involves attentive border work and policing. The levels of symbolic violence involved neatly scaffold and promote values of individualism and autonomy by making it a *moral imperative* that 'good' mothers should demonstrate their engagement in self-development and transformation. The 'right' pram, the 'right' attitude to an independent self, to the before and after pregnant body, and relationships all signal a morally coded care of the self – what Skeggs (2004) would also refer to as a self-*investment* – an imperative fuelled in part by a fear and disgust of dependency and poverty as embodied by the slummy mom (Lawler, 2005).

This border work deftly displaces the causes and solutions of poverty and class injustice from the structural (the organisation and ordering of society) on to the individual. This aspect of lifestyle, in relation to lifestyle media, will be explored further in Chapter 2, however, it's important to stress here that the 'Just do it' mentality and the blank slate thinking on which it depends and supports imagine poverty as a choice, a failure of will and as a lack of self-determination (Cassiman, 2008, p. 1693). It's possible to imagine how this mentality energises the motivation to navigate one's way towards the Yummy and to the 'OK' and 'normal' while denigrating those who fail to make this journey. It is imperative then that the slummy is *always* found lacking – that she cannot be easily transformed by practical time-management or by replacing her unglamorous training shoes with trendy ballet-style pumps – although it is equally as important to the purported universality of middle-class values, that, at times, she tries.

Situating the self

It's possible to argue that the universalised, blank individualism of Giddens' self is conjured with scant account of *context* – that is, the social, political, economic, cultural, temporal, material and spatial forces and resources in which selves are, as Plumridge and Thomson have it, 'always already situated'. There are two useful points to draw out here. Firstly, to regard the self as situated is to claim that there is an environment of (structural) opportunities and restraints within which we all have to negotiate. With this in mind, while 'the self appears in Giddens as a *neutral* concept available to all' Skeggs argues that the making of a self and the reflexive production of a self-biography is 'dependent on access to discourse and resources' which are not equally accessible (2004, p. 53). When we account for contextual relations we start to see a constant scramble for those material and discursive resources, the imposition of group interests and the protection and contestation of privileges in the realisation of reflexive choices (Adams, 2007). The doing of a self then, in particular the doing of an *individual* self, might not be an achievement that is freely open to all but the very grounds and consequences of embattled power relations. It is here that we find class, gender and 'race' and so on far from being irrelevant, emerging as revitalised battle lines. At least, it may then be appropriate to argue for a *structured individualism* whereby individualism is mediated through existing social and cultural divisions (Roberts et al., 1994).

Secondly, to regard the self as 'always already situated' invites us to regard contexts not as backdrop or even as a playground for a self, but the very media thorough which the self is possible and viable. As Foucault (1988) argues, the self as a historically specific category cannot pre-exist the discursive mix that generates it and breathes life into it. For Judith Butler (2005) advancing Foucault's thinking, a legitimate and culturally recognisable self is one constituted through social norms. The self is produced and imagined in contexts that sociologists sensibly argue bear the markings and consequences of class, gender and 'race'. To be *in* context, to be only *known* and to *know* through contextual relations raises major challenges to Giddens' image of the self, which as Skeggs (2004) puts it is somehow able to *step outside* of itself to regard contexts as merely a site of resources to be picked over. We are left then with strong suspicions that resources required for self-build may not be freely or neutrally available to all, and too, that the plays of social divisions mean that not all selves are positioned equally or neutrally in relation to them: a suggestion then that the maldistribution of resources is accompanied by a mal-construction of selves. Attention is then beckoned towards the ways cultural representations of the self and its realisation and intelligibility through transformation are constructed and with what consequence. Lifestyle media starts to look like an important site of inquiry for critical concerns about the self and its biography.

Complicity, choice and blank slate thinking

Skeggs' (2004) forensic attention to the decontextualising nature of Giddens' work and of the individualisation thesis more widely delivers a further devastating blow to any suggestion of neutrality. It is through her work that we can see that the trick of the 'blank slate' is like all other tricks, an effect of labour and concentration. It is not an accidental or clumsy starting point for theorisation, but rather it is the materialisation of a particularly imagined self, carefully conjured in the cultural domain. Pertinent questions may well gravitate around issues of what the 'blank slate' thinking misses out in terms of the context-specific power relations sketched out above, but Skeggs also demands attention to just what this thinking obscures and with what consequence. The salience of these questions is perhaps best evidenced in Helen Mirza's (1997) critique of the power and consequences of Whiteness as an unmarked racial category:

> Whiteness that powerful place that makes invisible, or re-appropriates things, people and places it does not want to see or hear, and then through misnaming, renaming or not naming at all, invents the truth – what we are told is 'normal', neutral, universal, simply become the way it is.
>
> (Mirza, 1997, p. 3)

The seeing/not seeing and naming/not naming/misnaming that Mirza pinpoints here are the cultural labours of the blank slate and the unmarked. To name and remain unnamed, to inscribe and remain unmarked are 'the effects of...domination' (Frankenberg, 1993, p. 6) – a domination that is secured through processes by which the unmarked aims to be the unthought, *habitual* normalised referent against which all Others are defined and known. More specifically it is the herding of the unmarked's investments, anxieties, panics and desires into specific inscriptions on Others that force homosexuality, the working classes, femininity, ethnicity, *inter alia*, to oscillate between culturally constructed poles of the fantastical and the patho-logical (Hill Collins, 1990). For Skeggs there are two upshots of this. The first is that such projections, significantly repeated, are distilled and condensed so that they appear as *essential* characteristics of the Other. On one hand, this severely constrains the mobility and access to resources required by the self-authored self, because the Other is *fixed* by the binds of essentialised traits, which may be variously and interchangeably culturally coded as say, 'cool', 'authentic' and 'dan-gerous' (none of which she argues serves well in a job interview). On the other hand, Skeggs argues that these distillations can them-selves be resources and playthings for the privileged self who can pick them up, try them on, experiment and dally (albeit with a range of intentions), with little sacrifice to their own unmarked status with its 'non-stick' surfaces of class, 'race', gender and sexual privilege.

The second upshot for Skeggs is that blank slate thinking reflects the epistemic and cultural privileges of their authors. Those who enjoy social mobility and the freedom of reinvention; who are best placed to flourish in a world of fragmentation; and who are already unmarked have created a theory in their own likeness to explain their own lives. From a position of privilege, it is all too easy to deny the gritty relations of class, gender and so on. Ros Gill (2008a) also draws out the bitter consequences, accusing such social theory of being *complicit* in the very neoliberal social and economic power relations and rhetoric it should be critical of. For Gill, this complicity abounds in the seemingly casual ways in which some social science research equates 'agency' with 'empowerment'. She argues that once arguments around women's wearing of the veil or their objectification in the sex industry, for example, were highly complex and politically charged. Yet now, there is a tendency to read agency as flowing from freely selected choices. Further, she notes in such research an increasingly pernicious equation that converts the making of choice into an act of empowerment. As political cartoonist Elena Steier illustrates below, it now seems that it is women's *choice* to engage in practices that were once deemed objectifying – indeed, there is a prevailing sense in some social theory and in the popular imagination that exploitation is no longer exploitation if it is freely chosen – it may even be empowering (Negra, 2009). Steier isn't] convinced!

The state of empowerment

Skeggs and Gill lend their voices to a growing chorus of concern that the enthusiastic and uncritical celebration of choice and individual agency effectively purge both from the contextual relations which shape 'doing' (Brannen and Nilsen, 2005; Gordon et al., 2005; Wray, 2004). It denies the ways contextual power relations not only outline *which* choices are made available and specifically directed along gendered lines, for example, but which also frame choices in such ways that they are only intelligible and accessible to select groups. There is a neglect too of the realisation that *a lack* of material resources may force some choices and that the taking up and living out of others requires certain material means not readily accessible to all: as Bauman argues 'all of us are doomed to the life of choices, but not all of us have the means to be the choosers' (1998, p. 86). It's important to stress that to advocate that contextual forces are considered and exposed by social theory does not deny the complexities of agency nor does it suggest a return to so-called victim theorisations, whereby models of repressive power negated the creativity of agency (McNay, 2000; Raisborough and Bhatti, 2007). It is, however, to argue for a political sensitivity to the contexts in which agency is realised and expressed.

Before we leave this chapter it is important to note how the term 'lifestyle' is conjured from the same trick of de-contextualisation already noted in relation to the self. Neil Maycroft (2004), for example, argues that the ubiquitous use of 'lifestyle' (from health to cultural diversity to consumer choices) denies it any definitional clarity but nonetheless enables it to convey an abundance and freedom of choice and to equate choice to quality of life. This gives 'lifestyle' a certain 'lightness' which exfoliates 'social differences of wealth, opportunity, class, gender, ethnicity, as well as obscuring global and historical inequalities' (2004, p. 61). Maycroft's is not a lone voice. Feminist scholar Diane Negra notes with some despair how the consumer spectacle of lifestyle choices serves to 'neutralize and camouflage looming crises of natural resources and the persistence of poverty' (2009, p. 118).

Additionally critical disquiet has gathered around the presumed ease of choice-making; health care and national health promotion, for example, utilise notions of 'lifestyle' to suggest that, say, healthy eating and safe sex are choices within anyone's power to make. The

Nike call to 'just do it' would not be out of place in the recent UK £75 million 'Change 4 Life' health promotion campaign which encourages the population to exercise their bodies and their intellect by making the 'right' (healthy) eating choices. Leaving aside the doubts cast upon the bio-medical evidence linking lifestyle with health, there is much concern that many of the causes of ill health are by-products of unjustly stratified social organisation not of poor individual choices (see Fitzpatrick, 2000; Roy, 2008). The aggressive nature of agribusiness, the existence of 'food deserts', where healthy food is inaccessible in areas of social deprivation, combined with financial obstacles and cultural patterns around food preparation and consumption, all conspire to make the 'right' food choices difficult at best and unimaginable at worse (McEntee and Agyman, 2010; Probyn, 2008). Similarly, empirical explorations of sexual practice cast further doubt on the ease of choice-making. The question of whether to use condoms or not may seem a straight-forward personal and intimate choice, but when raised in heterosexual relations it is one that demands careful negotiation within a discursive nexus of risk, sexual scripts, notions of romance and desire, and prevailing gender norms (Gavey et al. 2001; Vitellone, 2002). In short, there are degrees of contextual complexity tied into any choice-making which are effaced under the term 'lifestyle'.

Summary

Lifestyle media is saturated with the implication that 'just living' is not enough and with suggestions to make life better. Processes of social change have jostled the self out of once pre-given trajectories, creating a self that is forced to embark on a journey of its own making and lifestyle options offer handy anchor points for a self-in-the-making. While the image offered in lifestyle media and accredited by some social theory is that of a de-contextualised, supernatant self, this chapter has gone someway to argue that the self and its reflexivity are only intelligible and possible through historically specific and contextually sensitive relations. The self is then 'always already situated and in relationship' (Plumridge and Thomson, 2003, p. 221). What this chapter has argued is that context *matters* – a realisation that opens up ways for us to seriously consider the plays of social divisions and inequalities, in short, power relations in those contexts.

In conclusion, this chapter has argued that not everyone can be the selves Giddens imagines. If the English adage has it right, only the *clean slate* is considered to be the start and pre-requisite for a journey of self-transformation. Marked slates, those marked by strategic inscriptions of class, are culturally fixed by, and harvested for, the identity work of the unmarked. Social divisions then still matter and the trick of the universal self-authored self is to hide, yet re-circulate relations of privilege and disadvantage. The 'get going' mentality chanted through Fat Face and Nike advertising may look like rallying cries motivating the individual to do more than 'just live', but we may hear them as invitations for the unmarked self to flex the privileges of its mobility and a call of judgement which finds those fixed by symbolic systems of constraint as lacking – as 'not enough'.

From here a different approach to lifestyle media is possible. Far from a trivial and popular parade of lifestyle options and consumer choices, from the yummy mummy to the ambitious go-getting sofa, questions can be raised about its neutrality and its consequences. We are encouraged to ask questions concerning what self is being imagined, sold, shaped and normalised within the symbolic repertoires that make up what Gill calls our 'cultural habitat' (2008a, p. 434). Following on from Gill then, cultural representations *matter* because 'their relationship to subjectivity is too important' to ignore (p. 434) and as lifestyle media has been defined as that concerned with the management and betterment of the self (Lewis, 2008) it offers a fertile space to chart that which matters.

2
Makeover Culture: Becoming a Better Self

> Self-improvement is a continuing process that lasts a life-time. Be good to yourself. You deserve to be the best you can be.
>
> Thompson (1999, p. 1)

Introduction

Cecily Mwaniki's self-help book *Becoming the Better You* hit the shops in 2009 to fight for a share of an annual $13 billion US market. It jostles for shelf-space among a host of other titles enticing readers onto the path of becoming a better parent, lover, friend or *Becoming the Best Version of Yourself* – the title Matthew Kelly's (2002) motivational CD recording. Like the others, Mwaniki's book facilitates the process of becoming a better you through encouragement and an expert-designed action plan of visualisation, practical steps and rules. It's clear that becoming better requires work and a campaign strategy. These points are most dramatically underscored in Gael Lindenfield's (2000) *Self Esteem: Simple Steps to Develop Self-Worth and Heal Emotional Wounds,* who encourages her readers to 'survey the enemy field', 'fly the flag and declare war', 'sharpen your weapons' and 'lay plans for victory day'. These battle rally–cries indicate something of the heroic effort involved in becoming a better you, and of course, it's the skirmishes of these battles that make up most Lifestyle TV programming. Shows, in particular the makeover show, are filled with often unflinching detailed commentary on the labours of becoming thinner, uncluttered or fashionable. *What Not To Wear*, for example, devotes more airtime to the trails of becoming appropriately fashionable than it does the end result. What these lifestyle shows and self-help books share with the Fat Face buttons discussed in the previous chapter is the conviction that 'being' is not enough; but they also suggest something else: they celebrate and promote the importance, vitality and heroics of a project of *becoming*.

It's worth thinking about the word 'becoming' – it mingles a sense of movement and transformation to be an improved self with ceaselessness. It takes another word to mark an end to that movement – 'becoming' has its own internal momentum. In English usage 'becoming' also refers to appearance and manner. It indicates the 'decorous' and 'aesthetically pleasing', and also the 'suitable' and 'appropriate' (Allen, 1990). There is something interesting held in these different usages; there is a play of endless movement and yet, a certain fixity that comes from a sense that something has to be *in place* to be coded and recognised as 'suitable' and 'pleasing'. Mary Douglas' (1966), and more recently William Miller's (1997), argument that dirt and the disgusting are merely 'matter out of place' underscores the importance of 'place' in its widest terms – not only as physical, but as a positioning within culturally specific codes, frameworks of recognition and commonsense knowledge. The word 'becoming' then beckons attention towards those codes and contexts, to encourage this chapter to explore how particular journeys of self-transformation and their happy endings, as variously narrated through lifestyle media, become suitable and appropriate – how they are *in place*.

This chapter does so by situating lifestyle media specifically within what Meredith Jones (2008) identifies as a 'makeover culture' – a cultural ethos and logic that privileges processes of becoming over being. If the previous chapter argued that being was not enough and thus recast the self as a site of labour, this chapter makes the stronger claim that those labours, and 'being' itself, are increasingly intelligible as ceaseless projects of becoming in neoliberal Western democracies. Once this claim is made, this chapter moves to unpick two specific themes of lifestyle media, 'the mundane' and 'efficiency' which promote and entice the self into certain modes and practices of becoming. In short, this chapter is about situating lifestyle media and then explaining its own particular shape and characteristics in relation to a neoliberal project.

Makeover culture

'Becoming' preoccupies Meredith Jones (2008) whose notion of a makeover culture leads us in to a consideration of the social and political contexts in which lifestyle media flourishes. Jones' realisation of the makeover culture occurred during what she calls her 'Jerry Springer moment', which is worth recounting here:

> The programme [Jerry Springer] was about friends and family telling their loved ones how embarrassed they are because they dress inappropriately. In most cases the problem was that an overweight middle-aged woman was 'dressing like a teenager'. An obese woman appeared on stage wearing a micro-mini frock and high heels. Her waiting family members shook their heads in disgust and the audience booed and jeered. But then Springer said she had recently lost 100 pounds and the audience boos changed to cheers, and the woman sat down proudly, ready to defend her right to wear skimpy clothes.
>
> (p. 11)

The sudden sea-change from jeers to cheers led Jones to reflect that what was praiseworthy was not just the loss of weight, but the fact that the woman was in process of losing it. The visual result remained the same – still an overweight woman in 'inappropriate' clothing – but the woman was recast, through Jerry Springer's commentary, from a figure of ridicule to a woman in the process of transformation: from (fat)being to one engaged in the process of becoming (thinner). Jones' 'Jerry Springer moment' furnished her with two important insights. The first is that becoming better is valorised over a final completed project and secondly that the labour of becoming better (in this case the battle involved in losing weight) is integral to its valorisation. Both are clearly evident in makeover TV shows. *Ten Years Younger*, a show which aims to reduce a participant's visible age through cosmetic surgery and less-invasive techniques, is taken up with identifying the 'problems' of age (in many cases, the causes are poor lifestyle choices), the solution (expert intervention) and in filming the pain, misery and sheer determination of the participant to survive the process. The end result is only screened in the final minutes of the show's airtime. Joanne Morreale (2007) has observed the same narrative device in the show *Faking It.* Airtime is devoted to displays of the participant's 'painful labour' as they learn to 'fake' a new identity (2007, p. 99), but Morreale adds that these labours are further emphasised as the show includes footage of participants intimately confessing their struggles, doubts and pain into hand-held cameras. She concludes that evidence of a participant's suffering adds a vital patina of authenticity to the labours of becoming. Meredith Jones would argue that what we see across these shows is a spreading open and slowing down of the gap between the traditional 'before' and 'after' shot. This leads her to conclude that what is important, entertaining and audience-pulling is less the result, but how that result was achieved. Her definition of makeover culture is then 'a state where *becoming* is more desirable than *being*' (p. 12, original emphasis).

That there is a morality involved is evident in the ways that pro- cesses of becoming are judged. By way of example, Carnie Wilson, the American singer, and Anne Diamond, the UK newsreader and TV pre- senter, both faced public outrage when they resorted to gastric band surgery as a solution to their weight gain. Analysis of the media cov- erage of Wilson's televised surgery has offered instructive contrasts with the media coverage of Tracey Gold, the US Actress who was hos- pitalised when her weight dropped to 90 pound through anorexia. Ferris (2003) argued that while Gold's publicised battles with will- power and strength of character won the hearts of her viewing public, Wilson's surgical move was deemed a cheat. Ferris concluded that while Wilson's body looked the part, it was regarded as 'rude and arro- gant by skipping all procedures and protocols. It took on a surgical action, skipping the culturally condoned steps of diet, physical stress and strain and consumer related weight loss' (2003, p. 270). Similarly, Anne Diamond, one of the celebrity contestants on the 2006 edition of the UK weight-loss show *Celebrity Fit Club,* was condemned for her surgery while her fellow contestants underwent the pain and hard- ships of a military regime of exercise, diet and lifestyle changes. What we can draw from this is that the 'easy' route and the self who under- takes it is a cheat: only hard labour and effort secure a respectable, authentic and morally praiseworthy process of becoming. Inciden- tally, this goes someway to explain how the contemporary popularity and growing acceptability of cosmetic surgery has involved gruelling in-surgery footage and why painstaking and gory recovery periods are aired on shows like *Extreme Makeover* and *Ten Years Younger*. While the shots of blood and gore might be expected to put people off, instead it serves to elevate the moral acceptability of surgery as it reveals its own laborious journey. This is a point not lost on Anne Diamond's publicists who over 2008 and 2009 released the 'full story' of Anne's long battles with weight and her survival from 'botched up' surgery to restore her to the public's affections.

To return to Jones, she is not suggesting that 'being' is replaced by 'becoming', but rather that *'becoming' increasingly becomes the ways in which 'being' is done.* For our purposes, this means that the taking up of a lifestyle, such as the yummy mummy, is not an end in itself, but rather that lifestyle options become sites for the expenditure of continuous energies and concern. As this chapter's opening quote illustrates, betterment and self-improvement are endless. Indeed, for Jones, the activities of becoming are increasingly coded as the activities of life itself: to stop, to have reached betterment and perfection, to be the best you can be, to be a 'finished product' relegates the self *outside* of intelligible life. If life is the activity of becoming better, then being better can be understood as moments where energies are forcefully stilled, where life is 'not enough' and the self occupies what Jones likens to a 'still life' and spaces of the 'living dead' (p. 147). The fact that many makeover shows have 'revisits' where presenter-experts surprise past participants to see just how they are 'getting on' with their 'new look' testifies to the expectation that ongoing labours are necessary. 'Revisits' also suggests that lifestyles are themselves launching pads for new ventures beyond simply maintenance. The point here is that the happy endings offered by journeys of transformation may be momentarily experienced, but more often than not they are deferred – or more correctly, they are points of entry for new journeys.

There are two related lines in Jones' argument that I wish to take further over this and the next chapter. The first is the heightened need for visibility. In order for 'becoming' to be recognised, it must be seen, displayed and known by others. As we might conclude from the cautionary tales of Carnie Wilson and Anne Diamond there has to be a 'visible act of labouring' (p. 57) to becoming – a sudden transformation is a cheat. There is then the vital dimension of 'public performance of moving from one self to another' (p. 57) and this will occupy the discussion of the next chapter. The second, explored here, is that visible performances of becoming are neatly enfolded into contemporary constructions of the 'good' citizen. In the makeover culture, good citizenship is forged from the self-determination, discipline and labour necessary for an endless project of becoming better: 'good citizens of makeover culture effect endless renovations, restorations and maintenance on themselves and their environments, stretching and designing their faces, their bodies, their ages, and their connections with technologies and other bodies' (Jones, 2008, p. 189). So strong is the connection between becoming and citizenship that Jones argues that the makeover has left the realms of aspirational, wishful thinking to become increasingly etched as a cultural imperative – as that which must be done.

Becoming and the self

The ideal citizen of the makeover culture is clearly premised on the enterprising, calculating, highly individualised self required by neoliberal organisation and rationality. Neoliberalism has been introduced in the opening of this book as referring to a 'retreat of the state' and the heaping of responsibility, often bundled with packages of 'rights', on to the individual. One manifestation of the displacement of state responsibility to the self is a cultural politics imagining the self as obliged to improve – a self often referred to as the entrepreneurial self – for whom biography is a project, improvement is the goal and who will bend the body and mind to the self-discipline and increasing self-surveillance demanded (Roy, 2008). Widely understood as a means of 'governing at a distance' (Miller, 2007), these activities are argued to create a self who is flexible, adaptable and mobile enough to meet the demands of an ever-changing, fluid labour market; a 'Jack of all trades' (Bauman, 2007, p. 9). While there is some scope here for an enterprising self to find places and resources to position themselves more favourably in discourses and traditions of class, gender duties and racialised expectations, we need to exercise care here to avoid replicating the 'blank slate' thinking discussed in the previous chapter. Critic Toby Miller (2007, p. 5) cautions against any easy celebration of an enterprising self by stating that the United States with its advanced neoliberalism 'has become the least socially mobile advanced Western economy. Frankly, it is a not a First World country for a fifth of its inhabitants'.

The previous chapter went some way to argue that while some were free to engage in a mobile selfhood, others were culturally fixed. Valerie Walkerdine (2003, p. 239) is among those who have dissected the norms of neoliberalism to argue that the autonomous, entrepreneurial self is 'made in the image of the middle class' and constructed in relation to a 'deficient' Other – the working class. This awareness invites us to be alert to the ways that normalised neoliberal rationalities are so strongly classed as to afford middle-class values a certain universality, which, in turn, effaces their classed heritage (see Savage, 2003). Judith Butler (2005, p. 7) is clear that universality is not 'by definition' symbolically nor ethically violent – but rather that there are conditions and contexts 'under which it can exercise violence'. These conditions, for Butler, are found in the effacing and invisibility of the ways the self is shaped and imagined. She reminds us that 'there is no "I" that is not implicated in a set of condition-ing social norms' (p. 7), indeed it is those norms that render the self an 'I' – that is, as culturally recognisable and *valid*. The concern here is not just that specific contour lines emerge around the valid/invalid self which necessarily become lines of symbolic violence and exclusion, but that, for Butler, they create the means by which the self is possible and thus create points of entry to and rejection from humanhood itself. Butler understands this as involving a dual pro-cess of *doing* – taking on those norms and *undoing* – making the self *fit*. Here, Butler nudges us out of a solely class emphasis to consider the ways that humanhood is defined, naturalised and accessed along intersecting lines of gender, ethnicity, sexuality, nationality *inter alia*.

In terms of the makeover culture, it's the manufacture of the partic-ular into universal norms of conduct and personal worth that create a specific cultural climate whereby we are *all* increasingly morally obliged to engage in the performance of becoming. As Meredith Jones says of the makeover culture, it has become a 'mode of being' (2008, p. 55) – the means by which we claim a culturally intelligible self. Yet, this manufacture favours those whose lives it speaks to and from (Palmer, 2004) and while policing those serves to exercise violence on those found lacking – or as Fat Face buttons, in Chapter 1, have it – as 'not enough'. Butler (2004, 2005) would go further to argue that the plays of social norms on the constitution of the self demark those who can access *liveable lives* and force Others in to unlive-able margins. It is the political passion of such realisations that lead sociologists like Mike Savage to argue that social scientists should take up 'a kind of forensic, detective work' that enables 'normality…to be carefully unpicked' (2003, p. 537) – in other words, not to produce a complicit, uncritical social theory that Beverly Skeggs and Ros Gill were so critical of in the previous chapter. I want to start some forensic unpicking by suggesting that there are two aspects of 'becoming' in the journey of self-transformation; *becoming a citizen*, which via Jones we could argue is achieved though the visual displays of transformation, and that of being *a becoming citizen* – one who is 'in place' – who belongs and is deemed 'appropriate' – in short those wider usages of the term 'becoming' in terms of current social norms. Both are evident in Jones' 'Jerry Springer moment', so it's worth a revisit.

Revisiting the Jerry Springer moment

Social psychologists Hélène Joffe and Christian Staerklé (2007) have identified self-control as the core component in Western individualism. They argue that 'crucially, being a socially respected "self", western style requires maintaining active control over one's desires, emotions and actions' (p. 402). Theorists of the body concur, finding that, in Western influenced cultures, the fat or fleshy body is often coded as excessive and 'out of control', both of which signify a 'failed individual morality' (Dworkin and Wachs, 2004, p. 611). This coding takes on added significance in societies facing the so-called obesity epidemic which tend to present the 'problem' of fat in terms of the perceived economic costs of an ailing and unproductive fat population; as sociologist Lee Monaghan argues, in such social landscapes 'the fat body' constitutes 'a personal and social liability' (2007, p. 585). Thinking about how values of control frame bodies and morality allows us to suggest that the overweight woman in Jones' Jerry Springer moment was cheered because she presented as a 'socially respected self'. The overweight woman did not just lose weight; she wasn't just becoming thinner – although this activity is deemed praiseworthy through biomedical discourses that forge equivalence between 'fat', 'disease' and 'dependency' – something else occurred too. By presenting her 100-pound lighter body, she placed herself within a culturally valorised rhetoric and display of transformation, a body in process of becoming, *and* she presented her allegiance to neoliberal values of self-control and its associates, self-discipline, self-responsibility and self-management: she presented as *a becoming citizen* – as one 'appropriate' and in place to prevailing social norms. As such, she was cheered by an audience ready to condemn an inappropriate body and self.

Interestingly, her placement in the rhetoric of transformation recoded her body from 'fat' to 'becoming thinner' and shifted her body and moral self from the 'margins' of cultural acceptability to having a claim on the 'centre' as Alice Jones (1993) would put it (see Chapter 1). I would argue that her fat body was *temporarily* rehabilitated by this positioning work (I stress the temporal condition here, as the 'fat body' even recoded, can only be rehabilitated to the degree that it can align itself to respectable, and what Skeggs (2004) would call *respectablising*, practices and values of becoming better). It's this rehabilitation, the public occupancy of social norms, that gives the woman the *legitimacy* to tell her story – in Butler's (2005) words to 'give an account' of herself *as a culturally intelligible self*, in ways acceptable and intelligible to the audience. The overweight woman is able then to defend her right to wear skimpy clothes – at least for the time being. Before I leave this, I want to quickly add that while the visible effort to secure a temporary rehabilitation deserves cheers, we might also want to think about the ways this supports the construction of those who are structurally and culturally disadvantaged (those who are 'fixed' as Skeggs would say), as blameworthy for being unrecuperable and irredeemable individuals – *for not making the effort.*

My point is a simple one – there are specific, socially sanctioned, ways of becoming and of 'being' a self. It is not *any* transformation, nor any labours of becoming which themselves are the key – 'any-old' change, effort or presentation of these will not do: only those which are deemed 'appropriate' by the (middle-classed)norms of neoliberalism are deserving of cheers. Following from Butler, the acts of becoming have to be related to prevailing social norms so that a self in process of being better can be recognised and appraised. There are issues of identification at work in this line of argument, but I want to place these on hold until later chapters. For now, playing with the different meanings of 'becoming' allows me to focus on the question of 'what' are we becoming, what are we working towards and what is shaping the ways we imagine and practice the journey of self-transformation. I want to make more headway in unpicking the neutrality that accompanies highly individualised accounts of the self as this chapter now leads into a breakdown of the key features of lifestyle media with an exploration of the relationship of becoming and consumer capitalism. I do so to further stress the deeply social specificity of selfhood.

The self goes to market

Neoliberalism is not, of course, just about social norms and values directing 'becoming'. It is, in essence, an expanding, colonialising economic rationality which philosopher Axel Honneth (2004, p. 475) describes as causing 'the creeping metamorphosis of the whole society into a market'. This 'creeping' depends on a rampant individualism, discussed in the previous chapter, and a valorisation of choice. As Clarke and Newman (2007) note, many models of choice exist, but the choices which lubricate the 'creeping' of neoliberalism are economic ones. The prevailing, hegemonic model of 'choice' is that which speaks to a 'competition between providers' – be they fashion gurus, surgeons or primary schools for one's kids – and also to the needs and agency of a 'sovereign consumer in pursuit of individual wants' (Clarke and Newman, 2007, p. 741). The important relations of marketisation, individualisation and choice are acutely realised by Neil Maycroft (2004) who reminds us that 'lifestyle' is primarily a marketing term created to help advertisers target and direct our choice-making in consumer culture. He uses this to extend the argument that 'personal identity is bound up with the regular acquisition of material possessions' (Billig, 1999, p. 316; Wee and Brooks, 2010), to claim that life itself is increasingly resourced, expressed and experienced through consumer culture. The current popularity of 'lifestyle', he argues, forms part of a wider shift to the greater *commodification of life*. Maycroft's concern is that the commodification of life denies other ways of living 'it acts as a consumerist carapace, resisting and defending against the possibilities of a life lived away from consumerism' (p. 62), and that it does so by exaggerating the aesthetic pleasures of choice-making in consumer culture. These pleasures, as Marx has argued in terms of the commodity fetish, are dependent on the masking of necessarily exploitative relations of Western consumerism. In short, for Maycroft there is a naturalisation of consumer capitalism working through lifestyle, which he argues is the very means of 'handing over of life to the market' (p. 62).

Nick Fox and Katie Ward's analysis of what they call the pharmaceuticalisation of everyday life concurs (2008, p. 856). Since the 1990s they have noted that drug companies sell their products less on their ability to cure a disease and more on improving quality of lifestyle. Linda Blum and Nena Stracuzzi's (2004) analysis of the psychopharmaceutical Prozac offers a useful illustration. Not only is Prozac 'sold' through magazine covers *(Vanity Fair)*, news reportage, TV talk shows and other popular media, but it is framed as an alternative to the sedation offered by drugs like Valium. Prozac promises to restore and enhance an individual's mood and self-esteem. More specifically, the drug is touted as a means of improving one's disposition to the demands of work: subsequent increased productivity and efficiency are all linked to Prozac. This 'sales pitch' is clear to see in two vignettes pulled by Blum and Stracuzzi from national media:

> James', a 41-year-old ex-lawyer, realised 'his mood, not the original job', was the problem. 'Back on the job and on Prozac, James recalled a 'particularly busy spell', when 'he paused mid-frenzy and thought 'God, I'm so efficient. I've never been able to handle this much work' *(New York)*...'Helen', a public relations executive, who had been 'paralyzed' by 'looming deadlines' but found on Prozac, she 'juggled' competing priorities 'gracefully', 'with a more buoyant personality'.
>
> *(Newsweek)* (2004, p. 278)

So successful is this pitch that some corporations have encouraged 'sluggish workers' to take Prozac – a buoyant over-efficient worker seems too good an opportunity to miss (Blum and Stracuzzi, 2004). What we can add here is that an individual's 'choice' to seek such a remedy to a problem of work is a rational one in a makeover culture. Under the guise of getting one's life 'back', or enhancing the activities required by 'becoming' in order to 'be' a self, the choice to medicate is culturally intelligible: the Prozac-self, like Jones' overweight woman, might attract social approval (cheers) for a return to a viable life and taking control. We can also see a shift here from dealing with the illness of depression to dealing with one's faulty 'mood' for life.

Rather than sedation (allowing one to step back from life to deal with illness) the favoured solution is now one that not only allows a continuation of life but enables one to *become better* at it. As Maycroft would lament, these choices may attract cheers, but poor managerial practice, exploitation and the serious issues of overwork all pass by without comment. It's not to say that these issues are ignored – that James and Helen experience overwork is part of the 'pitch' – but the problem and solution are presented as individualised ones: there are readily purchasable lifestyle pharmaceutical cures if you can't be adaptable enough. I don't think that we can underestimate the sheer cultural labour needed to allow one to realise, like James, that the problem isn't the job but with one's mood.

From the discussion so far it's possible to regard lifestyles as contrived entry points into consumer culture. They herd together and then present expert-selected consumer choices to the self and direct the further acquisitions of goods and services necessary for the maintenance of a lifestyle identity. Lifestyles then are not just the means by which commodities are sold, but the ways we are positioned to appreciate and desire their utility to our project of becoming through self-transformation. Lifestyle media presents, displays and markets these entry points, and through melodrama, infotainment and entertainment serves to familiarise, naturalise and quietly valorise the logic of makeover and an ethos which is consistent with the rationalities of neoliberalism. As this logic slips into commonsense imaginations of the self, Jones predicts that soon the question will not be why one had a nose job (or take Prozac) – but rather why one didn't.

Becoming in a society of consumers

It's this positioning that draws the attention of the sociologist Zygmunt Bauman. His aptly titled *Consuming Life* (2007) argues that society is increasingly shaping up as a 'society of consumers' in which we are steadily encouraged to actively market the self. He states that the normative self has, in order 'to be admitted to the social prizes' of a society of consumers, to recast itself as a commodity, 'that is, as products capable of catching the attention and attracting demand and customers' (Bauman, 2007, p. 6). Whether it's about attracting and collecting 'friends' on social network sites or convincing an employer we are right for a job, the self has to market and *sell* itself (Wee and Brooks, 2010). Such selling demands repackaging, transformation, self-surveillance and, importantly, a market-literacy in order to know how 'value' is assessed and how to improve one's value-rating. Bauman would argue that there is a hard-edge commodification at play in Jones' makeover culture, as would Laurie Ouellette and James Hay (2008) who see in lifestyle media an aggressive promotion of the self as its own 'branded commodity' in need of constant rebranding to keep a market viability. Additionally, it's possible to see how the 'ordinary' becomes commodified in lifestyle TV; ordinary lives, problems and stories are converted into commodities in lifestyle TV, which in turn helps networks sell airtime to advertisers (Illouz and Wilf, 2008).

The movement that pulsates through Jones' makeover culture, where 'becoming better' is a ceaseless endeavour, also thumps through consumer capitalism. While it is argued that consumer culture becomes the main site where citizenship is established (Vidmar-Horvat, 2010), Bauman argues that being a valued citizen of the society of consumers rests not just on 'acquiring and possessing' goods and services, rather is it 'about *being on the move*' (p. 98, original emphasis). By this he means that being up to date, being fashionable and, we could add, being able to hedge and trade on futures markets in terms of fashion and skills are necessary labours if the self is to maintain and improve market viability. This movement is driven by a constant state of dissatisfaction. Miller and Rose (2008) have argued that the continuation of consumer capitalism rests on its skill in persuading the self that it is in some way deficient and in need of a consumer fix. Its success lies in the endless cycle of lack, needs and fix. The consumer who is *satisfied* constitutes a threat. Bauman claims that 'individuals who settle for a finite assembly of needs...never look for new needs...are *flawed consumers* – that is, the variety of social outcast specific to the society of consumers' (2007, p. 99). The necessity of movement in Bauman's formulations stress 'becoming' over the stasis of 'being'. There are clear echoes between Bauman's outcasts and Meredith Jones' 'living dead' – those who stop becoming and are still (2008, p. 147).

It's tempting to slip into the seductive sedation of 'blank slate thinking' by assuming a neutrality in the society of consumers: market viability spun through aggressive individualism rests on the ability of the self to consume *and* to demonstrate its allegiance to prevailing norms through choices made – in other words to consume *right*. However, both of these rest to different degrees on a politics of recognition: 'individuals not only recognise themselves, but are crucially *recognised by others,* through their publically visible consumer choices', argues Keith Haywood (2004, p. 144, original emphasis). By considering recognition, Haywood brings us squarely to the interpretative criteria of normative selfhood. And it becomes quickly clear that not every self is equally or fairly positioned or favoured. Bauman, for example, notes that structural poverty excludes many from exercising choice in consumer culture. Yet 'creeping' market rationality displaces structural explanations for consumerist ones. The poor become constructed as 'failed consumers': 'in a society of consumers – a world that evaluates anyone and anything by commodity value – they are people with no market value' (Bauman, 2007, p. 124). Without the material means to demonstrate flexibility, to enact transformation or to perform allegiance to consumerism, the poor are rendered worthless and useless.

Furthermore, thinking about recognition allows us to perceive other forms and degrees of exclusion. Keith Haywood and Majid Yar's (2006) discussion of the cultural representations of the white, working class in the United Kingdom note how this group are denigrated not through their inability to consume, but by the ways they *do* consume, through an excessive, tasteless and 'vulgar' consumption (p. 14). Recent sociological inquiry has pulled upon the work of Pierre Bourdieu (1984, p. 66), who argues that 'taste' becomes the 'ideal weapon' in forging distinctions between those with the 'right' taste and those who are defined by their lack. The operations of taste allow an expression of middle-class distaste for working-class lifestyles (Raisborough and Adams, 2008). This distaste is readily apparent in the proliferation of terms for sections of the white, working class like 'chav', 'ned' and the incredible, 'white trash' (McRobbie, 2004; Skeggs, 2004). These are culturally marked, rendered visible and necessarily misrecognised (see Skeggs, 2005), through consumer choices in clothing (sports clothes, baseball caps and 'hoodies'), music (R&B, hip-hop), jewellery (so-called bling), strong sun-bed tans and through excessive behaviours – promiscuity, aggression, binge drinking and so on (Haywood and Yar, 2006, p. 14). In short, certain sections of the white, working class are identified as culturally distinct through a tasteless consumption that is coded as reflecting a morally reprehensible, unrestrained and out-of-control lifestyle (McDowell, 2006). As such, they provide an instructive lesson to other consumers; the poor are 'walking symbols of the disasters awaiting fallen consumers and of the ultimate destiny of anyone failing to acquit herself or himself of the consumer's duties... They are the yarn of which nightmares are woven' (Bauman, 2007, p. 124).

We can conclude here that the need to overdraw and over-determine flawed and failing consumers is necessary on two grounds. Firstly, the creation of such a strongly drawn Other deflects criticism from the workings and logic of consumer capitalism itself – consumerism cannot help those who do not help themselves: consumers have failed not the market. Discourses of aspirationalism and 'becoming better' escape critical attention when we focus blame on those excluded and marginalised – those whom Bauman caustically refers to as the 'collateral casualties of consumerism' (2007, p. 117). Secondly, the vilification of the Other helps to remind and instruct 'normal' selves of appropriate consumption behaviours. Rather like the health warning stamped on alcohol sold in the United Kingdom – 'drink responsibly' – the ideal consumer-citizen is one who not only exercises control and restraint, *yet still consumes,* but for whom responsible (read 'tasteful') consumption is part of the wider project of self-investment and enhanced marketability. In other words, the correct practice of the self is to turn to the market to help the project of 'becoming better' and to exercise and enact independence and self-management through the flexing of choice. Consumption and consuming *right* are then the keys to viability and market worth. This demands not only the economic means to consume but also *taste* – a tan but not a sun-bed tan, jewellery not 'bling' and so on. In sum, the self is expected to look to the market to solve problems of living (e.g. over work), map out its biographical trajectory (becoming better) *and* secure citizenship. To avoid the zombie, nightmarish state of a flawed or failed consumer, the good citizen is 'someone who actively participates in social and economic life, makes rational choices and is independent, self-reliant and responsible' (Galvin, 2002, p. 108).

Lifestyle media is especially interesting in this context because it presents as a voluntary and individualistic choice *itself:* the decision to watch the makeover show, buy a self-book and then *engage* with them are personal and individual consumer-decisions. Lifestyle media are also commodities, bought and sold and wrapped in their own dramas of rebranding and holding market share (Ouellette and Hay, 2008). A reasonable question to pose here is, how does lifestyle media, itself part of the market, fit into the project of the 'handing over of life to the market'? In what ways are lifestyle TV, self-help books and advertisements, amongst other things, implicated in this 'handing over' and in shaping specific forms of citizenship? This chapter has already suggested that lifestyle media helps normalise and valorise transformation by casting it as both infotainment and melodrama. We could say that lifestyle media sells the idea of transformation and educates us in the various fashions and technologies available (Jones, 2008). But, leading from Fox and Ward (2008), I am interested in the ways lifestyle media sells transformation by recasting ordinary life as a series of problems with market solutions. Such a recasting, I argue, dislocates and fragments the 'ordinary' in very specific ways to then *re-locate* it in with a logics and rhetoric of consumer-choice and neoliberal flexible, self-transformation. One of the ways this occurs is through lifestyle media's focus on mundane, everyday life.

Lifestyle media and the mundane

It's fair to say that something happens to ordinary life in lifestyle media. The makeover show, self-help book and talk-show are visible attempts to translate the normal and mundane aspects of everyday life into problems or potential risks for which there are specifically shaped, temporally bound, solutions (a permanent solution, as we have seen above, is as problematic in the makeover culture as no solution at all). Stress provides an instructive example here. Stress, or rather the encouragement to understand life events as stressful and thus in need of stress-control and management intervention, occupies the attention of the psychologist Steven Brown (2005). He argues that stress has in recent decades become 'the pre-eminent term for describing a huge range of experiences and conditions' (2005, p. 232) and looks to the ways that self-help books not only aid the 'popularizing' of stress discourses but how they attempt to recruit individuals to assess their lives in terms of stress-risks.

One of the key popularising and recruitment tools is the check-list questionnaire. A popular self-help device, check-lists contrive to diagnose likely problems through direct questions; answers are awarded 'points', which when totted up into a 'total score' by the reader lead to an authoritative, quantifiable, diagnosis. Brown's point is that these check-list questions speak to such mundane aspects of life and encompass such broad categories that any reader would find it hard to escape a score that places them at risk of stress-related illnesses and dysfunction. Very few of us, he argues, could not confess to some interruptions or changes to our sleeping patterns, appetite or sexual desire. Changes and fluctuations are the very rhythms of life – yet, despite this, check-lists are presented in self-help literature as 'robust and straightforward means for learning the "truth" of one's personal distress' (p. 240). For Brown no such truth can be secured. The sole purpose of check-lists is to present stress as a neat, over simplified, highly individualised explanation for existing problems and any potential risks lurking in the very unfolding of life itself – the only possible diagnosis is that 'everything is a source of stress. And everyone's life is stressful' (p. 242).[1] The reduction of life into a simple diagnosis not only air-brushes the complexity and messiness of life away, but it also invests the mundane with increased significance – it is where perils and salvation lie and ongoing vigilance is demanded.

The issue here is not just that everyday life is recast as problematic, but rather the individualist ways these problems are understood. As Debbie Epstein and Deborah Steinberg's (1998) analysis of the award winning *Oprah Winfrey Show* demonstrates, structural causes for distress are deftly avoided and problems are quickly related to failings of an isolated self. For example, institutionalised heterosexuality is not called to account when *Oprah's* resident expert Dr Phil teaches women to better adapt, and indeed to find success and security in fitting with its demands. The answer to why some moms yell at their kids (in the *Oprah* show 'Why you behave in ways you hate') is located firmly in the individual – we are mimicking the behaviours of our own parents – moms are encouraged to 'break the cycle' and 'don't be afraid to apologize'. Rather like the Prozac-using James cited above, problems of life stem from the failure of an individual to adapt and master situations, not from the situation of exploitation itself. 'Stress' has an added utility here because it serves to place the failings of the self in already highly individualised discourses of pathology, self-disorder (the 'break down' and 'burn out') and disease (Keane, 2000). These discourses reverberate in the solutions offered by lifestyle media. Drawing heavily on treatment models of addiction and compulsion (such as the 12 Steps of Alcoholics Anonymous), self-help books, talk-shows and lifestyle TV present expert-designed steps and rules that allow the self some mastery over a problem sliced up into identifiable components. What the problem shares with the solution is its individualised, personalised, nature.

The processes and tactics that enable problems to be detached from everyday life take up different guises. Many self-help books beckon the reader to places of reflection and meditation, to quiet and 'alone' moments – they are encouraged to move out of life in order to reflect upon it. In the makeover show, participants are often 'handed over' by family and friends at the start of a show that returns them at the reveal. One of the most successful shows, NBC's *The Biggest Loser*, for example, sends its participants to a California ranch to live for 3 months, while the C4 *Supersize vs. Superskinny* imprisons it's participants into a food clinic for five days. It may seem somewhat contradictory then to observe that many makeover shows spend time getting to know the life and personality of the participant. *What Not to Wear* experts spend a day living the life of their transformee. They feed their family, go to their work and dress in their clothes (the latter for comic appeal). The getting to know, to really know, the participant is displayed in confessions in front of mirrors (*How To Look Good Naked*), on therapy couches (*How to Dump Your Mates*), through interviews with friends and family (*Ten Years Younger*) and CCTV footage (*SuperNanny*); further, the extent of the 'problem' is known and applied to individuals through test swabs (*How Clean is your House, Embarrassing Illnesses*), stool analysis (*You are What You Eat*) and medical tests (*Honey, We're Killing the Kids*). However, this 'getting to know' is not an exercise in contextualisation but a means to convince the participant and viewer that expert solutions are bespoke, carefully crafted, individualised remedies for highly personal problems. It helps *sell* the expertise of the hosts as they scrutinise, analyse and bring their professional knowledge to bear upon a single life. Further, the personalised nature of the problem/solution is reflected in the ways that shows like *Ten Years Younger* title episodes with the name of that week's participant – in many ways it is *their* show. So convincing is this personalisation that it seems unaffected by the endless repetition of the same steps and rules for different individuals over successive shows. In short, throughout lifestyle media we are reminded that the 'problem' is one that is socially recognised, even shared by others, but still necessarily an individual one – it is *yours*.

Control and efficiency

Given the importance of self-control to Western-style individualism (Joffe and Staerklé, 2007), it may be unsurprising that many of the problems and solutions paraded across lifestyle media reflect its significance. Self-control takes up many forms across lifestyle media but is most apparent in a general emphasis on 'order' (both the ordering of emotion and of things) and in 'efficiency' (doing things better). A mundane example can be found in clutter. There is a wide portfolio of self-help books and lifestyle TV dedicated to organising, decluttering, cleaning and ordering the home: *How Clean is Your House*, *Clean Sweep* and *Hoarders* feature among the TV shows while the recent additions to the anti-clutter movement include the self-help books, *Clutter Busting: Letting Go of What's Holding You Back* (Palmer, 2009) and Barbara Tako's (2010) *Clutter Clearing Choices: Clean Clutter, Organize Your Home and Reclaim Your Life*. What is clear from the always explicit titles of self-help books is the immediate logic that equates the organisation of one's things with the organisation of one's life.

Clutter is interesting because normative consumption is premised on the acquisition of goods – surely the more the better? However, the normative plays of self-control and, following Bourdieu (1984), the operations of taste, both serve to complicate a logic whereby a self succeeds merely through the collection of stuff; the turnover, use and disposal of goods are part of the *movement* in Bauman's society of consumers. In lifestyle media excessive consumption is distasteful – Belk and his colleagues go as far to say that clutter is deemed 'dirt', it is 'out of place' in Mary Douglas' terms, and thus 'provokes disgust and precipitates guilt, shame and embarrassment' (Belk et al., 2007, p. 134). This disgust is intensified when the *home* is cluttered. Media scholar Kirsten Seale (2006) explains that property ownership is a cornerstone of aspirational consumer culture – this is often expressed through the rhetoric of the 'home'. There is then a sensationalised jarring when the valued (home) is contaminated with 'dirt' (clutter). She would conclude that lifestyle TV focuses solely on the cluttered home because the audience's shock and reactions of disgust at a *transgression* serve to renew and re-energise the normative status of home/property ownership and, in so doing, also neatly deflect any critique of conspicuous consumption.

What we might refer to as 'clutter porn' also reinforces a now-blatant individualism. Personal misfortunes are presented in shows like *Life Laundry* as causal explanations for those whose lives are besieged by clutter (bereavement, illness and divorce feature highly). These quickly slide into discourses of addiction ('clutteraholics') and mental health. By way of example, the executive producer of the Canadian show *Hoarders*, Jodie Flynne sees her show raising awareness of clutter as a sign of 'mental disorder' (CBS News, 2008). Online posted comments to her views indicate the appeal of this explanation: 'the show has opened my eyes to an issue that I had no idea was such a terrible disability' (Will2Change, CBS News, 2008). This has little to do with clutter now, and everything to do with the cultural dexterity of neoliberal values normalising their worth by pathologising all else.

What is especially convenient about perceiving the cluttered as mentally ill or as addicts is that these problems can be worked upon by experts *and* there is a possibility of rehabilitation (see Chapter 3 for further discussion). Control then is the means of demarking the good from the failed in terms of citizenship, but also provides the means by which individuals who 'fail' can be explained away (ill) and also the grounds on which they can enjoy repatriation (get better). This aspect of lifestyle media is explored further in the next chapter. Roy (2008, p. 468) notes in lifestyle media the repeated use of words like 'need', 'should' and 'must' and the use of often 'cautionary tales' of those who fail to take advice. It is clear for her that problems and solutions are both situated at the level of individual – and, of course, discourses of culpability attach to those who fail to take up the opportunity to do what they 'should'.

The value of self-control is also expressed in terms of efficiency. Time is often used to signal the efficiency of lifestyle experts in enacting any transformation. From *Sixty Minute Makeover* to *Extreme Makeover: Home edition* when a house is demolished and rebuilt in a week, there is an urgent percussion to many Lifestyle TV shows. Wheeler Dixon (2008) notes how production and editing techniques are used to communicate the essence of speed; time-lapse photography and speeded-up motion are used alongside the cheaper method of hosts literally shouting-out time deadlines.

Time may add to the drama of 'will they, won't they finish' but perhaps best operates to showcase the skill of experts in controlling and mastering hectic timeframes in their confident handling of problems and obstacles as they arise (hosts are perhaps fortified by Prozac). In such a light, experts lead by glamorous example. The efficiency of lifestyle solutions also serves to reduce any resistance or excuse. It would be hard to argue that one doesn't have the time when Richard Wiseman's (2009) *59 Seconds: Think a Little, Change a Lot* promises so much in less than a minute. For the more time-pressed Blair Singer's book offers to transform life in 30 seconds *or less*. A more sedate challenge is offered by Mylene Kluss in the Pantene Pro-V ad 'Healthy-looking hair in just 10 days? Go on I challenge you'. In these examples there is a presumption and constitution of an already-efficient consumer who 'on the move', as Bauman has it, relies on the promise of time-frame to realise the results of their investment. Efficiency sells to the efficient *and* sells efficiency.

A rhetoric of efficiency also underpins good design in the home makeover shows. Homes are zoned into kitchen areas, play areas and family areas. *The Home Show* through its efficient use of space not only imagines a specific family life but prescribes and serves to control it. George Clarke, the celebrity architect, when selling his design to the show's contestants explains that *this* is where adults will relax, and where they will entertain and *here,* as he moves to an adjacent 'zone' signalled by a differently shaped and coloured rug, is where the children will play. He designs the home for at-home working *and* for 'family time' and neatly reproduces the ideal of work:life balance. Design not only divides the house into functional spaces – spaces for animals, for sitting, for plants, for guests – but it dictates how they are used and approached with built-in paths, walkways, gateways and focal points. The key is an efficient space for the multitasking, flexible family: taste is not just signalled through the highlighted 'interest pieces' but in the ability of the house to be flexible and to grow with the expected changing demands of life – to be a *becoming* home.

Summary

This chapter has through Meredith Jones' makeover culture shifted the book's focus from the labours of being to those of becoming. This has forced attention more specifically to question what counts as appropriate self-labour and to what/whom the self is encouraged to aspire. Through Jones and Bauman's 'society of consumers', this chapter has explored how 'becoming' involves the necessity of turning the self into a commodity and necessary labours of rebranding to attain and improve market value. The conclusion is that the self who can take on neoliberal repertoires enjoys recognition (cheers) and moral self-worth. Lifestyle media through repetitious imagery, themes and technologies such as the check-list, steps and rules, and use of injunctions 'must' and 'ought' help define the personal as a moral sphere for the pursuit of self-worth and self-development – as a site of becoming. What we can take from this chapter is the idea that makeover culture is not simply a promotion of various lifestyle options to be taken up, but ways of doing life itself. It is about movement and progression – about opportunities and enterprise. It is about the increasingly moral imperative to be seen labouring not just at 'being' but *'being better'*. Simply put, makeover culture speaks to an ethos and accompanying collection of discursive and material resources to keep working on, and within, lifestyle choices, and also, an interpretive framework that recognises, appraises and rewards the labours of becoming, through which we can all stake a claim on life itself. Jones' makeover culture also serves to throw visibility and recognition into critical light – an exploration of these makes up the next part of this book.

Part II
Framing the Self

3
Living Autopsies: Visualising Responsibility

> In the quest for happiness and peace the first and most important key is to take personal responsibility for your life. I believe that we are 100% accountable and responsible for everything in our lives, even if we don't like it.
>
> Julie Way (2009) *Inner Self*, http://www.innerself.com.au

Introduction

Stewart's drinking was getting out of hand. He was starting to feel the impact on his health, but it was his family and partner who'd had enough of him being a 'bad drunk' and they wanted him to quit, 'if he doesn't do that, then I will have to seriously review the situation of our relationship, because he is going to lose everything if he doesn't stop', warned his partner. A wake-up call was needed. Successfully nominated for the BBC Three makeover show *Make My Body Younger*, Stewart finds himself strapped into a bodysuit nervously gripping the sides of a hospital gurney in a pathology suite. His family watch on as the show's presenter, George Lamb, invites a pathologist to assess what damage Stewart's lifestyle has exacted on his 'insides'. The light dims; the pathologist steps forward to draw his hand down Stewart's chest which slices open in response. 'So what is happening now is that the primary incision is occurring, coming down the skin of your chest', explains the pathologist, who gestures at the incision making it slowly retract, 'pulling the skin back and we see your heart and lungs', and then 'your liver and intestine – all beating away'. Stewart looks down in stunned silence; his family is clearly shocked at the verisimilitude of the visual living representation of his inner body projected on his chest. The living autopsy has started.

The screening of autopsies and representations of internal organs is not new. TV's *Silent Witness, The Expert*, the *CSI* franchise, and projects blurring art and science like Gunther von Hagen's *Köperwelten* and The Visible Human Project, all indicate a robust interest in 'insides'. What *is* new is the increasing popularity of the 'insides' in lifestyle media. Not only does the 'inner self' circulate in self-help books, but flick through TV channels: there are adverts inviting us to visualise and then assess the age of our heart (What's your heart-age? asks *Flora Pro-Activ*), to score our blood cholesterol (*Benecol* ads), and to imagine a disgruntled gut ('Give yourself some tummy loving care with *Activitia*'). Pick up a glossy magazine: skin care cosmetics and anti-wrinkle developments like Botox are *mining* the surface of the skin to exploit new territories of cellular vitality, musculature and structure. And there's more to come; industry giants, L'Oreal, Shiseido and Kose are pumping funds into the research and development of nanotechnology to work on appearances from *beneath*. All in all, something is happening to surfaces. Not only is the 'inner' enjoying heightened visibility but it's taking on a very active relationship to the external: 'when you're feeling good on the inside it shows on the outside' is the gleeful message of Danone *Activia*. Pro-Biotic Yogurt and Danone are not alone in fostering a healthy relationship between 'insides' and 'outsides'.

The living autopsy could be explained as a shock tactic, or narrative gimmick to create a distinctive selling point for the show, and 'insides' may, more generally, offer a logical site for a marketing industry seeking out new niches and angles. Yet, this chapter argues that the recent visibility of 'insides' recasts them as the guardian of the self; organs, blood cells, digestive tracts and the inner self become surfaces for surveillance, risk-projection *and* sites for betterment. These surfaces emerge through a whole host of technological and professional developments allowing insides to be seen and more sharply imagined (from X-rays, ultrasound, CGI to psychotherapy). This chapter focuses on the ways 'insides' emerge through discourses of health. By discussing health I am not suggesting that one *shouldn't* care for one's health, what interests this chapter is how the injunction that we *ought* to drags the inners into a moral project of being and becoming. Principally, this chapter is concerned with how a particular visualising of the insides draws them into a project of citizenship-making through processes of responsibilisation. By drawing on Judith Butler's (2009) discussions on the mediation of visual imagery, this chapter argues that specific 'framings' of insides help to demark, and reproduce socially approved and socially disapproved lives in terms of their perceived ability to enact responsibility. This chapter extends this line of argument to claim that responsibilisation also creates surfaces and opportunities for rehabilitation – that is to say, the restoration of a disapproved life to a socially approved one. The operations and consequences of rehabilitation are charted throughout this part of the book to argue that the opportunity of rehabilitation is a necessary aspect of neo-liberal governance.

Back to Stewart

After the primary incision, the pathologist sifts through Stewart's body, assessing each organ in turn to track the cancers and diseases caused by poor lifestyle choices. To underscore a message of lifestyle-induced damage each organ is given a biological age based on its condition which when calculated produces Stewart's internal biological age. As with all cases on *Make My Body Younger,* a life of nutritional neglect and excess tots up to a shocking gap between the biological age of the inner body and the chronological age of the participant. Twenty-five-year-old Stewart has the internal organs of a forty-year old, the brain function of a pensioner and low sperm motility. Shocked into saving his own life Stewart, with the help of medical experts, turns things around. It's a hard and emotional struggle but new batches of medical tests some weeks later reveal a new 'brain age' of 18 years and a viable sperm count. Stewart is pleased that his 'hard work has paid off' and he has pleased his partner; 'I've got my dream guy', she said, 'hopefully we will have a really long and happy future together'.

From this book's discussions so far, we could say that Stewart's story, like many others circulating in lifestyle TV, is one of transformation that holds out the promise of a happy ending. Through expert assistance and his own labours Stewart is restored to a rightful life; he is now healthy enough to work, he is a 'proper' partner *and* he can declare his virile masculinity. His labours are affirmed and rewarded by his partner for whom Stewart has converted from a 'bad drunk' to 'my dream guy' and by medical science – he passes their tests and can claim youth as his reward. In common with other lifestyle TV formats, *Make My Body Younger* devotes more airtime to Stewart's 'becoming' than to the transformed Stewart. His suffering and his sheer hard work provide a prime example of Meredith Jones' (2008) argument that in the makeover culture the labours of becoming are always privileged over the result. On one hand, Jones argues that labours have to be visible 'public performances of moving from one self to another' (p. 57) in order for the new Stewart to have credibility and be recognised as authentic. On the other hand, 'labours of becoming' underpin and are constituted by the constant *movement* of the makeover culture. As the previous chapter argued, to merely 'be' or to be 'satisfied' in Bauman's (2007) terms is 'not enough'; to merely 'be' exiles the self to the nightmarish 'still life' – the living dead of the go-getting neoliberal makeover culture. Avoiding this exile requires the visible 'display of our ongoing improvement' (Jones, 2008, p. 57). Stewart's display is enabled through medical tests – these are the visualising technologies that allow us to 'see' and verify his transformation just as we can see a change when he picks up his roles of partner, father and citizen. But, as Jones would argue, this is just the start for Stewart: his transformation is the platform for more work at being a *better* partner, father and citizen. This point is not lost on his partner; she doesn't *guarantee* a long and happy future – she just has renewed hope for one.

However, there is an opportunity here to extend Jones' arguments by focusing on the visibilities and displays at work in *Make My Body Younger*. There are two movements at work. The first is an *awareness* produced through the visualisation of lifestyle choices that are literally written on body – this is Stewart's 'wake-up call', needed to kick start and sustain his labours. The second is that of *rehabilitation*, the explicit direction and goal of Stewart's labour, which is visually evidenced in his labours of becoming responsible, in the battery of medical tests and through the success of his 'new' life. This movement renders Stewart's labours intelligible. Both movements are specifically mediated through political orchestrations of responsibility. Bluntly put, Stewart moves from 'irresponsible' to 'responsible' by taking responsibility. It's helpful here to be reminded that, for Foucault, 'power works precisely because it enables rather than represses subjectivity' (Lunt and Lewis, 2008, p. 19). This nudge allows the question to arise of what self is enabled through mediations and movements of responsibility. This question drags another in its wake – with what consequence?

Responsibilisation and recognition

The previous chapters have argued that neoliberalism is characterised by a displacement of state responsibility onto the private individual. It may be ridiculous to argue 'against' self-responsibility (Butler, 2009), but it *is* important to unpick the relations of power operating through its rhetoric and its movements. This means regarding the shift of responsibility as involving more than an extension of an individual's duties and concerns, such as, say, being responsible for one's diet or exercise regime, or in Stewart's case, his drinking. Instead, the shifting of responsibility is perceived as involving a specific shaping of the self. The term 'responsibilisation' is useful here because it refers to the productions of the self through the dis- and re-placement of responsibility. It speaks to the ways that the shifting of responsibility firstly depends on imagining the self as capable of enacting and even as desiring responsibility – a self that *can* be responsible. Secondly, it depends on the imagining of a self *produced* through its own enactments and performances of responsibility – a responsible self. These imaginings circulate to ensure that moral, worthy selfhood is increasingly produced and encouraged in terms of these capabilities, performances and enactments.

Judith Butler (2009) reminds us that responsibility requires responsiveness; we have to respond to the call to take up responsibility and to enact 'responsible actions'. Yet, how we respond depends on the ways the world, the self and Others are presented to us; 'responsiveness is not a subjective state, but a way of responding to what is before us with the resources that are available to us' (p. 50). It is in thinking about what 'resources are available' that draws Butler's attention squarely to the media. Her explicit concern is to address the media which, as a powerful resource for knowing the world and its people, sculpts favourable perceptions of the so-called war on terror. Her argument is that mainstream media representations serve to justify, or at best render ambivalent, the violence and acts of torture enacted in the names of justice and security. She sees these media constructions as a concerted attempt to conduct certain responses not just to the idea of a 'war on terror', but certain responses of the self to the self and of the self to Others in support of the war. Lifestyle media may seem a world away from the news and war journalism that preoccupies her, yet it's possible to apply Butler's link between presentation (what she calls *framing*) and responsiveness. Do repeated framings circulate in lifestyle media to encourage certain responses to social issues, personal problems, to the self, to Others and even to our 'insides'?

Butler's work reinvigorates that of Erving Goffman who had earlier defined frames as a 'schemata of interpretation' that help individuals 'to locate, perceive, identify and label' experience (1974, p. 2). Butler sharpens Goffman's awareness that frames, while multiple, overlapping and divergent, are produced through a mustering and clustering of social norms so that frames are 'politically saturated' (2009, p. 1). In this claim she reiterates arguments that frames regulate perception; they train the eye and create an interpretative medium through which the world is known to us, producing a 'field of perceptible reality' (p. 64). To this, Butler adds the passionate claim that normative and normalising notions of a *recognisable self* are crafted and carefully maintained in the perceptible reality 'over and against' the self who is marked by misrecognition or non-recognition. For Butler, this is all about who gets to count as 'human' or not in that perceptible reality; who gets to access a liveable and viable life; who doesn't; and, crucially, *the price and cost of that access*: 'a life has to be intelligible *as a life,* has to conform to certain conceptions of what life is, in order to become recognisable' (Butler, 2009, p. 7) – there are then movements of productive power and symbolic violence as we are cajoled to 'fit' into prevailing conceptions of what life *is.* Her wider point is that recognition does not extend to everyone; 'recognition becomes the site of power by which the human is differently produced' (2004, p. 2) – which begs the questions of just who are the winners and losers in the recognition stakes and just how are these relational divisions drawn? What we can take from Butler is an urgency to expose the framings within shows like *Make My Body Younger* because the means through which the 'insides' are visualised and imagined are not neutral, indeed they may be operations of recognisability, through which ascriptions of humanhood are allocated.

Frames of healthism

It is not accidental that Stewart is transformed via his inners, nor it is coincidental that Danone's products claim that 'when you're feeling good on the inside it shows on the outside'. There is no surprise because processes of responsibilisation are most evident in discourses and practices of health. This is a consequence of neoliberal effects on health care and provision and also, related to that, increased attention to the somatic qualities of selfhood – whereby the body, or rather control over the body becomes a key recognition marker of moral selfhood (Heyes, 2007a; Newman et al., 2004). As such, *Make My Body Younger* and other media uses of the 'insides' are both tapping into and constituting wider, societal beliefs of a relationship between the corporeal body and personhood. Health, particularly *healthism* discussed below, becomes a very powerful frame, able to muster and weave together biomedical authority and 'commonsense' lay knowledge to such an extent that the frame itself can sink into the background; it and its cultural labours of mediation can become invisible influences of everyday experiences. It's worth then looking at health more closely.

Various commentators have noted, with varying degrees of acceptance and alarm, that health has undergone its own 'makeover' through the transformative policies of neoliberal organisation. Through processes of decentralisation, individualisation and marketisation, responsibilisation has been translated into a range of health technologies, vocabularies and expertise to reframe health as a matter of self-management and self-responsibility (Benford and Gough, 2006; Inthorn and Boyce, 2010). Sensitive to the directions of change, Robert Crawford in 1980 coined the term 'healthism' to refer to a 'new form of health consciousness' (p. 365). He was describing a growing ethos that redefined health from that relating to a state free from illness, to a perception of health as a precarious state under constant threat from external sources (such as contamination and infection) and through bodily betrayal (e.g. cancer and degenerative disease). This new consciousness has troubled once established divisions between health and illness, leaving the otherwise 'healthy' body as either asymptomatic or presymptomatic (Rose, 2001) – thus helping to create what has been called the 'worried well'.

Healthism, then, speaks to a sharp deployment of risk narratives whereby the body is imagined as at risk from illness/failure and, it should be added, *as* a risk to the self's ability to fully ride the changing fluctuations of neoliberal economy and organisation. For Crawford, and other critical voices, the labours to reduce or manage risks become defined as 'healthy': 'to be healthy is to live a balanced and controlled existence, valuing vigilance, self-restraint, and the avoidance of risk' (Hodgetts et al., 2005, p. 124). Of relevance to us here is the argument that 'being healthy' becomes imagined as a moral obligation. Nikolas Rose uses the phrase 'will to health' to describe the individual's responsibility to manage a body which is both a risk and at risk. He explains that the 'will to health' is a cultivated set of obligations for an individual 'not merely seek the avoidance of sickness or premature death but ... encode an optimization of one's corporeality to embrace an overall "well-being"– beauty, success, happiness, sexuality and much more' (Rose, 2001. p. 17). Being healthy is thus a crucial aspect of the imagined ideal neoliberal citizen, it is not just about being healthy – but being a *better* self and performing 'betterment' in a host of ways ('success') not just in improving the risk-status of one's 'insides'. It's unsurprising then that many critical voices have argued that the 'doing' of health stitches individual practices and values into systems of governance, whereby populations are governed through the 'conduct of conduct' (Howson, 1999; Murray, 2008).

As a consequence of its makeover, health becomes recast as a matter of choice.[1] But what does it mean to regard health as a choice? Firstly it means that health accrues a different value – a signifier of citizenship:

> A health that can be 'chosen' ... represents a different value than a health one simply enjoys or misses. It testifies to more than a physical capacity; it is a visible sign of initiative, adaptability, balance and strength of will. In this sense, physical health has come to represent, for the neo-liberal citizen who has 'chosen' it, an 'objective' witness to his or her subjectivity to function as a free and rational agent.
>
> (Greco, 1993, pp. 369–370)

The sociologist Monica Greco extends her point to argue that regarding health as 'choice' assumes a 'personal preventive capacity' to manage health – in other words, we can all do it. This neatly places health management within the personal sphere of lifestyle and within an individual's store of 'will-power' – the very narrative stuff of lifestyle TV and self-help books. If ill health can't be avoided through the regulation of lifestyle or 'sheer strength of will' then this is read as 'a *failure of the self to take care of itself* – a form of irra-tionality, or simply a lack of *skilfulness*' (Greco, 1993, p. 361, original emphasis). For fellow sociologist Sarah Nettleton, this 'failure' and 'lack' are spun into a 'new disease', a notion that grips professional and lay perceptions to such an extent that critical determinants of health, such as poverty, struggle to be heard over the strident claims for personal will: 'circumstances', she argues, are eclipsed by health explanations based on assumption of 'personal capacities' (1997, p. 214). This redefinition of health to personal choice, character and will-power creates what psychologist Darrin Hodgetts and his col-leagues describe as a 'morality of health' (2005, p. 124) whereby making the right health choices indicates moral character; 'in other words to be healthy is to be a good person' (Benford and Gough, 2006, p. 428). Those who reject or refuse 'correct' choices risk a stigmatised identity.

Secondly, as health becomes a matter of choice, a certain logic takes hold that spins individuals into health *consumers* who need knowl-edge, technologies and expertise to watch their bodies, monitor their health and reduce or avoid risks. State organised health care shifts from that solely concerned with care and cure, to take on the role of a provider of 'consumer' information through a multitude of agen-cies interested in the prevention and reduction of risk (Inthorn and Boyce, 2010). Within this reorganisation of health, 'empowerment discourses' take hold: consumers are empowered as they make choices because choice-making is performative of their citizenship and indicative of their rationality. Consumers are also empowered to make choices by consuming expert advice. Responsibility pul-sates through the different relations here; individuals are imagined as responsible for their choices and for seeking the right information needed to make them (Warde, 1994). At every step the possibility for empowerment is shadowed by accusations of personal culpabil-ity, error and failure: to be ill is to have failed – it is to have misread or wilfully ignored consumer advice. In short, the health choices forced upon the self through processes of responsibilisation are also those the self can use to manifest as recognisably 'responsible'. These choices are not, then, 'free'; for Rose, Foucault's theorising of power quickly denudes us of any illusion to the contrary. Instead we are invited to see what choices are made possible, what *they* make possible and the assemblages of power they are spun from and into. As Rose claims, via Foucault, within healthism 'the language of autonomy, identity, self-realization and the search for fulfilment forms a grid of regulatory ideals' (1996, p. 145) – where recognisable selves are produced and formed. What this means for Stewart is explored below.

Framing Stewart

In a critical extension of Goffman's work on frames, sociologists Robert Benford and David Snow (2000) have sought to unpack the mechanisms that organise perception. They identified three core functions of a frame: diagnostic (identifying a problem and attributing cause or blame); prognostic (identifying a solution and establishing a plan of remedial action) and motivational (what they describe as a 'call to arms', the execution of the plan). Each of these mutually supporting functions serves to recast an event or experience onto a very specific register and then works to keep it there. Necessarily there are acts of brutal omission, narrowing and masking as well as illumination and foregrounding as the frame is spun and sustained through acts of symbolic violence and exercises of productive power.

Benford and Snow invite a more nuanced approach to the living autopsy as a mediation of Stewart's 'insides' (and life) through a frame 'politically saturated' with healthism. In sum, in the living autopsy the pathologist draws on his visualising technologies to produce a diagnosis (Stewart's irresponsible lifestyle choices are killing him), the prognosis (a plan of action to achieve a more responsible and healthier lifestyle) and to motivate the execution of that plan (Stewart's labours of becoming responsible are spurred on by expert help and the threat of looming risks should no action be taken). A closer look at these functions can help dissect the insider workings of the story of transformation.

Diagnosis

The diagnosis involves more than a cataloguing of lifestyle-induced damage to Stewart's insides. Rather it operates a movement that lifts

Stewart from his social environment to relocate him in tightly regulated registers of healthism; a necessary movement if *Make My Body Younger* is to successfully present his problems and expert solutions solely in terms of lifestyle choices. This action rests upon a presumption that Stewart can be capable of, and able to, appropriately respond when his lifestyle and bodily insides are re-presented through that register. What are discernable here are the plays of an extant, off-screen interpretive labour that works to cast *all* selves as normatively (potentially) responsible: this is needed if Stewart is to be personally blamed for the poor health of his organs, and then rewarded for his specifically directed efforts. So strong is this presumption that it seems unintelligible that Stewart would not take up the invitation to change – his acceptance signals the enterprising spirit prized and *naturalised* by various neoliberal discourses. However, Stewart's own voice is not enough to convince of his potential to recognizable personhood: the dialogic nature of recognition (discussed in this book's introduction) is indicated and harnessed in most lifestyle TV narratives through the drama of the heartfelt testimony of families and partners in the 'before' sections of the show and in their euphoric reactions to the 'after' – the result of the makeover. The inclusion of Stewart's 'nearest and dearest' serves to convince the audience and possibly Stewart himself that he's worth redeeming and they also bolster the sense that Stewart has a moral duty to change: significantly, a duty to others neatly deflects any criticisms that Stewart is embarking on a journey motivated by narcissism (Hazelden, 2003).

The presumption of Stewart's potential for responsibility bleeds into the show to congeal through the various functions of the frame so that it becomes very difficult to perceive Stewart's insides as other than Stewart's responsibility and thus as an ethicalised site for his action. More specifically, the diagnostic function of the frame, as wonderfully dramatised through the pathologist's own diagnosis, deftly erases any non-personal explanations for Stewart's state. As the pathologist works his way over the surface of Stewart's insides he identifies, and delimits, Stewart's 'problems' in neat chains of causality or consequences; drinking causes *this,* smoking risks *that.* As the pathologist reads Stewart in this way a chronological narrative takes hold: Stewart's *past* choices are forcefully stamped onto his present body with an authority backed by medical science to firmly position Stewart as 'both the author and actor' of his own life (Rose, 1999a, p. 251). Here, risk plays a key narrative function because it allows a personalisation of epidemiological knowledge – these are *Stewart's* risks. Risk also beckons the authority and objectivity afforded by calculability and it provides a logical rationale for intervention: the pathologist is able to reconnoitre the inner terrain for future expert strategies. Further, the pathologist's actions offer a striking and current example of what Bryan Turner (1982) has called iatromathematics – the connecting of nature to numbers. By placing a biological age on Stewart's organs, the pathologist dissects the body into its component parts in ways that are more easily quantifiable and which serves to isolate them. A certain disembodiment takes place as organs receive their 'own' age from the pathologist. It's possible to suggest that as Stewart is decontextualised from his social and cultural contexts, and hence from the myriad of factors that comprise Stewart as a socially embedded and embodied life, so too are his organs disembodied and atomised as they are framed in terms of their own unique risk-factors and biological age: the processes of individualisation, then, work deep, politicising insides. In sum, the diagnosis works to suture Stewart and his insides into narratives of cause and effect allowing very specific solutions to glide forward on a lubrication of predictable logic: if Stewart's bad lifestyle is making him ill, then he needs a better lifestyle.

It's worth mentioning here that the diagnostic function of the frame, as dramatised in lifestyle TV and reality TV more widely, often involves its own reveal. It's commonplace to discuss the 'reveal' as the moment at the end of a show where participants are exposed to their 'new' self. However, this moment demands a narrative contrast – the 'before' to the 'after'. This is provided in an earlier reveal, the point at which participants are confronted with their 'old', 'faulty' selves. I described this above as a moment of awareness; it's a moment of consciousness rising where Stewart sees a very specific truth about his life. Of course, it's possible for Stewart to reject the call to change – and that possibility does add to the drama of the show. It would take a determined effort to break out from the narrative imperatives that seem to crowd around him, but, should he refuse there is little threat to the neoliberal project because its 'voluntary' and personalised nature seemingly allows Stewart to 'opt out' and to 'choose' the consequences of living an irredeemable and abject life – a discussion of which follows in the next chapter. It's timely to be reminded that this freedom is vital to the workings of neoliberal governance (Rimke, 2000): 'power is exercised only over free subjects, and only insofar as they are free. By this we mean, individuals or collective subjects who are faced with a field of possibilities in which several ways of behaving, several reactions are realised' (Foucault, 1982, p. 789).

It is upon Stewart's *free* self then that a whole host of visualising technologies are deployed to reinforce the 'wrong' choices of the past. Often in lifestyle TV shows, these visualisations are saturated with mockery, humiliation and in some shows, blatant denigration. *You Are What You Eat*, for example, shames their overweight participants by confronting them with a week's worth of their bad food choices. The pedagogical functions of lifestyle media (Ouellette, 2009) are driven home hard through the glutinous heaps of food – often presented as overflowing from rubbish skips – and in the contrasts between a mountain of fatty 'beige' food and bountiful assemblages of the colourful reds, greens and yellows of 'good' food. Again, 'insides' are deployed. The effects of bad food on internal health are dramatically visualised through a stool (faeces) analysis. The errant overeater has to present their stool to the host who mocks its texture and shape and is disgusted by its smell – all actions which strip the participant of any privacy or dignity and which elicit gut-churning reactions of disgust in the audience. The stool is treated as a direct communication from the 'insides' and is 'read' by the show's host to pathologise the participant's subjectivity: it's clear that if the stool is disgusting – in most cultures faeces are so considered – so too is the person who produced it (Miller, 1997). As the errant body is constantly fixed by repetitive visualisations of excess, waste and pathology (Skeggs, 2004), lifestyle shows are argued to visually produce a participant as an 'abject person with a mismanaged life' (McRobbie, 2004, p. 102). More particularly, as earlier chapters here have argued, this production redraws class divisions: the abject are those who lack middle-class values, tastes and natural restraint (Skeggs, 2004).

Prognosis and beyond

However, the prognostic and motivational functions of the frame suggest that Stewart is not left in a state of shock or shame. A seemingly obvious point to make perhaps – after all the show would be a short one if all it did was to point out the error of Stewart's ways. Obvious or not, it can be sidelined when critical attention is lodged against the standard narrative of humiliation, ridicule and shame of an 'abject self' in lifestyle TV (Mendible, 2004). Butler (1993) reminds us that abjection means 'to cast off, away, or out' (p. 243), yet it seems that lifestyle TV, with their attention to self-labour, are not always straightforwardly public spectacles of 'casting out'. Like other makeover shows and tales of self-transformation, *Make My Body Younger* devotes itself to *dragging Stewart back to a socially approved life*. The efforts involved and the (perhaps, temporary) results are what makes the story of transformation and the show's happy ending. Why is Stewart rehabilitated? Laurie Ouellette and James Hay (2008) offer an explanation that reflects their argument that lifestyle media are cultural technologies of neoliberalism. They argue that lifestyle TV diagnoses 'problems' in ways that enable individuals to be trans-formed into 'functioning citizens' (2008, p. 6). In that regard, we could say that through the prognostic and motivational functions of the frame Stewart learns skills and practical techniques from the experts and so does the audience. The audience, primed by their own various positions in and to discourses of healthism, find their own views of 'good' and 'bad' choices gently massaged and also learn the 'latest' health advancing technology, the 'latest' risk-scare, or have their own practices affirmed. The rehabilitation in this regard is about 'training' viewers and Stewart about the importance and rewards of self-responsibility (Ouellette, 2009).

More specifically, we are being 'trained' in a specifically formed responsibility: it is *classed*. Ouellette and Hay's term 'life interven-tion' (2008, p. 63) describes how shows like *Make My Body Younger* transform marginal, identifiably 'at-risk' individuals into success-ful self-mangers of their own lives. It is the 'bad drunks' and the overweight that are the fodder for lifestyle TV shows. But a closer look at just who gets to be identified as needing a makeover and who is deemed suitable for transformation reveals class relations at play. Previous chapters have indicated that citizenship is not a class-neutral term, but rather citizenship is forged and sustained through properties the middle classes have made their own and then spun into universal markers of personhood (Savage, 2003; Skeggs, 2004); accordingly the majority of programmes chart the story of 'less-educated, lower-income individuals' who are seen as in need of transformation and then being *dragged* up to middle-class standards (Ouellette and Hay, 2008, p. 7; Skeggs and Wood, 2008). Psychologists Jessica Ringrose and Valerie Walkerdine explain that class is heavily etched into the cultural imagery through subtle plays of identification, whereby we are enticed to reject the (working-class) self 'one shouldn't be' to embrace and embody 'generalized and normalized bourgeois' selfhood (p. 227). Class-making then is produced by attempting to forge complex discursive and affective equivalences between 'the working-class' and a 'life not worth living'.

What we can add to this via the specific framing of healthism is the way that middle-class standards of self-responsibility construct themselves as natural, essential features of citizenship by using the biological, living, easily visualised, 'proof' provided by 'insides'. Through framings of the 'insides' we are encouraged to see that the body's natural state is actually a contained, restrained and disciplined one – a 'truth' that is read from Stewart's blood tests and improved virility. The rehabilitation is then testimony to the transformative powers of neoliberalism and also to the 'natural' logic of its values and injunctions: it is biologically underwritten. If, as Butler argues, 'a life has to be intelligible *as a life*, has to conform to certain conceptions of what life is, in order to become recognisable' (Butler, 2009, p. 7) then Stewart's recognisability depends on his emulation of codes that are not his own (McRobbie, 2004), against which he is always placed at a disadvantage (Skeggs, 2009) but are nonetheless written on the 'truth' of his body.

But something else happens in Stewart's rehabilitation – he is transformed into a better consumer. In the dramatic revelation of Stewart's ailing organs what emerges is a prognosis and plan of action that gravitates around the problems of Stewart's *consumption*: the problem is not so much that Stewart is drinking – it is more that Stewart is drinking too much: he is a *bad* drunk. There are two related observations to make here. The first is that the living autopsy helps spin the lessons of citizenship into those of consumption. Similar to shows like *You Are What You Eat* and *Honey We're Killing the Kids*, citizenship is spelt out in terms of responsible consumption, defined as moderate, restrained, tasteful and importantly expert-sanctioned. Stewart is therefore re-presented not as a drunk but as a faulty consumer. Within the consumer logic outlined by Monica Greco above, Stewart's deviancy has to be presented as result of his being irrational, ill-informed, misguided, ignorant or as perhaps lacking the necessary skills to consume appropriately. It is important to the universality and essentialised nature of self-responsibility and the prevailing ethos of citizenship as enacted through consumption (Roberts, 2007) that Stewart's 'lack' is explained as personal but nonetheless as *surmountable obstacles* to consumption – as things he can learn about and learn from, thus advancing his market literacy.

There is a pedagogical dimension at work: Ouellette and Hay (2008) would argue that the pathologisation of poor consumption practices helps sustain the enterprise of existing citizens. The 'worried well' may be eating the latest in probiotic yoghurts and perhaps in the future using their IPhone to monitor their blood pressure but through stories of rehabilitation they also learn to be vigilant for diseases of consumption – those creeping signs of irrationality and compulsion that 'cause' excess, waste and tastelessness. Throughout the living autopsy any opportunity to criticise consumer capitalism is displaced by a framing that signals a moral approval by focusing only on the ordering of 'good' and 'bad' choices, and in so doing further promotes consumerism as a resource of life. It is only through aggressive framing that consumption can be a presented as a solution to the problems of consumption.

But what's important here is the momentum rehabilitation gives to the makeover culture. For both Meredith Jones (2008) and Zgymunt Bauman (2007) the endless labours of becoming a self demand a rebranding and refashioning; the ability to recreate and move through 'newly improved' selves provides the energy of the makeover culture and fuels consumer capitalism: 'you must keep going forward because there's no going back' is the encouraging message in self-help texts (Castillo, 2006, p. 235). To reiterate the argument made in the previous chapter, the consumer who is *satisfied* constitutes a threat. Bauman claims that 'individuals who settle for a finite assembly of needs . . . never look for new needs . . . are *flawed consumers* – that is, the variety of social outcast specific to the society of consumers' (2007, p. 99). So for Bauman, a constant state of dissatisfaction is important to keep consumers consuming. Yet, something is needed for dissatisfaction to spill over into action. That something is the belief that one *can* start again – no matter the past. In order for individuals to be cast as makers of their own destiny there has to be intelligible moments of awakenings, rehabilitation and *cleansing* built into the heroic narrative of the tale of transformation – if not, failure would write us out of the story and write us off the registers of personhood. Instead, failure, personal weaknesses and lack are actively sought by stories of transformation – to realise and embrace them as one's own signals a reflexive maturity and a rational ability to learn from the past and *move on*. Thus the currency of makeover culture depends on the belief that there is the potential and opportunity to start again: as Martina Navratilova's (2006) *Shape Your Self* repeatedly states 'defeat does not signal the end of dream'.

This is evidenced in *Make My Body Younger* when Stewart's labours virtually wipe the surfaces of his organs clear: the shadows retreat from his organs, his blood clears, his sperm is returned the motility levels Stewart enjoyed before his 'bad choices'. This movement of wiping clean is indicated by the title – *Make My Body* Younger (not, healthier) signals a form of time travel – the turning back of the clock to start again. Stewart's rehabilitation renders him, from the inside out, a blank slate on which he can now write the workings of his own self-authorship; as such his labours are not so much rewarded by a return to health, but rather through the access and mobility this new health affords him – the key to access new transformations and new re-brandings, new failings, new accusations and new starts.

Seeing the inner self

It is Stewart's 'strength of will' that the show works up and upon. Variously referred to as the 'true', 'subconscious' or 'authentic' self, the inner self is much harder to see than Stewart's organs, nonetheless lifestyle media prompt its *visualisation* by drawing on a range of what Rose (1999a) calls 'psy discourses'. 'Psy' relates to the spread and flowering of different forms of psychological expertise, especially their proliferation in popular culture and everyday speech. The 'heterogeneous knowledges, forms of authority and practical techniques that constitute psychological expertise' (Rose, 1999a, p. vii) construct, visualise and then enable communication with the inner self through a range of technologies and diagnostic methods. For example, the hypnotist, Paul McKenna's widely successful 2005 *Motivational Power* recordings use his variant of neurolinguistic programming to speak directly to the inner self. After inviting one to visualise a future self, he distracts the conscious self by asking it to count backwards, and then through a melodious mix of overlying voices and music speaks directly to the subconscious. Once the inner self is awoken and 'programmed' it can drive life-changes.

A more mundane example is found in the diagnostic quizzes in glossy magazines: *Psychologies* is an 'up market' monthly women's magazine, distributed across Europe, Russia and China. It's filled with battery of tests inviting us to communicate with the inner self and discover our real feelings and thoughts. One month you can be relieved to find upon toting up your test score that you can answer negatively to the question 'do you love too much', but find the next month that you have a borderline 'commitment problem' and a 'fear of rejection'. These tests offer a current example of the invasion of therapy in Western culture; as Steve Brown (2005) and Frank Furedi (2004) have argued every aspect of everyday life can be presented as an issue worthy of interrogation through diagnosis and thus as a site for intervention and betterment. That the tests are presented to us in the form of light entertainment indicates the subtle per-vasiveness of surveillance technologies and the popular currency of 'psy' in framing approaches to the self and self-understanding (Illouz, 2008). Nikolas Rose (1999a) concludes that visualisations and diag-nosis encourage us to imagine an 'interiority' 'behind our conduct' (p. 256) to reveal hidden 'needs and dependencies' (p. 255) that have to be seen, to be managed and 'sorted'.

Key to the visualisation of inner self is a wider imaginary that casts the inner self as a private store of positive power; one that's conve-niently attuned, or able to be tuned into the demands of neoliberal citizenry (McGee, 2005). The notion and action of tapping into this private store intensifies the individualisation at work in self-help nar-ratives and within the story of personal transformation more widely; as power is understood as being locked in the self, intervention and labour are devoted to unlocking it. However, self-help materials don't dismiss the hard work and struggle of maintaining and applying will-power, indeed they use these expected struggles as selling points. For example, Kelly Howell, author of over sixty audio books, explains in *Weight Loss: Brain Wave Subliminal*:

No matter how many times you've struggled to lose weight, you can do it now. Subliminal brain wave technology taps directly into the vast storehouse of creative energy that lies buried within the subconscious. In heightened states of receptivity, trigger words and phrases anchor a slim mind-set that eliminates self-sabotage and unleashes your most vibrant, vital self. Becoming trim, taut and terrific has never been easier.

(2003, back cover)

These alliterative qualities encourage the self to focus inwards and critical attention is dragged once again from social, structural explanations of personal problems to be hammered tightly into narrow explanations leading to personal-based solutions. Similarly, Brooke Castillo's (2006) best-selling weight-loss book, *If I'm So Smart, Why Can't I Just Lose Weight? Tools To Get It Done* makes clear the struggle of lifestyle change through will-power. Whereas Howell primes the will with key words and triggers, Castillo perceives the 'problem' as the individual's own *lack of trust* in the inner self: the 'problem' is not with the fantasy of will-power but a lack of faith. Her advice is to learn to re-trust the internal power of the self – to 'believe you are internally rather than externally controlled' (p. 131). Whether will-power is to be awakened (McKenna), primed (Howell) or just related to differently (Castillo) it remains an unquestioned force in self-help and is speedily accompanied by the injunction that it's the responsibility of the self to harness it and use it efficiently.

What is emerging from this discussion so far is the notion that each self is comprised of two selves. The external self is generally presented as the present, failing self which may jealously sabotage the intentions of the inner self or just gently thwart its potential through ignorance or indifference. The inner self is the real self – a self that needs to be realised. Interestingly and without contradiction, the inner self is simultaneously the self one has *always* been, the one Paul McKenna can awaken, *and* it's the new self that individuals are transformed into. The logic of the inner self being both past and future, the old and new, has a binding coherency in cultural frames that perceive a self searching *within* for resources of will-power and, as Giddens has it, regards identity as drawn from an ongoing construction of a consistent life narrative. It's the inner self that stitches life fragments and choices into a meaningful biography and from which choices can be made or rejected. As a *core*, the inner self lends integrity and sincerity to self-design projects, even if the inner self itself has to be reshaped and reformed as it spins through the unfolding of life. In this regard the inner has to be flexible enough to enable a sense of personal history and biographical-order without slowing or limiting the self's mobility – once it starts to do this the inner is re-orientated through the guise of being listened to more closely for what it *really* wants. Any inconsistency in the consistency of the inner is not a contradiction in self-help literature, instead they are starting points for new projects of the self, new refashioning and the creation of new problems for the self to resolve – in sum, it is part and parcel of the movement necessary for the makeover culture.

In common with Stewart's insides the inner self is ushered into discourses of healthism. Sociologist Rebecca Hazelden (2003) observes how self-help materials posit a relationship between the 'self' and the 'inner self' that is potentially risky if neglected or lost. The inner self is imagined as both robust and fragile. It cannot be completely lost, but it can be misplaced by the dull, mundane pressures of everyday life or neglected as the external self continually busies itself with the demanding impositions of others. The potential of the self as a whole is lost as a result. Once wounded, the inner self retreats with one's dreams and aspirations, but the cost of that retreat erupts 'behind our conduct' (Rose, 1999a, p. 256) bringing unhappiness and frustration to the external self's activities and feelings. Hazelden notes that this framing suggests that any problems of living are those caused by having a faulty relationship between the selves which risks a pathological identity: 'the reader is persuaded that it is her identity as an authentic self that is the issue and that she has an ethical obligation to this self' (2003, p. 416). The solution is then that of repairing the breach between the inner and external self: self-work that repairs the breach becomes an ethical project of autonomy, responsibility and control, and marks an 'effective, well adjusted individual in charge of her emotional life' (2003, p. 424). Once more the internal is ethicalised as a surface demanded of action and labour.

The emphasis on individuals as having responsibility for repairing the breach, or their insides, assumes that all are equally well equipped to do so. The presumption of reflexive rationality as a marker of normative personhood and citizenship is important to highlight here because it masks the reproduction of social divisions within self-help/transformational narratives. Not only are these attributes more likely possessed by those who made them their own and spun them into universal standards from which others are judged (Savage, 1993) but by casting rationality as an attribute of all and adding the notion that personal empowerment rests within, the production of winners and losers are skilfully presented as those naturally falling from either personal choice/determination or a pathology that derails or blocks the realisation of will. As a result, relations of class, gender, race and so forth start to leak explanatory efficacy and may lose creditability when individuals attach them to their own lives: the idea that the buck stops with the self makes other explanations look and feel like *excuses*. The idea that empowerment is self-generated suggests to the cultural imagination that disempowerment also lies within the remit of self-control, any excuses are thus indicative of a failure in self-design and the inability to learn from the past. To be a winner or loser is then to some extent, but with increasing degree, imagined as a matter of choice and will. Chris Haylett notes with growing alarm how the replacement of social and culture factors for personal ones also recasts those social and cultural factors *as* personal ones. She observes how the white, working class in the United Kingdom are repeatedly positioned as being in a state of 'cultural improverishment' – a poverty of identity based on outdated ways of thinking and being (Haylett, 2001, p. 352).

Summary

Sociologist, Raj Ghoshal (2009, p. 79) says of the process of framing that

> when one attempts to frame an issue in a particular way, one is making a claim about what the issue is 'really about'. This chapter has argued that frames in lifestyle media are 'about' the production of socially continent fields of 'perceptible reality' from which spin certain ideas and ideals of responsible citizenship.
>
> (Butler, 2009, p. 64)

It argued that lifestyle TV mediated 'insides' (bodily organs and the inner self) through specific frames of health and personal responsibility to firstly help us all picture an abject life and the 'type' of person who lives it, and secondly to celebrate the transformation of that life into that of a 'functioning citizen' (Ouellette and Hay, 2008). This chapter stressed that the rehabilitation from 'bad' to

'good' provides a crucial movement in the story of the transformation which fuels the incessant energies of the makeover culture and
its preoccupation with self-betterment. More specifically, this chapter
has argued that specific visual framings of the insides organise a
'field of perceptible reality' that re-orbits social, political and economic problems into the gravity of personal failing and individual
expert-guided solutions. Irresponsibility when refracted through the
mediations of healthism emerges as problems of skill and knowledge
(poorly skilled and ill-informed) enabling a targeted intervention at
an individual level: responsibility is taught and nurtured by providing the errant Stewart with the right knowledge and better life
skills.

The dramatisation of rehabilitation in shows like *Make My Body
Younger* could be seen to convey the universal inclusivity that stems
from, and enlivens, the blank slate thinking discussed in Chapter 1 –
anyone can be responsible – we can, no matter how errant our choices
to date, become recognisable through the labours, trails and sheer
graft of rehabilitation. Yet, the previous chapters have been attendant
to the dangers of the universality evident in blank slate thinking;
through its circulations, blank slate thinking presumes a socially
privileged self, effaces the material and discursive realities of people's lives, and ultimately masks the critical reality that some cannot
access, or are prevented from accessing, the various means to enact
normative selfhood in ways that others can. Indeed, Skeggs (2004)
argues that social privilege depends on this reduced and problematic
access. This begs the questions of what is happening in and through
rehabilitation – what cultural work is being done? These questions indicate that it's important not to refute claims that lifestyle
shows are 'about' abjection, nor to deny the reformulations of social
inequalities therein. What these questions *do* encourage is an exploration of the complexity and cultural ingenuity involved in the ways
selfhood is 'differently produced' in cultural productions that suggest
a universal inclusivity.

4
Headless Zombies: Framing the Fat Body

You have a BMI of 51.5. You are at a very, very high risk of death from your weight. So it is serious.

Dr Christian Jessen in C4's *Supersize vs. Superskinny*

They kill for one reason they kill for food. They eat their victims. That's what keeps them going.

Dr Foster in Romero's *Dawn of the Dead* (1979)

Introduction

There's a figure lumbering through the pages of this book so far that now demands attention. It's haunted the margins of previous chapters just as it's haunted the margins of Meredith Jones' makeover culture and Zygmunt Bauman's consumer culture; it's the figure of the living dead – the zombie. For both authors the monstrous living dead serve as a dire warning for those tempted to stand still in a social world morally underpinned by the movement of self-betterment. If the previous chapter was successful in arguing that rehabilitation was a necessary movement in the orchestration of transformation, then the zombie physically and symbolically marks the reach of those orchestrations: the zombie is one who won't rehabilitate or, for the reasons this chapter explores, *can't*.

The zombie helps this chapter further our discussion of framing. To reiterate, frames, as particular clusters of social norms, organise perception to ascribe personhood to selves capable of performing self-responsibility. However, frames also serve to unequally allocate personhood through plays of non-recognition or misrecognition (Fraser, 2000; Skeggs, 2004). This point is flayed open by Judith Butler who, in noting the slippery nature of the English language, observes that the word 'frame' enjoys a wide spectrum of meaning. She notes that 'to be framed' is to be 'set up'. By way of example she explains that criminals can have 'evidence planted' against them which 'proves' their guilt; if one is 'framed' then a 'frame is constructed around one's deed such that one's guilty status becomes the viewer's inevitable conclusion' (2009, p. 8). For the purposes of this book, Butler's observation creates a unique entry point into the current concern over obesity. This chapter explores whether the inescapable media attention given to the so-called obesity 'epidemic' and the spectacle of fat, overweight, fleshy bodies in lifestyle media suggest that some bodies are being 'set up' as the antithesis to a life defined through enterprise and self-improvement. The chapter starts exploring the problem of obesity before moving to examine how self-responsibility for weight is promoted through a raft of lifestyle TV shows devoted to weight-loss.

'Setting up' fat: the bigger picture

Fat is mainly framed in terms of neoliberal healthism. More specifically, weight-loss lifestyle TV shows and self-help literature all draw upon, and add to, prevailing constructions of obesity as an *epidemic*. The fact of obesity as both a 'disease' and one of epidemic proportions has been confirmed by the World Health Organisation (WHO) and a tsunami of supporting statistical evidence (Murray, 2008). For example, the Foresight Report (McPherson et al., 2007) indexed the levels of obesity in the UK adult population: this stood at some 7 per cent in 1980, had trebled by 2007 and is now predicted to reach 40 per cent in 2025, and 60 per cent by 2050 (McPherson et al., 2007). In the league tables the United Kingdom lags behind the United States, where 65 per cent of adults over the age of 20 are currently overweight or obese; Canada weighs in at 59 and Australia at 49 per cent (Inthorn and Boyce, 2010, p. 84). Additionally, the adult obese population was recently estimated as 56 per cent in Tonga, 29 per cent in Kuwait and 78 per cent in Nauru (BBC News Online, 2008). The global phenomenon of the obesity problem has been captured by the WHO's rather unpleasant sounding term, *globosity* (Murray, 2008).

The significance of these statistics owes much to links forged between overweight/obesity and the risk of debilitating and life-threatening diseases. Among these, cardiovascular disease, stroke, cancers, type II diabetes and osteoarthritis figure most highly (Salonen et al., 2009). As Sander Gilman notes just an increase of 1 per cent in obesity in countries the size of India or China would mean a staggering 20 million cases of these illnesses (2008). Further, theses illnesses are framed in terms of their economic costs: in news reportage, for example, a statement about the number of the obese is swiftly, if not immediately, followed by a declaration of the economic implications. Such reportage may state that the cost in terms of lost work-days due to sickness and cost of health care is currently argued to be in the region of $100 billion for the United States (Martin, 2007) and estimated to cost the United Kingdom's National Health Service some £49.9 billion in 2050 (McPherson et al., 2007). The United Kingdom's Department of Health has described the situation as a 'time bomb' (2003, p. 37). These figures cause increased concern for countries with ageing demographics: premature deaths due to obesity-related illness could reduce the retired population, but will also diminish the number of healthy workers needed to support them (McPherson et al., 2007). The need to ensure a healthy stock of future workers explains why government anti-obesity measures tend to target children and young people. In February 2010, President Obama established a taskforce to investigate childhood obesity. The 2009 UK health initiative *Change4life* initially aimed its national advertising campaign at families with children aged between 5 and 11 years old. *Change4life* encourages sensible eating and the uptake of active exercise. The current 'fun' *Change4life* slogans 'mind over batter' and 'don't veg out run about' are an early indication of the direction of these programmes: they locate the cause of obesity in diet and sedentarism, a framing that suggests its own 'cure' of reflexive, self-monitored actions – eat less, do more!

However, despite the authoritative urgency of these ever-escalating and horrifying statistics, there are grave concerns around the creditability of obesity science. These concerns cluster around specific 'truth' claims: such as the presumed extent and speed of the global problem (Gilman, 2008); the categorisation of obesity as a disease in its own right (Evans and Colls, 2009); the epidemiological evidence linking overweight with illness (Rice, 2007) and premature death (Campos et al., 2006); and even the connection between weight-loss and good health (Throsby, 2008). Blaine (2007) urges calm, suggesting that 'epidemic talk' is an overreaction to modest weight-increases over some 15 years that have pushed a small number of overweight people into the category obese. Others are suspicious about the vested interests insurance, drug and diet industries have in fuelling a panic about obesity (Oliver, 2006). Many food companies have, for example, lucratively rebranded their goods as 'low' or 'zero' fat whilst boosting the health claims of their products (Herrick, 2009). Further, Gard and Wright's (2005) oft-cited analysis of obesity science notes the circulation of denigrating stereotypes associating fat with greed and sloth within the scientific enterprise. Similarly, others have argued that obesity claims are spun from a mêlée of cultural prejudice and economic considerations, with many dissenting voices and opposing evidence airbrushed out of overly polished epidemiological accounts (Campos et al., 2006; Rich and Evans, 2005). Many of these criticisms manifest in a growing suspicion around the ubiquity and authority bestowed upon what has become the main measurement of obesity – the Body Mass Index (BMI).

BMI

The BMI score is reached by calculating height and weight. This is the BBC's do-it-yourself- version

> If you'd like to calculate your BMI yourself, follow these three steps.
>
> 1. Work out your height in metres and multiply the figure by itself.
> 2. Measure your weight in kilograms
> 3. Divide the weight by the height squared (i.e. the answer to Q1). For example, you might be 1.6 m (5 ft 3 in.) tall and weigh 65 kg (10 st 3 lb). The calculation would then be:
>
> $1.6 \times 1.6 = 2.56$. BMI would be 65 divided by $2.56 = 25.39$.
>
> BBC Health Tools http://www.bbc.co.uk/health/tools/bmi_calculator/bmiimperial_index.shtml

The BMI is an important device in lifestyle media, used in lifestyle TV shows like *Honey, We're Killing the Kids* as both a measure and confirmation of fat/obese classifications and thus of the health risks listed above. However, it enjoys a much wider circulation especially in the form of the 'BMI calculator', where a computer coding does the maths for us: we can just enter our height and weight and our score is computed. The relative simplicity of the computer coding needed to produce a calculator affords the BMI its ubiquity. It can be found on most self-respecting health websites and those of glossy magazines (e.g. *Red* and *Men's Health*). Further, it's a component of the globally successful Nintendo game platform *Wii Fit* portfolio. There's an 'app' too – the IPhone application has the added feature of recommending an ideal BMI score for its user and recording their progress towards it (apple.com). The simple utility of the BMI makes it attractive to life insurance providers who base their premiums on its scores (Gard and Wright, 2005). As for those scores, a BMI of 25 is considered overweight; 30, obese; that of 50 plus can be fatal.

What's immediately problematic is the fact the BMI measures *mass* (bone and muscle) not adiposity (Monaghan, 2007), nor was it originally devised for its current use (Oliver, 2006).[1] This adds some disquiet around the relative ease with which the BMI sets its thresholds, especially when, in 1999, in a seemingly arbitrary move, the overweight threshold was dropped from a score of 29 to 25, instantly converting millions of people of 'normal weight' into overweight people with predicable health problems (Blaine, 2007). Yet, despite WHO acknowledging that the BMI is, at best, a crude measure (Evans and Colls, 2009) it has acquired what sociologists Alison Hann and Stephen Peckham call the 'gold effect' (2010). This is a term they reserve for ideas that take on the mantle of a generally accepted truth within lay and professional knowledges. Its capacity to pass as a truth is, in no small part, down to its ease of use and its cost; Bethan Evans and Rachel Colls (2009) explain that better measurements of fat would involve expensive equipment, such as DEXA body scanners, or technically difficult measurements using callipers (p. 1058). Regardless of its 'fit for purpose', the gold effect helps the BMI, and the obesity science it represents, to take on a life of its own as a way of translating the body into registers of normalcy and pathology.

The concern for sociologists is that the BMI rips the body from its cultural and embodied contexts, and hence from the associations, meanings, feelings and socioeconomic contexts that make our experience of the body. In so doing, it reduces the body to a stark, lifeless but nonetheless, politically laden measurement (Monaghan, 2007). It is politically laden because by isolating weight and height, the former is cast as the only variable that can be changed. Weight then is presented as *controllable*, and the health risks that are argued to accompany weight are regarded as *preventable*. The problem of fat thus becomes imagined as being within the personal capacities of an individual to manage. Given the personal health risks an overweight body is thought to recklessly flirt with, and the social and economic *burden* of fat bodies, it is no surprise that obesity discourses have a moralising tone; the fat body constitutes both 'a personal and social liability' (Monaghan, 2007, p. 585), and, as such, it is to be managed, contained or preferably re-aligned to the norms of healthism and prevailing social aesthetics (Bordo, 1993). It's possible to conclude that the BMI operates as a very specific visualising technology through which all bodies, not just 'fat' ones, can be monitored and surveyed. We are all called to monitor our bodies because they may drift from the safety of 'normal' into the troubled water of 'overweight' if we are not bodily-vigilant, aware that our lifestyle choices are written both within (as the previous chapter argued) and on the very contours of the exterior flesh. The BMI, then, no matter its accuracy, is a device of responsibilisation because it recasts the exterior body as an ethicalised surface on which we are all obliged to work *and* to publically parade that work to others. What's important here is a very subtle shift from 'treating or controlling obesity as a disease' to 'controlling fatness (as abnormality)' (Evans and Colls, 2009, p. 1060).

Mind over batter: self-control and literacy

The shift from disease to a control of fatness indicates something about the shape and concern of prevailing social norms. Social psychologists Hélène Joffe and Christian Staerklé (2007) argue that contemporary Western societies are characterised by what they call a self-control ethos. The self-control ethos speaks to a bundle of family values including self-discipline, restraint and self-management. These are found across many other cultures, but are increasingly valorised in highly individualised societies, where 'a socially respected self' is recognised through maintaining (and exhibiting) 'a control over one's desires, emotions and action' (2007, p. 402). As self-control provides a 'normative benchmark' of 'respectable' personhood it also serves to mark Others or out-groups, considered such because of their supposed violations or rejection of the ethos. For Joffe and Staerklé, this goes someway to explain why the content of so many denigrating stereotypes, which isolate and then attempt to exclude Others, focuses on a *lack* of control. In particular, the body of the Other is regarded as excessive, uncontained, undisciplined and in many cases contaminating – a common trope in stereotypes which denigrate the working class, homosexuals, women, people with disability, the aged and ethnic minority groups among others. When directed at weight, the fat body is believed to be produced though greed (excessiveness) and laziness (ill-discipline). In contrast, the thin/fit body 'symbolises the mastery of mind over the body, signals virtuous control' (p. 405).

The self-control ethos aids the enduring everyday 'commonsense' and professional explanations that regard weight as a matter of self-control. It's clearly evident in the public health initiatives and associated technologies discussed above: just as the BMI places monitoring at our fingertips, the *Change4life* slogan 'mind over batter' presents weight very definitely as a matter of will-power. Although belief in self-control may be tempered with a realisation that wider forces may work upon the body – namely acknowledging the role of fast food or advertising industries – the 'blame' still sits with the fat individual who cannot or will not take responsibility for itself and who allows itself to be manipulated. However, this allocation of personal blame does little to explain why obesity and/or the repercussions of an anti-obesity moral panic are unevenly distributed (Campo and Mastin, 2007). The controversial nature of obesity science may dog any confident straight-forward declaration that the fat body is also a classed one: obese and overweight bodies inhabit most social classifications, and there is some variance in how class is defined and operationalised in epidemiological studies (see McLaren and Godley, 2009). Yet, the risk of obesity falls more heavily upon poor or socially marginalised groups (Drewnowski, 2009; Salonen et al., 2009), and risk- talk, and accompanying intervention strategies are more busily engaged around these groups too, rising their all ready problematic visibility.

Explanations and theorisations of a clustering of obesity risks to those inhabiting lower social-economic classes range from the cost and accessibility of 'healthy' food (Drewnowski, 2009; McEntee and

Agyman, 2010) to explanations which highlight the psychological stresses of living out a stigmatised identity, be that of class, sexuality or ethnicity. Becky Thompson (1996), by way of an example of this second point, argues that overeating may be a 'survival strategy' – a way of coping in a racist and classist social world. Thompson, in this light, regards food as a *calming drug*. This explanation draws attention away from the individual body towards the social body for the determinants of obesity (Lovejoy, 2000).

However, the depoliticising, decontextualising imperatives of healthism tend to distract from the social body by placing the individual centre-stage. This is nowhere clearer than in health promotion policies. Michael Gard and Jan Wright state the consequences:

> Health promotion strategies locate the responsibility with all individuals to monitor their behaviours and those of others in keeping with desired health outcomes. In doing so, the specific social, cultural and material conditions of people's lives are ignored.... The strategies that are often employed in these programmes assume that individuals are free to make decisions and choices in relation to health.... This means that people who do not exercise their 'freedom' to choose in ways that are productive to health, can be categorized and stigmatized as lazy, undisciplined, lacking in will-power or just downright 'bad.'
>
> (2005, p. 183)

As Gard and Wright argue, processes of decontextualisation make the step from a cultural valorisation of self-control to accusations and blame a very small and easy one to make. What is variously referred to as 'sizeism', 'weightism', 'fatism' or 'fatphobia' describes how fat bodies and the selves who inhabit them are heavily stigmatised (Warin et al., 2008). Roberta Pollack Seid helps reiterate points made earlier by identifying the 'root' of weight-prejudice as,

> Our belief that the fat are responsible for their fatness. We believe people have absolute control over their body size. Even the most liberal, compassionate people will cluck their tongues about overweight friends and ask why they 'let themselves' get fat. Our belief leaves no room for the sympathy we extend to other abnormalities or illnesses.
>
> (1989, p. 22)

The real effect of this belief is evidenced in personal testimonies and a range of research concluding that fat/obese people are more likely than non-obese people to face institutional discrimination and everyday 'interpersonal mistreatment' (Carr and Friedman, 2005; Cooper, 1998; Murray, 2008). So strong is this belief that weightism[2] is generally perceived as the most *acceptable* form of prejudice, if it is considered prejudice *at all* (Martin, 2007). In exploring the acceptability of weightism many scholars have turned to the visual presence of the fat body.

Unlike other stigmas which may be hidden, or presented in such ways so that they can 'pass' daily public scrutiny, the fat body has a physical presence and an exaggerated visibility. Charlotte Cooper (1998) and Samantha Murray (2008) enliven their work by drawing on their own lived experiences of inhabiting a fat female body. From their work and others, it's possible to see how the physical environment, the size of changing cubicles, seats in public places, washrooms and so on create situations where the fat body is constantly caught in moments of unease and difficulty. The *lack of fit* (in all its meanings) pronounces the visibility of the body as it tries to fit into a landscape that conspires to make it clumsy, worthless and idiotic. Further, Susan Bordo (1993, p. 94) has argued that the fat stomach is 'most targeted for vicious attack'. This may not be surprising given how images of bulging stomachs saturate the mediascape and seem to be the sole staple visual tool in news reportage of the obesity crisis (Murray, 2008). For Bordo and others, the stomach operates metonymically signalling a blatant disregard for self-control and stands as a symbol of personal failure. Interestingly, the denigration of the weighty is so readily familiar that it has a transportability: Tanya Lewis (2008, p. 236) notes how lifestyle TV shows about climate change use 'fat metaphors' to describe over-consuming villains as 'carbon fatties' while urging the nation to 'slim down' carbon wise. The link between 'fat' and 'carbon' hints at the way the fat body's excess is framed as a *threat* and in need of management. It's hard to dismiss the importance of these cultural representations when theorists like Elizabeth Grosz stress the implications; 'representations and cultural inscriptions quite literally constitute bodies and help to produce them as such' (Grosz, 1994, p. xi). What we see then in media representations of the fat body are not descriptions but *productions*.

The exaggerated visibility of the body is a product too of an everyday cultural ability to read fat bodies in ways that reflect and reproduce the prevailing frame outlined thus far. Murray argues that Western cultures have a 'well-developed and readily deployable "literacy" when it comes to reading bodies' (2008, p. 13) and cites Graham's (2005) term 'lipoliterate'. Lipoliterate refers to the cultural meanings that a perceiver can directly fix to fat bodies so that they are understood through a matrix of historic cultural prejudices, financial burden, self-control violations and healthism. Lipoliteracy circulates everyday tacit knowledge about what the fat body *is*, how it was *caused*, and can immediately index its risks – we have the 'know how' to authoritatively conduct our own mental living autopsy on the bodies of Others, and a moral legitimacy for any discrimination/dislike that may follow. Like Grosz, Murray is clear that these readings are not descriptive – a reading *off* a fat body – but active productions of 'fat' as problematic – reading *of* the fat body. Indeed, the power of such framings and accompanying literacy foreclose the ways the fat body can be intelligible if not through risk. What we can draw from this discussion so far is that the fat body is 'always visible and always already constituted as health offenders' (Tischner and Malson, 2008, p. 26).

Televisual fat

Lifestyle media is, of course, part of this cultural habitat. Accordingly, obesity 'truths' and values of self-control trample throughout, generating and depending upon certain levels of audience lipoliteracy. It's worth mentioning then that as thin bodies tend to populate the mediascape (Gill, 2008b), it is significant that the fat body is over-represented in the lifestyle genre and mainly within weight-loss shows (Sender and Sullivan, 2008). Before we conclude that the increased visibility of fat and fat bodies testifies to a wider, positive *democratisation* of the media, it's important to reflect that while there may be *more* fat bodies, they are presented in contexts that aim to reduce that body and expel fat – the fat body thus overpopulates media spaces designed to transform it in something else. That said, the dramatisation of transformation takes many various and novel forms; taking lifestyle TV shows as an example, *3 Fat Brides, 1 Thin Dress* surprises three brides-to-be and sets them in competition for a designer wedding dress of their dreams – the thin dress of the title. Weight-loss alone doesn't guarantee success; the host,

Gillian McKeith, rewards the prospective bride who best combines a commitment to the McKeith 'way of life', the 'right' attitude *and* weight-loss. The competitive aspect of weight-loss is currently fashionable. The latest US show, *Dance Your Ass Off*, hosted by once-Spice girl Mel B, fuses the competitive dance show with formats like those of the hugely lucrative *The Biggest Loser* where contestants race to lose weight for a cash prize:

> Twelve finalists, nearly 3,000 lbs, one goal – to go from an eating machine to a dancing machine in Oxygen's new dance/weight loss competition series *Dance Your Ass Off [...]* Bringing dance and diet together, *Dance Your Ass Off* features talented, full-figured contestants who will have to lose to win. Each contestant is paired with a professional dance partner who will train him or her for weekly stage performances – ranging from Hip Hop, to Ballroom and even Pole Dancing! Then they shake and rattle their rolls in front of a live studio audience and a panel of expert judges. The judges score the routines, and then the contestants weigh in to reveal their weekly weight loss. The dance score and the weight loss are combined for an overall score, which determines who is sent home each week.
>
> http://dyao.oxygen.com/about-dyao

The mix of exercise and diet also feature in the UK's *Too Fat to Walk* and the US version, *Fat March*, in which 12 obese people vie for a pot of cash at the end of a 500-mile walk. Not all shows are so energetic, a more sedate *Supersize vs. Superskinny* requires a severely underweight and overweight participant to swap diets for five days while imprisoned in a food clinic. These shows may differ from those adopting a more traditional makeover format (*You Are What You Eat*) where individuals receive dedicated expert attention in diet and exercise as they are propelled to the show's reveal as lighter, empowered and radiant individuals. However, despite their diversity, it's possible to distinguish shared characteristics across weight-loss lifestyle shows.

Primarily, all recognise fat as an issue of diet and exercise and thus as an individual problem demanding a personal solution. That this is a blatantly obvious statement testifies to the ways that the healthism frame circulates, often without comment, in the cultural imaginary. From this, other characteristics fall; firstly, lifestyle TV and media more widely draw disproportionately on the most extreme fat bodies. The circulation of only a narrow-range of fat bodies is argued to exaggerate the scale of the obesity problem (Blaine, 2007). Secondly, shows tend to delimit the subjectivity of their participants to the matter of their weight (Sender and Sullivan, 2008); participants are first and foremost *fat*; their biography, emotional state and wider life are all refracted through this prism so that problems with weight are deftly translated into the cause of problems in all other spheres of life. Thirdly, all shows are unstinting in their visualisation of fat bodies. Not only are participants viewed in their underwear or swimwear so that all is exposed, but unflattering camera angles, unflinching close ups and 360-degree panning shots across the body tend to linger on dimpled bellies, thighs and flesh spilling out from drab underwear. Accompanying soundtracks play a part – *Supersize vs. Superskinny*'s errant bodies are screened against an unforgiving clinical backdrop while the Talking Heads repeat their line 'how did I get here?' (Talking Heads, 1984). Most shows accompany the visualisation of the body with expert commentary which is variously shocked, mocking, humiliating and disparaging – all helping create what sociologist Karen Throsby describes as the 'enfreakment' of the large body (2008, p. 121). Fourthly, there is an overarching message that losing weight is an expression of personal empowerment (Guthman, 2009). Weight-loss is dramatised in the theatrical and often highly public 'weigh-ins', where participants are called to account or rewarded for their efforts to reduce their weight: their body weight is unequivocal proof of their determination, hard work and will-power.

The fat body in contrast

Many of these characteristics can be glimpsed in the dramatic use of contrasts in TV weight-loss shows. We might immediately think of the contrast between the 'before' and 'after' shots, but strings of contrasts thread through the shows to position fat bodies as deviant in order to then construct fat as a problem to be managed. *3 Fat Brides and 1 Thin Dress*, for example, starts with footage of large women in a bridal shop trying on dresses. It's immediately obvious that the dresses are too small for them, but nonetheless they struggle, providing ample opportunity for the camera to linger on material straining over flesh, fastenings that cannot fasten and on any rolls of fat which distort the shape of the dress. The contrast between large (bodies) and small (dress) creates something of a comedic moment which affords the expert, Gillian McKeith, some space of mockery ('you'll need a posy the size of a beach ball to hide that belly'; 'you're like a beached whale'). These humiliating barbs are thinly disguised as humour which affords the women little recourse to challenge them. As Charlotte Cooper (1998) notes, fat women are expected to 'get the joke' and understand themselves to be a fair target. Struggle over, the women stand in dresses that gape at the back and await McKeith's judgement; the camera lingers on the flesh escaping from the too-small dress and upon the distance between the sides of fabric that can't reach across what McKeith calls a 'flabby back'. This prolonged focus on the 'gap' is interesting because the body is presented as a very tightly framed text intended for a specific reading from an audience – it is a surface inviting lipoliteracy. On one hand, it affords McKeith more material for her 'humour' that helps direct the audience's reading of the body (she jokes that one bride will have to wear her veil back to front so that it covers her back). On the other hand, the gap indicates the women's irrationality and perhaps deluded state (does she not know *just* how big she is?). It also dramatises the distance between the fat body and that of ideal femininity. As the bridal dress symbolises successful heteronormative femininity, the contrast of 'flabby backs' with the pure white, but ruined, fabric is so striking that the brides-to-be often collapse in humiliation and shame. Tellingly, the blame is their own: the dress serves as a 'wake-up' call for the women to claim that culpability before the transforming work can start.

There is a clear resonance with the ethos of self-control at play throughout these shows, and a determination to isolate fat as an individual problem with social implications. Many shows such as *3 Fat Brides* start off with jaw-dropping statistics and a scare-mongering list of ails and illnesses before presenting weight as the direct consequence of greedy overeating and lazy lifestyles. Secret footage of the brides snacking suggests daylong compulsive eating. Similarly, the entire premise of *Supersize vs. Superskinny* is based on the equivalence between over-eating and fat. While the skinny participants are filmed struggling with food, doing their best to be 'good', the overweight are pictured gorging and expressing with a childlike glee their shame at 'naughty' eating habits. The contrast between the mature body and the immature fat body plays through *Supersize* even as it presents two polar examples of extreme eating. So formulaic are the shows, it's possible to hold one show as a fair representation of the rest. Julie and Jade, the respective 'size' and 'skinny' of one episode, are filmed before their arrival at the food clinic. Jade is pictured playing with her child in her own home. She is deeply anxious that her eating problem will affect her son, or that he will develop a similar eating disorder. She wants to beat her problems so that she can be a better parent and have the energy required. Julie, however, is unemployed and lives with her parents. She expresses a deep love for food and is filmed being served mountainous plate loads of food by her mother (filmed pouring in a quart of cream into Julie's food). Julie talks enthusiastically about her mum's shepherd pie while her mum beams with a nervous pride, 'I like food because I like eating. I'll eat anything I can get my hands on basically', she says. That Julie has already been presented to the audience as 24 stone serves to orchestrate an unfavourable reaction towards her. She is presented as unaware, selfish, lazy, greedy and child-like – a melodramatic contrast to the guilt-ridden Jade. The immaturity of the fat body is further underscored when a thinner Julie receives warm congratulations for leaving home and for living an adult (self-responsible) life in the show's reveal.

What we can draw from the discussion so far is that lifestyle media play out (and upon) a bigger cultural background that attempts to limit the intelligibility and possibility of the fat body to the obesity epidemic. As such, lifestyle TV shows like *The Biggest Loser* are prime examples of what media scholar Jack Bratich has called 'instructional devices' (2006, p. 67). He is not referring to the ways shows may educate viewers in diet tips and exercise plans. Along with others discussed so far in this book, he critically situates lifestyle media as a cultural technology of neoliberal governance to argue that lifestyle media is about the 'making' of subjects through their conduct. In other words, what happens in, around and through innocuous pieces of advice about exercise and weight-loss are highly politicised injunctions which nurture and further responsibilisation (discussed in the previous chapter) and which promote self-enterprise, choice and personal accountability as the markers of recognisable and moral citizenship. Further, what is happening in the making of citizenship is the attempt to establish a moral economy where distinctions between a 'good' and 'bad' self are forged and circulated. What is of importance then are the ways that weight is framed and what relationships between the self and its (fat) body are imagined in that framing as it manifests in lifestyle media.

This brings me to explore the two fat figures conjured up in lifestyle TV shows; the rehabilitating fat body and the zombie fat body. The first is the initially reluctant, but later, plucky fat body, afforded a self-dimensionality. By self-dimensionality I mean that the fat body is re-presented with *makings of a self*. We know something about a person 'trapped' in the fat body. We know their motivations and struggles and can feel involved when they 'dig deep' and we, the audience, can follow their 'ups and downs' throughout the show. Their efforts to become better and thinner afford them a stronger stake on personhood – even if they fail – for then they can testify to self-development, lessons learnt and a renewed commitment. What we see is a determined but nonetheless cheerful engagement with the process of change. The rehabilitating fat body dominates much lifestyle TV, however is haunted by the second fat figure, the zombie. Before I explore this further, it's instructive to take a slight detour and examine the zombie more closely.

Zombies and TV decapitations

Zombies are thought to originate in the Vodoun religion of Haiti. Belief has it that Vodoun priests awoke the dead, lobotomised them and then trapped them in an infinite existence of unthinking slave labour: the zombie slave was 'speechless, incapable of emotion, slow moving but diligent, and utterly beholden to his or her "master"' (Gunn and Treat, 2005, p. 150). These defining characteristics largely held as the zombie entered Western popular culture. What's believed to be the first Western zombie film *Das Kabinet des Doktor Caligari* (1919) depicted a dastardly stage hypnotist who used his unthinking zombies to murder in accordance with his stage predictions. Later, Victor Halperin's *White Zombie* (1932) told the tale of a factory owner replacing his workers with the lumbering zombies made from his former enemies. Both films were thinly veiled critiques of global capitalism and master/slave nature of class relations, but the symbolic versatility of the zombie is evident in later films that cast Nazis as instigators of fiendish plots to bring about global fascism on the backs on their zombie armies (e.g. *Revenge of the Zombies*, 1944). From their potted history, Joshua Gunn and Shaun Treat (2005) identify two enduring features; firstly the zombie is always unthinking, and secondly it is controlled by a higher fiendish force or authority (p. 151). Thus zombification, the process through which one becomes a zombie, is one where an individual is *taken over* by something bigger than itself, so that the mind (imagined as the house of rationality, affect and reflexivity) is short-circuited leaving a mindless body.

The notion of being 'taken over' is one that preoccupies the modern zombie film. George Romero's (1968) *Night of the Living Dead* is argued to herald a new sub-genre of zombie apocalypse horror where zombies are taken over by their insatiable cannibalistic *appetites*. Although not the first to do so, Romero successfully recast the zombie in terms of excessive, mindless consumption – a notion cemented in his *Dead* portfolio (*Dawn of the Dead* (1979), *Day of the Dead* (1989), the 2005 *Land of the Dead*). The zombie 'taken over' by appetite has a wide currency, found, for example, in the multi-million *Resident Evil* franchise and in the newly spun 'zom-rom-com' sub-genre – the zombie romantic comedy – exemplified by Edgar Wright's (2004) *Shaun of the Dead*. In these films, hoardes of zombies take to the streets, threatening civilisation in search of food. Alongside the shift from zombies as slaves owned by masters to zombies as slaves of their own appetites there is another change. Fiendish masters are not needed to 'make' individual zombies, zombies increase their numbers by zombifying others through a single bite (an interesting textual borrowing from vampire myths – also enjoying current popularity in the West) or through contamination often through bodily fluids (e.g. vomit in Oliver Hirschbiegal's (2007) *Invasion*) – zombieness can thus be caught!

There are striking similarities between the fat body, as drawn in the cultural imagination through media representations, and the modern zombie and I am not alone in observing them. Others have noted how fat bodies are portrayed as the living dead. Media studies scholar Deborah Morrison Thomson (2009) notes that television reports of obesity represent the fat body through the girth of the stomach – rarely are the face or head shown. In what she calls an act of 'spectacular decapitation' (p. 8), fat bodies are filmed neck to knee, and in ways that allow weight to fill the screen. She speculates that decapitation may be an attempt to protect the privacy of a person filmed without their knowledge, but she is more interested in the symbolic violence enacted once a body is rendered headless; personhood, subjectivity and individuality are removed alongside the head. Kirsty Fife (2009) adds that decapitations remove the mouth, a symbolic act that denies the fat body a voice: the voiceless body is then unable to defend, protect or account for itself. It can only be spoken and regarded by others. There are many parallels then between the fat body and zombie – an appetite unhinged from rationality and self-control, a self 'taken-over' so that no face or voice is needed and also a sense of monstrous threat that the zombie/the obese poses to civilisation. Just as zombies unthinkingly 'take over' through ever expanding numbers, so too does the fat body swell in number and significance with each additional condemning statistic. Both zombies and fat bodies are a risk that must be managed or if not, extinguished because they are beyond repair.

Within weight-loss TV shows, the zombie fat body is presented in two discrete ways. Firstly, it is the 'before' body in the narrative device of 'before' and 'after' and is thus portrayed as an abject body to be cast off and escaped from (Morrison Thomson, 2009). As a body and state to be refuted, the zombie is used in lifestyle TV to incite 'manic desires for changing the self' (Ringrose and Walkerdine, 2008, p. 235). As a 'before' body it is presented as imprisoning and 'taking-over' a normal life, reducing it to a life lived on the margins. It has no motivation or agency – *it just is* – there are no desires to be filled through discerning consumption, rather, as the glistening mounds of food in *You Are What You Eat* indicate, the zombie fat body eats *anything*.

Secondly, the zombie body, when reduced to bulging, escaping stomachs and backsides, serves as a stock visual display in a TV show's reportage of obesity truths. In *Supersize*, for example, statistics are superimposed on a backdrop of various oversized bellies and butts. As such, the zombie fat body represents a homogenous mass from which the participant's body has been plucked and offered a chance of redemption. Further, if the zombie fat body represents a past it also stands for the future. Like a Dickensian ghost, it stands as a threat and warning of what's to come if opportunities to change aren't realised. *Supersize*, for example, conjures the zombie body through the testimonies of six severely obese people who embody a warning to the show's participants. This is one of the few cases where the zombie body actually speaks. Filmed naked on a bed, its immobility underscored by footage of teams of people turning an impossibly distorted body to clean its hidden crevices, the body is denied dignity or privacy but nonetheless it is given a head and a voice from which it issues pitiful laments and warnings – it's too late for me, don't be like me, make the change, take responsibility. As such, the zombie who *is* afforded a voice does so to articulate the ideals of self-responsibility, other zombies are left voiceless. That one of the people died during filming of *Supersize* adds to the urgency of their message and the presumed sad waste of their (unchanged) lives.

Honey, We're Killing the Kids provides a further example of the zombie as a 'future threat'. Using time-progressed, enhanced pictures of children *Honey* illustrates what a families' children would look like when they reached 40 years old. The primary point of the shocking visualisation is to demonstrate the impact of poor lifestyle choices on children currently enjoying their pre-teen years. However, what's striking is not just the catalogue of health risks that accompany the pictures, nor the tired, disgruntled, ill, bloated faces that stare out from under lank hair – but their *lifelessness*: these kids clearly got nowhere in the get-going neoliberal economy. Significantly lifelessness is read from a register of neoliberal values of self-managed health and social mobility. These static, dead-eyed bodies seem to represent a known social type and conjure up images of its habitat (Khatib, 2004). The lifeless life as coded here is that of the white, working class. It forms part of a cultural repertoire of stereotypes that draw similarities between the 'fat' unhealthy body and the working-class body across the mediascape.

As Bev Skeggs has argued, 'bodies are the physical sites where the relations of class, gender, race, sexuality and age come together and are embodied and practiced [...] Class is always coded through bodily dispositions: the body is the most ubiquitous signifier of class' (1997, p. 218).

Skeggs encourages a comparison between the zombie and classed body: both bodies are read as threat and risk through their refusal to be neatly contained – the fat body spills out of the respectable lines of deportment, just as the white working class threatened to spill into 'respectable' spaces of gated communities and shopping malls (McDowell, 2006). They are both bodies that are marked by lack *and* excess and through these are rendered a homogenous *mass*: the

parade of indistinguishable fat stomachs to the 'uniforms' of baseball caps and 'hoodies' of the 'chavs' stand in contrast with the
'individual look' wrought from personal choice in consumer culture
(Haywood and Yar, 2006). Ringrose and Walkerdine (2008) are critically sensitive to the ways class is reproduced here by equating a life
that 'shouldn't be' with stereotypical notions of working-class life.
They are clear that life while 'coded universal, normal and attainable
for all' is 'bourgeois' (p. 228). The zombie fat body is then abject,
threat and warning and also heavily classed.

The Zombie and the self

This chapter started with Judith Butler's interest in framing. More
particularly, it began with her observation that to 'be framed' means
to be 'set up', to have evidence planted against one, so that one's
guilt is an inevitable conclusion. In what ways then is the fat body
'set up'? What we can conclude so far is the fat body is framed
through the gradual devolving of state responsibility to the self
(responsibilisation), a process most graphically illustrated in the ways
individuals are rendered managers of their own health (healthism),
buttressed by the prevailing self-control ethos which defines and
allocates personhood on performances of culturally boosted values of self-discipline and self-management. As health is increasingly
translated as a matter of choice (Greco, 1993) and personhood as self-
discipline, weight manifests as matter of will-power and self-control,
marking *over*weight as a consequence of personal failure and an irrational risk-taking which has financial consequences for all. That the
fat body is so overdrawn raises questions of what function it serves in
the formation of self. To recap, the zombie refers to those representations of the fat body that are either cast outside of rehabilitation
narratives (this body isn't going to change) or depicted as the body
and *state* that one needs to change from.

Despite its different manifestations it's possible to argue that the
zombie is clearly cast as the bodily Other in the weight narratives
weaving through contemporary lifestyle TV. Othering has been mentioned earlier in this book (Chapter 1), but it's worth reminding
ourselves that it refers to the construction of points of difference and
distinctions between groups or identities, in such ways that protect
the privileges, exclusive membership and values of a dominant group

(Wilton, 2000). As such, Othering is both product and constitutive of dominance as it forges neat, cauterised, but nonetheless culturally *fictive*, divisions between self and Other. As might be expected from my emphasis, these divisions are not neutral; the self constructs itself as socially worthy and authentic *at the expense of the Other* (Prokhovnik, 1999). This is how feminist scholar Evelyn Glenn explains it;

> The dominant group's self-identity (e.g., as moral, rational and benevolent) depends on the casting of complementary qualities (e.g., immoral, irrational, and needy) onto the subordinate 'Other'.
> (Glenn, 1999, p. 10)

This dependence means that any assertion of what we are is at once a declaration of what we aren't: 'we know what we are by what we are not' (Shildrick, 2002, p. 17). The upshot, as sociologist Stevi Jackson argues, is that the self 'can only exist in relation to the other' (1999a, p. 17). In other words the Other haunts the self because it is only through the Other that the self can be possible and intelligible. For our purposes this means that fat bodies *have* to endure heightened visibility in the cultural imaginary for there to be a notion of a 'normally-weighted' body; further, the association of the fat body with negative values and behaviours, even lifelessness, is necessary for the 'normal body' to be read in ways that allow its inhabitant to claim socially approved personhood: the zombie fat body then 'rings the margins of the good self, haunting them as it helps create them' (Kent, 2001, p. 136). That said, it's important to the viability of the 'normal' body, dependant as it is on current neoliberally infused values, that some 'abnormal' bodies do attempt and even succeed to rehabilitate. The meritocracy suggested in the stories of transformation, paraded in lifestyle media, masks the intimate power plays and psychological investments in the self-controlled body. However, it's *as* important that the zombie fat body doesn't transform, seeming to place itself outside of rehabilitation – so that the self has it's necessary Other.

Additionally, the self's disruptive desires, non-compliant behaviours or poor attitudes, all of which threaten its integrity are, through the process of Othering, attached to the Other and presented as its essential characteristics (Joffe, 2007; Skeggs, 2004). For us, this means that the 'normal' sized body is 'set up'/framed to be read by the light of its alignment to the self-control ethos and any temptations or obstacles that threaten to destabilise or 'take-over' its project of becoming are cast onto the Other. The fat body is thus targeted with fears of laziness, greed, inefficiency, and, tellingly of our time, dependency and immobility – all fears of a situated self. Drawing on psychodynamics, Joffe (2007) notes how the projection of the self's anxieties and fears onto the Other serves to condemn the self to a constant vigilance against the return of those projections – often understood in terms of contamination – and to an enduring apprehension, unease and even fear of the Other: for the Other threatens to *undo* the self. So, while the 'normal' body can't 'catch' fat, it is fearful of the contagious 'diseases of will' so imaginatively and intensively housed in the body of the Other. As these anxieties are the self's own, it is no wonder that the non-obese body can so easily, and with authority, read the zombie fat body – it has the advantage of familiarity. This goes someway to explain what seems to be a cultural acceptability of fat prejudice. The fat body is then a predictable casualty and construct of the strident, at times exuberant, calls to self-discipline and its hyperbolic drawings are highly indicative of the way self-control has shaped-up in Western neoliberal democracies.

Cultural theorist Margrit Shildrick (2002) is interested in the intense cultural work that goes into constructing what she sees as the *illusion* of a secure discretely bounded selfhood, the kind nurtured in Western accounts of autonomy and self-realisation. Her work on monsters (deformed, disabled and mythical bodies) charts how this illusion has been manufactured across various institutions, from the Church to biomedical science, each attempting to identify, rationalise and then expel the monster (a literal expulsion in the past and an often surgical reconstruction today), She takes these labours of rationalisation and expulsion as her starting point to militate against the possibility of cauterised self/Other separation. Instead, she argues that when we look at the monster – in our case the zombie fat body – we see and realise our own vulnerabilities, our own 'leaks and flows' of our 'embodied being' (2002, p. 4). Although the zombie fat body, like Shildrick's monster, is sanitised by medical discourses and contained in discrete parts of TV narratives and thus 'safe', it tends to move into more troubling water in those long-lingering, repulsive yet fascinating, camera shots on bloated, naked, zombie bodies. This close exposure to the televised body causes some self-anxiety, just at the point where we might conclude a self-security, an affirmation of the self, by virtue of the sharp contrasts between living dead/dead; mobile/immobile; responsible/culpable and so on. Shildrick explains that this anxiety is a consequence of the self encountering resemblance and familiarity within the Other.

For Shildrick, this encounter provides a politically charged opportunity that could allow all bodies to slip and slide within and from their social classifications, producing, she argues, a realisation of the vulnerability of the self and of all bodies. This realisation through resemblance is politically important for it reveals that what passes as normal, such as the BMI score of below 25, is actually *normative*. There is an opportunity then to expose and critique more fully the pervasive, invasive shaping of the self (the normative) and, in so doing, to realise as Foucault had hoped, that we are freer than we may think (Foucault, 1982). For Shildrick, the political and life-defining moment lies in embracing, not projecting, vulnerability and anxiety, to allow us all to recognise the 'interrelatedness of social life' (p. 85), the necessary fluidity of all bodies and the rhythms of embodiment which are currently exorcised or denied by socially constructed notions of 'normal' (Murray, 2008). In such recognition there is the potential to detach ourselves from normative dictates – the zombie can thus free the self.

To be sure, this potential exists in the shows described thus far. As diligently as the zombie is dehumanised, it has to retain some echo of resemblances to the self to function as the monster we ought to orchestrate our biographical trajectories *away from*. As the zombie has to be so drawn, it may well spark a politically important encounter borne from a realisation of the impossibility of self/Other binaries, of the consequences of denying the body's, all bodies, vulnerabilities and of the importance of interdependency and interrelatedness. While that reading exists, it is limited, or at worst erased, by the existence of that first fat figure I identified earlier, the rehabilitating fat body. This plucky body helps tease our recognition to a body that materialises through the same effacing, cauterising, values that create self: Other relations. This *becoming* body, as it dominates the airtime of the weight-loss show draws our attention, may grab our sympathies and serves to retrain any errant gazes back from the body to the action of transformation. Interestingly, the narrative structure of weight-loss shows actively encourage moments of recognition of resemblance in those painfully loitering shots of the 'before' body, and then with narrative dexterity orientate those onto the rehabilitating fat body. It is not incidental then, the rehabilitating body starts off as the zombie body, the body the show is devoted to casting off. We are left then with a further encounter of 'becoming' not of a politically charged undoing; the self is thus once more 'set up' for its life of self-betterment.

Summary

This chapter has expanded on a previous discussion of framing to specifically focus on weight-loss TV shows and, particularly, upon the ways the fat/obese body is represented within them. It has shown that weight-loss shows are deeply situated in wider social and economic constructions of an obesity epidemic, the rhetoric of which stubbornly locates the cause and cure of 'fatness' within an individual's personal remit. The repeated insistence that fat can be controlled is evident in the BMI calculator's ubiquity and in the 'commonsense' injunction to exercise and eat well. It also enjoys heightened cultural circulation in lifestyle TV, which tends to cast the problem of individual weight as lack of motivation (hence the 'fun' competition of *Dance Your Ass Off*, and the 'boot camp' survival competition favoured by *The Biggest Loser*), or lack of nutritional knowledge and skill (*Supersize; You Are What You Eat*). The chapter discussed two representations of fat body in weight-loss shows: as the headless zombie that signalled the abject, operated as a threat and served up warnings and as the plucky, rehabilitating body. This latter body caught the attention of Meredith Jones in Chapter 2, who observed how the fat body was recast from worthy of 'boos' to 'cheers' as it moved from 'being' fat to 'becoming' thinner. However, that the plucky body materialises through the values of normative selfhood was argued to erase a potentially radical encounter with the zombie body. To conclude, an opportunity to image bodies beyond risk and self-control is foreclosed by a frame 'politically saturated' with healthism.

Part III
Before and After

5
Being Worth It: The Deserving Self

We're off to Mineola, Texas to help another amazing family. Mike and Katrina Carr are loving parents to four adopted children who were abandoned in Kazakhstan. Two of the children, Ryanne and Rina, were born with Amniotic Band Syndrome which caused many physical challenges. And Mike has been plagued with diabetes since he was a child. Mike and Katrina have battled through their challenges to provide a loving home for their children. However, over $50,000 in repairs is needed and Mike was recently laid off from his job. The Carrs need help and we know a team that will step up to the challenge. *Extreme Makeover: Home Edition.*
http://abc.go.com/shows/extreme-makeover-home-edition/episode-guide

I want to give you the house that you deserve but unfortunately it all comes down to budget. How do you feel about handing over your money – everything really – to entrust me to do that for you? George Clarke *The Home Show.*
http://www.channel4.com/4homes/on-tv/the-home-show/

Introduction

As we reach the final part of the book it's worth taking stock of how it has unfolded so far. This book has placed lifestyle media within the specific imperatives of neoliberal governance. It has then sought to extend a critical awareness of the pedagogical function of lifestyle media by focusing more closely on how selves are formed through labours of 'being' and 'becoming' (Part I). Previous chapters concentrated upon rehabilitation. They argued that processes of rehabilitation provide the momentum necessary for a ceaseless makeover culture and they also highlighted the importance of the un-rehabilitated, the haunting spectre of zombie, to that movement (Part II). This brings us to this chapter, which furthers the theme of rehabilitation by exploring how selves are placed or judged as suitable for the specific journeys of transformation offered across lifestyle media. I am inspired here by Meredith Jones (2008) who makes an excellent case for teasing out the narrative spaces between the 'before' and 'after' stages of transformation. In this spirit, I want to pick at the 'before' moment to see what can be revealed when it is unfolded. Specifically, this chapter is interested in the cultural labours that present a self as worthy enough to *start* the journey of transformation.

This chapter argues that access to transformation depends on specific performances of worthiness and deservingness. It starts from the belief that the burden of proving worthiness is not equally distributed. Take the two home makeover shows quoted above as an example; the families who receive the charitable attentions of the *Extreme Makeover: Home Edition* team are presented as 'worthy' through their 'battles', insurmountable hardships and their determination, loyalty and family values in the face of these. In contrast, *The Home Show*, a show premised on family's ability to *pay* upwards of £40,000 to architect George Clarke to redesign their home, does not need to overstate the merit of the families involved – instead it simply *states* them. The ability to pay, more importantly to pay for *transformation,* signals the right aspirations and directions – these are then *already deserving* families: they need only to await the latest in mixer taps and open-plan living spaces. There are then two separate questions that inform these respective shows, 'do you deserve a makeover?' and 'can you afford what you deserve?' I am interested in the first question and explore it through a selection of lifestyle TV shows, variously described as 'feel-good TV' (Watts, 2009), 'good Samaritan TV' (McMurria, 2008) and as 'emotional pornography' (Dixon, 2008). I consider how a self is positioned in relation to the journey of transformation and how selves are enabled to *talk themselves into* that journey. My point is that the space between 'before' and 'after' is not the only space for transformative actions, rather how individuals are gathered at the 'before' stage demands an intense cultural labour which is indicative of the social forces attempting to form and shape contemporary personhood.

'Feel-good TV'

There are an increasing number of lifestyle TV shows which can be described as 'feel-good TV' (McMurria, 2008; Watts, 2009). These include shows such as *Miracle Workers, Extreme Makeover: Home Edition, DIY SOS* and *Renovate My Family*. These different shows intervene in the lives of families and individuals who are beset by terrible and often multiple misfortunes, as these synopses demonstrate:

> In 2004 the five Higgins children, aged 14 to 21, lost their mother following her brave battle with breast cancer. Three months later, their father passed away due to heart failure. The kids used their last money to pay for their parents' funeral costs. In addition to going through their devastating loss, they had to figure out a way to stay together and continue living in the two-room converted motel/apartment that the family had shared. Phil and Loki Leomiti insisted that the five children come to live with them in their three-bedroom, 1269-sq. ft. ranch style house. With their own three children [...] that brought the total number of people in the small home to 11 [...]. The Leomiti family is willing to make whatever sacrifices are necessary to ensure that the Higgins have a brighter outlook in life *Extreme Makeover: Home Edition.*
> http://abc.go.com/shows/extreme-makeover-home-edition/
> episode-guide/leomitihiggins-family/68105

> The team is in Frimley in Camberley to help the Oxford family – Lisa, Andy and son Jordan. The Oxfords had just started a double-storey extension on their property when Lisa started getting terrible headaches. Shortly after she was diagnosed with brain cancer which left her unable to drive or walk. Husband Andy took two years off work to nurse her and look after Jordan. There was no time or money to finish the extension and without the extra space the whole family had to share the same bed. It was

time to call in *DIY SOS*. BBC http://www.bbc.co.uk/programmes/
b00k04j2#synopsis

The misfortune of others adds to the melodrama of lifestyle
TV makeover shows and heightens the urgency and significance
of lifestyle intervention, suggesting that makeover shows aren't
frivolous, rather that they help to rebuild lives. Additionally, in the
case of home makeover shows, the knowledge of the participant's
misfortune tightens the moment of suspense around the 'reveal'. The
question, slowly building through any show, often pondered by the
hosts, of 'will they like it?' is answered in the overwhelmed, emotional reactions of the participants. Through their tears, captured by
close-up shots, a show's participants testify not just to the sensational
makeover of their homes, but to the restoration of their lives. This is
only intelligible if, as Cressida Heyes (2007b, p. 20) argues, the home,
its decoration and layout are imagined as an 'extension of the personality and status of their occupants'. The new home doesn't promise
a new life to come – it *provides* that new life in the instant of the
reveal, hence the joy of the recipients who don't just get a life *back*,
but a better start in a new life. The audience's tacit knowledge of the
link between appearance and the interiority of the self, when combined with the contrast between the horrifying events which brought
a family/individual to apply to a lifestyle show with the joy of the
reveal, produces the show's feel-good factor.

There are a number of home makeover shows, many of which have
grown from the instructional 'how to' DIY shows of the 1950s, but
have moved away from the practical skills of repair to showcase the
skills and creativity of the expert-presenters and their teams. The
'action' rests not in craftsmanship but in what can be produced in
a limited amount of time. Currently, the US show *Extreme Makeover:
Home Edition* is one of the most successful, harvesting a crop of
industry awards and attracting lucrative sponsorship and advertising sales (Dixon, 2008). *Extreme* as the title may suggest does not
repair a home, rather it demolishes it and rebuilds within seven
days (a time limit that might be intended to spark off some religious connotations). The United Kingdom's *DIY SOS* is more modest
in scope than *Extreme*, the DIY team mostly repair, renovate and
re-energise what they find over a few days. However, it shares with
Extreme a focus on helping deserving families, and what the show
may lack in the frenzied action of *Extreme* it more than makes up

for in its pathos. By presenting brief video clips of deserving families, *DIY SOS* invites the viewing audience to vote for who will receive the team's attentions the following week. In so doing, *DIY SOS* can exhibit more hard-luck stories than the show actually needs – a voyeurism that encourages scholars like Wheeler Dixon (2008, p. 56) to describe the increasing parade of misery in lifestyle TV as 'emotional pornography'.

Yet, this 'porn' is not a recent narrative invention. Amber Watts (2009) is among those who discern precedent in 1950s American shows such as *Strike it Rich* and *Queen for a Day*. *Queen*, for example, comprised of housewives who presented their misfortune to a studio-audience's judgement and made a plea for the one consumer good that would improve their otherwise sorry lot. The most deserving of stories, as voted by the audience's volume of applause, was rewarded with a new washing machine, tumble-dryer or Cadillac convertible (Dixon, 2008). This 'merchandise-based relief' (Watts, 2009, p. 303) has stood the passing of time and circulates in many makeover shows, with at least two consequences. Firstly, it turns contemporary shows like *Extreme* into lengthy commercials for the goods 'donated' by Sears and other sponsors. This takes the practice of 'product placement' to new levels under the guise of corporate philanthropy and happily compensates for viewers who use their home technology to 'skip' the traditional space of advertising – the commercial break (McMurria, 2008). Secondly, it reinforces a central motif of lifestyle TV that this book has been unpicking thus far: the notion that problems of 'living' can be resolved through recourse to the market and consumer culture. Speaking of *Queen*, Watts argues its message is that consumer goods bring happiness 'and ensure that her problems would not resurface' (2009, p. 312).

'Feel-good TV' is not without its critics. On a practical front, Wheeler Dixon (2008) is sceptical of the effectiveness of *Extreme's* market-based intervention. He reports on poor standards of building work that later needs costly repairs and he has concerns about the scandalous property and utility taxes due when properties are transformed from affordable homes into real estate with million dollar property values (one family ended up with a six-figure tax bill). However, a more pertinent line of critique for our purposes is provided by John McMurria. He moves away from the show itself to consider the wider social context that, for him, produces the need for *Extreme's* intervention. Far from seeing hard-luck stories of the families as exaggerated and perhaps rare, he is more inclined to view them as indication of the 'precarious living conditions that many experience in neoliberal policies that champion "free market" principles and diminish government social services' (2008, p. 307). Hard-luck stories of costly health-care, unemployment, poverty, crime and so on are not personal misfortunes but, he argues, are direct consequences of the reduction in the scope and depth of 'social safety nets' (p. 306) through neoliberal reform. Laurie Ouellette and James Hay (2008) have described this context as a 'post-welfare society', arguing, with no small amount of concern, that lifestyle media becomes one way in which social services can be delivered – the makeover becomes something of a *substitute*:

> It is the sign of the times that hundreds of thousands of individuals now apply directly to reality TV programs not only for medical needs, but also for decent housing (*Extreme Makeover: Home Edition, Town Haul, Mobile Home Disasters*), tuition and income assistance (*The Scholar, Three Wishes*), transportation (*Pimp My Ride*), disaster relief (*Three Wishes: Home Edition*), food, clothing, and other basic material needs (*Random One, Renovate My Family*).
>
> (Ouellette and Hay, 2008, pp. 32–33)

For whom does lifestyle TV serve as an intelligible substitute? Ouellette and Hay (2008) report that *Extreme* receives some 15,000 applications *per week*. As the applications for *Extreme* come from existing home-owners (an application criteria), applicants tend to come from what can be described as lower middle class or aspiring working class. They are often 'junior' public sector workers (nurses, police officers) who have a precarious hold on the 'American Dream' and are exposed to the vagaries of an expanding and contracting labour market, yet are vital to the reproduction and security of the neoliberal way of life – enforcing law, advising on health and so on. They have, in the cultural imagination, something to *lose* – their home and the respectable way-of-life they have been striving towards. This makes their story of personal misfortune more dramatic for American viewers who may be making the same investments, and helps *Extreme* to focus on personal hard-luck stories while ignoring any political or structural explanations for hardship.

However, *Extreme's* application process immediately disregards a whole swathe of the American public. McMurria argues that less than 50 per cent of Hispanic and African American communities own their own home, and are under increased financial pressure to pay rent due to ex-President Bush's strategy to encourage home ownership by, in part, cutting the funding for rental assistance and public housing schemes. Although McMurria argues that many Americans can find themselves living in poverty at some stage of their life, the burden of poverty falls most heavily on those systematically denied the means and resources to escape, yet are blamed for not so doing – the working class. It is not coincidental that the groups who are over-represented in lifestyle TV are also those who bear the blunt of many reformist neoliberal policies. While *Extreme's* application process may operate as a filter to exclude the most vulnerable, it's far to say that across the board it's the lower classes who must present themselves as needing, but more importantly as *worthy* of assistance and intervention (Ringrose and Walkerdine, 2008; Skeggs, 2009). If we must regard lifestyle media as one of an increasing number of substitutes for social service provision, we must be crucially aware of the uneven access to these 'services' and also to their discriminating attentions.

Couches and life stories

An individual's access to the journey of transformation depends on their success in convincing the producers and then the audience that they *deserve* the makeover. This 'pitch' tends to take the form of personal tales of hardship as the earlier synopses have illustrated. These personal tales form part of the application process of all shows but can also form part of the show itself. For example, both *DIY SOS* and *What Not to Wear* screen the video applications of want-to-be participants. *What Not to Wear* goes further and makes the selection process, including a probing interview conducted by the host, a lengthy segment of the show. Interestingly, the interviewee reclines on a therapist's couch, the host sitting alongside armed with a thoughtful expression, pen and clipboard. The therapist's couch as a prop and setting for the intimacy of the personal story is also used by TV psychologist Geoff Beattie in the example that started this book. In *How to Dump Your Mates*, a cherry-red couch is transported to Adam's housing estate. Not only does its colour make a striking contrast with the

drab gray of the rundown estate, it serves to suggest that the therapeutic encounter is the only possible reflective, meaningful space
for Adam, and as Beattie only doles out his advice while near it,
the couch seems an island formed by his authority in an unruly
and unpredictable habitat. In both examples, the couch suggests that
therapy, confession and testimony are the only vehicles for change
and are the only route of escape from the events and circumstances
of hardship.

On those couches or in the alternative confessional spaces of
lifestyle TV (in front of mirrors, home video cameras and so on), the
personal story of hardship is normally presented in the form of a life
narrative, *not as a singular current event*. In *How to Look Good Naked*, for
example, a specific focus of bodily discontent is presented as emerging through the life course to taint every aspect of life; stomachs
that produced acute self-consciousness in the teenage years become
unbearable disabilities in adult life. In *Embarrassing Illness* some people have experienced painful conditions for many years, if not all of
their lives. *What Not to Wear's* participants are encouraged to recount
their lives to seek the origin of their present suffering. The use of long
time frames serves as a dramatic device to satisfy Aristotle's point that
suffering, in order to receive the required response of compassion,
has to be perceived as 'serious' (cited in Williams, 2008); a lengthy
time span of pain/misery or suffering communicates the extent of
a problem and its seriousness to the audience because it suggests a
stoic struggle and a brave, if misguided, *coping* on one hand, and an
anxiety and fear on the other.

However, the life narrative is of additional interest to us here
because of its inability to be a factual recording of a series of events:
any life story is a *framing* – the generation of a specific story from
a mass of experience through selection and omission. Frames have
been discussed in the previous section of this book, but it's worth
explaining here that as a frame, a narrative is produced through the
presumed expectations and values of the audience and the intentions
of the speaker. It is necessarily a product of its cultural context – as
such it bears all traits of its contextual 'cultural, interpersonal and lin-
guistic influences' (Bruner, 2004, p. 694). The ways we generate and
communicate life stories 'speak' to the prevailing social values which
shape ideas about who speaks to whom, in what ways and for what
purpose – and which also influence which stories can be told and
which will be listened to (Epstein et al., 2000). Jerome Bruner adds,

Given their constructed nature and their dependence upon the cultural conventions and language usage, life narratives obviously reflect the prevailing theories about 'possible lives' that are part of one's culture. Indeed, one way of characterizing a culture is by the narrative models it makes available for describing the course of a life.

(Bruner, 2004, p. 694)

For Bruner then life stories reflect a culture's aspirations and idealisations of 'possible lives'; stories are told in terms of which lives/ways of living are valued and recognised in a given culture in a given time. This returns us with some force to the necessarily contextual, embedded nature of selfhood and of recognition. Butler argues that the self 'has no story of its own that is not also a story of a relation – or set of relations – to a set of norms' (2005, p. 8). As we have seen, these norms pester, prod and produce hegemonic frames of recognition so that to have self-recognition and to be recognised by others always entails a relation and negotiation of normative and normalising frames that persist in their insistence of carefully delimited 'possible lives'. To tell a life story then, especially in the heightened judgmental scene of an application or supplication, is not to describe a self, but is an active production of selfhood – in the telling of the self, the self is made (Murray, 2008). This argument gives added impetus to question the shapes life stories take on lifestyle TV and to explore what 'makings of the self' are being attempted.

Being worthy

Lifestyle TV shows such as *Extreme* favour life stories of suffering. Suffering is usually the means through which a problem is presented for the experts to 'fix' and is often 'fixed' through forms of therapy from the 'retail therapy' of the home/garden/wardrobe makeover to the emotional therapy of weight-loss, clutter-busting, esteem-enhancing shows and self-help books. While 'there is no single way to suffer', stories of hardship have to appeal to an audience on both emotional and moral grounds (Kleinman and Kleinman, 1997, p. 2). In short, this means that someone else's hardship/suffering has to perceived or *felt* on some level, in the stirrings of empathy, sympathy, concern or indeed, as Shildrick (2002) would have it, in the recognition of resemblance. Further, it means that suffering has to be presented in

ways that prompt or suggest a sense of injustice, and perhaps a remedial action, or in the case of lifestyle TV shows offer the satisfaction of
watching the remedial actions of intervening parties. The 'feel-good'
factor depends on a sense that it is right to intervene and 'good' to do
so. But there are further plays of morality – an audiences' feeling and
recognition of someone's suffering depends on whether the sufferer
is deemed to be morally culpable for their fate or not.

These points are developed in Christopher Williams' (2008) analysis of suffering. He extends Aristotle's observation that compassion
for another's suffering depends upon three related judgements; that
the suffering experienced by another is serious, undeserved and
the misfortune that befalls another *could* fall upon one's own self
(a belief that it could happen to me). Williams focuses on two of
these observations to claim that there are 'compassion filters', two
forms of related judgements, which someone has to pass through
to have their suffering recognised and to be deemed worthy of
compassion. He identifies the compassion filters as 'appraisals of
desert and responsibility' and 'perceptions of likeness and difference'
(2008, p. 5).

Diane Richardson and Helen May's (1999) analysis of crime victims
may seem a departure, but is helpful in expanding Williams' filters.
Starting with 'the appraisals of desert and responsibility', Williams
argues that the types of suffering we regard as deserving of compassion are 'wedded to prevailing social attitudes' (2008, p. 10). As Joffe
and Staerklé (2007) have already argued in these pages, current attitudes tend to reflect and reproduce a family of values (autonomy,
self-discipline and self-responsibility) that are housed in what they
term the 'self-control ethos'. If that's the case then violations of these
cardinal values are unlikely to incur sympathy or compassionate
understanding. Accordingly, Williams states that a perception that
suffering is caused by 'malfeasance, negligence' or 'dangerous risk-
taking' (p. 10) seldom elicit a compassionate response. Richardson
and May concur, stating that the designation of 'victim' rests on these
very judgements of culpability and self-responsibility. In other words,
in the course of any judgement a question is asked of whether the
misfortune could have been avoided. However, they extend the point
to argue that there are context-specific influences at work when making a judgement. Via an example of sexual crime, Richardson and
May note how women are less likely to gain a conviction for sexual

assault if they are unescorted and if the attack occurs at night, outside the home. What's clear here is that notions of gender appropriate behaviour, tacit knowledge about male sexuality and cultural notions that bind normative 'respectable' femininity to the private sphere, all swirl into an interpretive moment to confuse a woman's claim to victimhood.

Williams second compassion filter is 'perceptions of likeness and difference', by which he means that we are more likely to respond compassionately to another's plight if they are presented as 'like us', and sharing a similar moral code, and less likely if they manifest as different. Again, this is a point Richardson and May can expand upon in terms of their victimhood studies. Their main argument is that a claim for victimhood rests on the *social status* of the person claiming to be a victim. More specifically, they utilise the concept of 'right to life' to explain how circulations and sedimentations of social discrimination in the wider cultural imagination attach to bodies/selves. These attachments produce a general working belief that some people 'not like us' have less personhood – less right to life – than others. For Richardson and May, personhood is socially defined, and those regarded as having less personhood are less likely to be recognised as victims/sufferers and *more likely* to be regarded as complicit or responsible. For example, enduring, persistent homophobic stereotypes inform what Murray would call a 'negative cultural knowingness' (2008, p. 4) about the gay body that troubles the victim status of gay men. Both the gay man and the woman out at night invite this 'cultural knowingness' rendering them both, albeit to differing degrees depending on context, 'deserving victims' and the acts of violence they experience *could* be regarded as 'intelligible violence' (Richardson and May, 1999, p. 309). By virtue of *being*, in the tight discursive and material spaces afforded to them, some selves and identities are always *already* culpable.

If we broadly accept the existence of compassion filters, we can make two points. The first is that we can expect the burden of proving worth to fall most heavily upon those groups with little or precarious social status. The second is that these groups and individuals, in order to be successful in lifestyle TV shows, will have to remove any suspicion of their own culpability in order to have their misfortune and suffering, *their victim status*, legitimated and recognised. In many ways, the self will have to present as an ordinary 'blank slate' discussed in Chapter 1, as one untouched by the taint of class, race and gender. These, of course, are the very means that position the self at the mercy of many neoliberal policies, yet, in order to avoid incurring any 'negative cultural knowingness' that attaches to these readable, visible 'known social types' they must remain unspoken or carefully managed. This is especially true of class, were an abundance of stereotypes about working class *lack* conjure up notions of laziness, poor attitudes, lack of pride, and uncontrollable, uncontained excess and waste. All of these code some sections of the working class as culturally retardant in a progressive neoliberal context and render them 'deserving victims' (McDowell, 2006). This is important, because to reiterate, 'individuals are less likely to feel empathy for targets to which they have attributed blame ... and conversely, more empathy for targets they perceive as innocent' (Pizzaro, 2000, p. 363). Some selves are not, then, likely candidates for the *Extreme* or *DIY SOS* teams without intense cultural work.

I want to focus on two examples of that cultural work; the use of *bad luck* stories in the 'before' segment of a show and the use of *discourses of addiction* which progress the rehabilitation movement required by the makeover culture. Both, I argue, help position the self as worthy of change by enabling their suffering to pass through the 'filters' of appraisal identified by Williams.

Victims of circumstance: the right kind of 'bad luck'

Does your home *desperately* need some attention? Then print out the application form and send it and you may have the *Extreme Makeover* team knocking at your door! If you are, or know of, a family who has fallen victim to circumstances beyond their control that truly affects their home or the condition of their home, download an application for now!

Please note we are *not* looking for families who:

1/ bought a fixer-upper and can't afford to fix it
2/ have outgrown their home
3/ Own a home larger than 2,000 square feet.

http://a.abc.com/media/primetime/xtremehome/
apply/EMHEApplicationS7.pdf

As this application form for *Extreme* makes clear, it is important that a families' misfortune is not 'self-afflicted' through risky purchases (buying a property that one can't afford to restore) or wrong purchases (a house that no longer fits). Rather than being a consequence of poor financial management or lack of forward planning, misfortune is immediately defined as something that is unexpected and unlikely ('circumstances beyond control') and which could not be reasonably avoided. If suffering can't be regarded as a consequence of one's own actions, it has to be presented as the result of some event or *happening* to the self such as illnesses or unemployment. It adds to the melodrama of a show if one of these serves as a trigger event to a calamitous chain of circumstances. A very crude approximation of a premise for an episode of *Extreme* could look something like this: illness leads to unemployment, financial hardship means that insurance payments aren't made, house burns down or is destroyed by flood or earthquake and there's no money to rebuild it, the family are reduced to living in one room and the future of the family is at stake.

As misfortune is so tightly defined, what counts as suffering also becomes quite limited. Lifestyle TV shows don't tend to present suffering as that *caused* by an illness or unemployment, although there will be mention of pain and difficulty. Rather, the *real suffering* is reserved for the implications of that illness/job loss to one's role and social standing. In the lifestylemediascape suffering is saturated by a powerful narrative theme of loss that speaks directly to the threat or reduction of one's *viability* in the makeover culture. Property makeover shows express this loss most graphically because they play on the symbolic importance of home ownership in neoliberal Western democracies (Seale, 2006). The home is not only equated with financial success and social status but it also acts as both a reward and right of neoliberal citizenship (Negra, 2009). To misquote Gareth Palmer (2004, p. 181) the home is an 'opportunity for self-staging' because it stands as an immediate marker of one's taste, role and aspiration. As such, the privately owned home is an extension of the responsible, mature and desiring self (Silva and Wright, 2009), and thus presents the ideal melodramatic setting for lifestyle media stories of loss and restoration. As Jerome Bruner argued earlier, the stories we tell of our lives reflect cultural definitions of what he called 'possible lives'. These are the lives that count and *matter* in the material and discursive orchestrations of neoliberal societies. Presenting the loss of the components of these lives *as a cause of suffering* is to further naturalise these lives as worthy and 'right'. In terms of the pedagogic function of lifestyle TV (Ouellette and Hay, 2008), stories of loss serve to highlight and valorise that which is lost and the depth of suffering testifies to its desirability.

However, it is not just the 'right' kind of loss that makes for a successful application. What are also important are the ways individuals and families *cope* with their loss. Ouellette and Hay provide the following quote from the executive producer of *Extreme*, Tom Forman;

> We look for people who deserve it. It's tough to judge. It's people who have given their whole lives and suddenly find themselves in a situation where they need a little help. Most of the families we end up doing are nominations. The kind of families we're looking for don't say 'Gee, I need help'. They're quietly trying to solve their problems themselves and it's a neighbour or a co-worker who submits an application on their behalf.
>
> (cited in Ouellette and Hay, 2008, p. 48)

Forman's phrase 'find themselves in a situation' serves to remove any suggestion of the families' culpability: they are victim of circumstance. His mimicry of 'Gee, I need help' serves to mock and denigrate those who *expect* that some form of help will be forthcoming and who turn to others in askance. In contrast, the *deserving* family may need 'a little help' but their first response is not to ask for it but to try to solve their own problems. Forman's use of 'quietly' is important here; these families are not creating a fuss by 'moaning', picketing their old employee or starting campaigns for health-care reform. They are not railing against a system that has let down the people 'who have given their whole lives'. No. Instead, the 'ideal' family *looks within*, no doubt adopting the self-reflexive, mature stance favoured by self-help books to reflect upon errors made, lessons learnt, and to pull upon their own personal will-power to puzzle out their return to viability. Because it is 'quiet' the struggle is a private one, but nonetheless recognised by others who, in turn, feel moved to nominate them for the show. It's suggestive of the cultural appeal of 'feel-good TV', and of the perceived failure of more traditional welfare support, that concerned co-workers would *think* of contacting a TV show to help someone in need. But the point I want to draw out here is Forman's suggestion that families are considered 'deserving' *because they don't ask for help.*

John McMurria's (2008) argues that what we see in *Extreme* is the presentation of deserving families who are *already* model neoliberal citizens; they work hard, don't complain, and when misfortune hits, they rely on their own resources not on the state. McMurria shares the example of Carrie, one of *Extreme's* lucky recipients. Carrie, a florist, struggled to hold down a job because she had to provide care for her young son. Her son, who suffered from a series of allergies and a rare blood disorder, needed constant care and expensive medication. Rather than castigate the failings of the health-care system, the inflexible nature of employment or present the need for decent child-care, *Extreme* instead heaps praise on Carrie for her own resourcefulness in continuing to find work and for growing medicinal herbs for her son. Other episodes of *Extreme* praise this level of self-reliance, but that's not to say that the show denigrates dependency. While dependency on the state, on the 'hand-outs' of welfare aid, is not to be encouraged and are seldom highlighted in the show, a dependency on local communities, neighbours and extended families each 'helping their own' invokes notions of an authentic spirit of community and suggests something about the pride and determination of families that help their claim to be the *deserving* poor. Dependency is thus recast as resourcefulness when it takes these forms and is to be supported and championed.

In sum, these are ideal citizens *despite* their circumstance because they have the right 'attitude' and demonstrate the same cultural moral code presumably shared by the producers, audience and sponsors/advertisers (Pizzaro, 2000). They are 'like us'. The result of such a compelling narrative spun from very selective definitions of misfortune is a tightly defended notion of what constitutes 'a deserving self'. A story of bad luck is not simply presented (an event happened to me), it has been reworked so that it is wiped clean of culpability (I am not responsible for the event). Further, it has to be tightly located in the personal (I am not blaming society) and in so doing already signals a certain allegiance to normative citizenship (I will exercise my responsibility to help myself).

There are a number of issues here. The first is the problematic assumption that all are positioned to help themselves. This presumption is directly drawn from the 'blank slate thinking' discussed in Chapter 1. That chapter argued that the ability to 'just get on', to reflect and to take up a favourable strategic position to the world depends on access to, and the skilled utilisation of, a range of material and discursive resources that class analysis clearly demonstrates are not in reach of everyone (Lawler, 2005b; Skeggs, 2004). There are a number of practical questions that can be posed; what happens to those who aren't nominated/selected? What does it say about the moral fabric of society that care of the vulnerable can intelligibly fall on the grace and favour of TV production companies and their extravagant gifts of transformation? What kind of solution is the makeover?

It is this last question that drags attention to the alarming depoliticising movement that is achieved when the makeover is paraded as rescuer and redeemer. The deserving family has an *under* whelmingly apolitical reaction to their misfortune and an overwhelmingly joyous reaction to the reward they get for their apolitical stance. In terms of the pedagogical function of lifestyle TV, the lesson to be drawn here is akin to that drawn from the passive female form in classic, Western fairy tales; the Cinderella who quietly gets on will be rewarded as long as she doesn't abandon her duties or her dreams. We also learn that misfortune is isolated to specific families, drawing the eye away from systematic inequalities, and we learn that those personal problems demand personal, bespoke, market-based, expert-endorsed solutions which like Cinderella's prince will lead to a happy ending (or at least, within the logics of makeover culture, allow one to start working towards a new happy ending).

But we learn too that the appropriate performance of that passivity is communicated in friendly, measured, paced, 'reasonable' tones. What a sharp contrast with angry and inarticulate outbursts fuelled by injustice and sheer frustration that fill other media spaces such as news reportage and Jerry Springer-like day-time talk-shows! Even in suffering, distinctions are forged between those who can talk themselves into transformation and those whose behaviours suggest a lack of 'self-knowledge and self-reflection' and so casts suspicion on their 'true' intentions and thus upon their deserving status (Aslama and Pantti, 2006; Lawler, 2005b, p. 118). Feel-good TV warns its citizens not to be complacent – misfortunes can hit and when they do, they hit hard – it's best to be ever vigilant. But should bad luck occur, then shows like *Extreme* and *DIY SOS* leave no doubt as to the best way to cope and of the rewards that might follow.

Addiction

If the bad luck story erases any suspicion of culpability by presenting already ideal neoliberal citizens for the *Extreme* makeover, other lifestyle makeover shows manage the relationship between culpability and deservingness in different ways. Individuals are often herded into the 'before' stage under the guise of addiction. A growing number of addictions crowd lifestyle media: from the perhaps more familiar 'workaholic' to the newly spun 'clutteroholics' discussed in Chapter 2, to 'chocoholics' 'spendaholics' and 'fast-food junkies'. These labels mingle with descriptions of caffeine 'fixes', sugar 'buzzes', retail 'highs' and consumer 'cravings' across lifestyle TV shows and self-help books. As Robin Room (2003) argues, it matters little whether there is any truth in whether people are 'addicted' to clutter or not, or indeed whether there is any 'truth' to addiction itself (there is some contention around its designation as a 'disease'). What *is* important is the way addiction operates as a cultural frame, shaping contemporary storytelling and thus enabling specific stories of the self to be told. What is pertinent then is the *currency* of addiction discourse, what it allows to be said and what space it affords the self.

As a frame, 'addiction' reveals its own cultural contingency. Just as Berridge and Edwards (1981) argued that opium use turned from a 'habit' into an 'addiction' in the nineteenth century as a consequence of wider class frictions and the demands of an emergent pharmaceutical profession, Robin Room starts by arguing that 'addiction' is a historic and cultural concept deployed at specific cultural junctures. He uses the example of drink to argue that the problem of alcoholism emerged through wider concerns about social control and self-discipline in times of rapid social change. He states, 'as an accepted way of understanding human behaviour, addiction concepts are a phenomenon specifically of the late modern period' (2003, p. 222). Eve Kosofsky Sedgwick (1993) concurs, using the term 'epidemics of will' to describe the range and spread of addictions and addiction discourses that spin, she argues, from general anxieties and fears associated with the heightened free will and choice-making in neoliberal societies.

As Sender and Sullivan (2008) argue, the ideal neoliberal citizen as imagined through rational, tasteful and discrete consumer lifestyle choices is haunted by the relational construction of the addict who is 'unable to cope with the endless freedom on offer' (p. 580). The inability to make tasteful choices, to consume correctly and to responsibly *cope* with choice, as we've seen in previous chapters, is repeatedly associated with certain segments of the working class (Hayward and Yar, 2006). Addiction discourses when targeted at the 'less–educated, lower-income individuals' who overpopulate lifestyle TV (Ouellette and Hay, 2008, p. 7) parade as a seemingly neutral (non-classed) address but serve to effectively re-circulate class divisions and distinctions. As the choosing self needs its nemesis, 'addiction' is largely an 'invented' term that manufactures the 'addict' and which aids the medicalisation of non-appropriate and *strongly classed* behaviours of 'excessive consumption, loss of control and inner conflict' (Benford and Gough, 2006, p. 429).

For Room, the cultural anxieties around self-control figure more highly than those around choice. If ideas about normative selfhood are as deeply embedded in notions of self-control and personal responsibility as this book has argued thus far, then addiction looms large in the cultural imagination not just because one has lost control over a certain substance or experience but rather because this indicates that one has lost control over *one's life* (Room, 2003). It is telling, he argues, that addiction is referred to as 'dependency' in the Diagnostic and Statistical Manual of the American Psychiatric Association. Dependency, as we have seen, is recast as troubling, threatening and rather *distasteful* in the neoliberal rhetoric spiralling from Thatcher/Reagan administrations of the 1980s, setting dependency and vulnerability as markers of an illegitimate subject (Haylett, 2001). However, while the addict is a figure of disgust and denigration (Murray, 2008), the addict does not simply slip into the living-dead status of the zombie (see the previous chapter). Instead a belief in self-control works alongside the belief that one can be 'taken-over' by desire and craving, to offer redemption. As Kosofsky Sedgwick puts it, the addict is 'propelled into a narrative of inexorable decline and fatality, from which she cannot disimplicate herself except by leaping into that other, more pathos-ridden narrative called *kicking the habit'* (Sedgewick, 1993, p. 131).

'Kicking the habit' makes up much of lifestyle makeover shows and self-help books. Participants in weight-loss shows are encouraged to 'kick' their addiction to fatty, sugary snacks (*You are What You Eat*) while most self-help books start by asking readers to confront and then 'kick' the self-destructive habits of poor time management or the habitual faulty thinking that has been holding them back (Covey, 1989; Field, 2004). While 'addiction' may position one as in *need* of a makeover, it doesn't necessarily convince or interest a viewer that a makeover is *deserved*. How then does the addict manage the appraisal filters? I want to explore this through a brief example from *Supersize vs. SuperSkinny* (C4, March 2010) below.

'It's not longer what you eat, but what's eating you' Dr Jessen

The show's 'before' moment is quite a lengthy one; 'at-home' footage of the participants cross cuts with health messages about weight-related illnesses. These both intermingle with soft-focused, speeded-up footage of celebrity Dr Christian Jessen, weighing and measuring this week's errant bodies. The action slows for a consultation in Jessen's surgery. Twenty-four stone, 'food addict', Julie has just been weighed and Dr Christian has told her she has a fatally high BMI score. He moves from this blunt, seemingly objective statement to ask a more subjective question (signalled by his leaning his head to one side and softening his voice): 'Have you always been overweight? What happened?' This may be kindly said, but behind this question towers a wider social intolerance for the non-conforming body; normalising process is immediately swept up into the assumption that something must have *happened* to cause Julie's body to deviate from the ideal, natural, but importantly, *normative* body. The question 'what happened' effaces the body's normative condition and the conditions of its normativity. The self housed in the deviant body is then dislocated from other frames of reference and left to account for itself within this newly arrived therapeutic encounter.

So, in this moment there are two movements: Julie is called to account for her body but in response to a very specific register of cause and effect, and Jessen shifts from his objective bio-medical stance to take up a more therapeutic one – he is now *counsellor*. The ease with which he can slip between the two is indicative of the spread and flourishing of therapeutic or 'psy' discourses across disciplinary and professional bodies of knowledge (Rose, 1999a). Julie explains that her weight piled on when she started secondary school where she was relentlessly bullied:

> *Dr Christian*: Do you think bullying caused you to eat more?
> *Julie*: I don't think so. I wouldn't say I comfort eat as such. I eat because I like food
> *Dr Christian*: There's two things, there is what we call emotional hunger and physical hunger and I bet you haven't felt physical hunger for a long time and I think, although you say you don't comfort eat, that there's a large amount of emotional eating in you
> *Julie*: yes

It's not clear here whether Julie is acquiescing or agreeing, and there's a degree of confusion in the show's wider narrative of whether Julie was bullied because of her weight, or gained weight through bullying – however, as Room (2003) argued above, the key here is not the 'truth' but the production of a truth. The truth is that Julie has been wounded and it's only fair to heal the wound. Paula Reavey and Brendan Gough (2000) argue that locating current problems in identifiable childhood events elbows out any other explanation, leaving an unrelenting stress on the personal; the personal narrative, when mediated by the expert, is transmuted into the truth. In the example above, this truth is presented *back* to Julie for her acceptance. This truth is not always simply accepted in the therapeutic encounter (Brownlie, 2004), Julie sensing the direction of Jessen's thinking tries to forestall him (I don't comfort eat, I eat because I like food), but the momentum of the show's narrative depends on her acceptance so that the show can slide into an intervention based on self-esteem building, confidence and weight-loss. As the show is only calibrated for the personal, Julie has to be recast as emotionally 'ill' and thus currently 'in denial' (a strongly suggested reading encouraged by the show). Indeed, the show progresses by linking Julie's acceptance of the 'truth' into her progress through transformation. The show's narrative momentum 'leaves few participants able to defend their bodies as not in need of transformation' (Skeggs, 2009, p. 635), or indeed, as able to talk *against* the registers which position them as worthy of this intervention.

'Kicking the habit' or rather kicking the habit caused by an *identifiable emotional wound* enjoys such currency because it neatly houses both a problem and solution. In a narrative flourish, 'inappropriate behaviours' are immediately conjured away to reappear as problems of the wounded self. Deviancy is thus neatly pathologised and causes little threat to the logics or ethics of the makeover culture. This framing then not only renders redundant the explanatory efficacy of structural determinants (such as inequality or injustice), but also defuses any political threat inappropriate behaviours could potentially pose. Further, the stealth-like dislocation and relocation provides a powerful rationale for the 'cure' – for that too resides at the level of the individual and personal (Hazelden, 2003). This relocation swiftly moves addiction into the territories of expert knowledge and assistance, for it is only the expert who can awaken and mobilise an individual's will-power (see Chapter 3). Robin Room appreciates that this way of understanding addiction allows for the failure of the experts and of neoliberal governance. If an addict *fails* to transform, the failure is their own: a result of lack of self-will and self-belief (Room, 2003) – of course, the possibility of failure adds to the melodrama of a makeover show's reveal – particularly in the latest twist of the revisit show, when experts surprise participants to inspect how they are keeping up with their new lives and looks. This melodrama is heightened by our tacit knowledge of the zombie fate that awaits the failed. It also allows the 'good' citizen the comfort of knowing that such a fate is *chosen.*

While the families in *Extreme* are 'worthy' through their quiet, apolitical, gritty determined response to the 'right' kind of problem (loss of neoliberal viability), the 'addict' is also recast as having the 'right', if different, kind of problem. It is the right problem because it enables the flexing and exercise of individualism and responsibilisation by sharply translating problems of living, *and of class,* into problems of the self; a sleight of hand that sparks the restoration function of the makeover culture. As Rose (1999b, pp. 231–232) argues

Selves unable to operate the imperative of choice are to be restored through therapy to the status of a choosing individual. Selves who find choice meaningless and their identity fading under inner and outer fragmentation are to be restored through therapy to unity and political purpose.

Summary

Williams' (2008) conclusion is that compassion filters *block* the potential of compassion to bring about better relations between people. Compassion, he argues, can destabilise the damaging, disparaging nature of self/Other relations and limit the reproduction of misery and suffering which he sees as their consequence: he claims 'where our interpersonal realities are defined by difference and dissimilarity, the promise of injustice is amplified' (2008, p. 7). Williams' plea for the potential of compassion offers some overlap with that of Margrit Shildrick (2002). Shildrick, in the previous chapter, nurtured hopes that a recognition of *vulnerability* as a characteristic of being human could potentially revolutionise relations and experiences of our humanhood by dissolving the fears and anxieties fuelling current self/Other relations. In terms of the mediascape, claims for the so-called democratisation of the media, often made in light of the opening-up of celebrity culture and from the wider and fuller representations of once invisible or disparaged groups (Mitchell, 2005), may suggest some space to seek out a more compassionate and more meaningful relations across culturally fictive social divisions. Christine Marshall and Kiran Pienaar (2008, p. 526), for example, hope that as suffering is something all people share, the display of a suffering person on lifestyle TV and talk-shows should help us all 'emphasise our shared humanity and potential victimisation'.

However, this hope may seem naïve when one accounts for the mediating frames which as Butler argues are 'politically saturated' with context-embedded norms, values, and prevailing cultural ethos (2009, p. 1). At the level of representation in lifestyle media, selves are only transformed if certain stories can be told of them, or if they are positioned to talk themselves into certain narratives. By arguing that narratives and life stories are frames, this chapter has suggested that far from destabilising compassion filters, lifestyle TV shows reinforce them through performances of worth and desert which resonate with prevailing neoliberal ideas and values.

What's suggested here is that class relations are not necessarily reproduced through overt demonstrations of class antagonisms in lifestyle TV shows. In the framing and performances of 'worth' a more subtle but no less aggressive practice of symbolic violence is achieved. The 'before', by highlighting the (addiction) errors associated with (working-class) lifestyle and attitudes, echo wider, insistent constructions of the working class as an obstacle to the mobile, progressive neoliberal economy (McDowell, 2006). The working class may then 'appear ripe for the possibilities of transformation' (Skeggs, 2009, p. 633), yet their own culpability and lack are indelibly marked by the way they are presented for this journey. This creates an impossible tension for some selves; for to be rehabilitated involves a detachment of culpability from the self, but this action of 'wiping clean' is only really possible for those with the cultural and economic privilege of invisibility and the mobility to reinvent themselves (Negra, 2009). Indeed, only some selves can be *restored*, Others need to be *re*invented, *re*translated into the values that are not their own but are nonetheless imposed upon them (Ringrose and Walkerdine, 2008).

6
Repatriated and Repaired: Gender's Happy Ending

David, do you like the new you, David?
Yep. Better than the old one. *Ten Years Younger.*
Cultural literacy is intimately linked to visual media.

(Mitchell, 2005, p. 1052)

Introduction

It's fitting that this book summarises and concludes with a discussion of the 'after' stage of the journey of transformation. The 'after' is the conclusion of a self-help book or the surprise 'reveal' of the makeover TV show. The 'after' appears as a solid and unproblematic moment of success where dreams come true, where the inner self beats the external self into compliance, bodies are sculpted, esteem is supercharged and people get the look/home/confidence – *the self* – they always wanted. Yet, this success is only short-lived because the 'after' is temporally fragile; the ceaseless momentum of the makeover culture rolls these moments into new beginnings and new projects of the self. As Meredith Jones has argued, successful selfhood lies not in 'being' but rather in 'becoming'. She says, 'in the makeover culture the process of *becoming something better* is more important than achieving a static point of completion' – good citizens are always on the move, engaged in 'never-ending renovations of themselves' (2008, p. 1). The 'after' then maybe fleeting and momentary, but it's interesting because it is the point where bundles of desires, aspirations and needs, the fuel of transformation, are most densely concentrated. It is the moment when we can see *who and what counts as a self* and how a desire to be that self is orchestrated in lifestyle media and in the wider cultural imaginary. With a focus on gender this chapter continues this book's focus on the journey of transformation to question just what we are being encouraged to transform *to*.

Revealing empowerment

> When you say 'Yes' to a private Makeover Session, you are saying 'YES!' to yourself as your personal source of empowerment.
>   http://serenitymatters.com/sessions.html

The UK show *How to Look Good Naked* demonstrates the skill of its host, Gok Wan, as he transforms a woman barely able to look at her own body in private, to a catwalk-model confident enough to bare all in front of a large crowd. Gok's 'confidence boosting arsenal' of makeup, hair styling, self-esteem building 'Gok shocks' and fashion tips produce, without fail, a 'reveal' of overwhelming confidence and bodily celebration that the participants themselves can hardly believe it ('I can't believe that's me'). The show ends with Gok asking 'tell me, do you think you look good naked?' The participant, beaming with pride, screams to the affirmative and often qualifies her joy with a declaration of womanhood: 'I feel like a woman'; 'I am a real woman'; 'I am all woman'. It is hard to not to feel emotionally moved by the obvious delight of a woman once socially and psychologically crippled by body hatred. So, it seems somewhat churlish to dismiss Gok's claim to be 'all about empowerment' (www.ivillage. co.uk); it's better to question what empowerment *is* in the lifestyle mediascape.

'Empowerment' is a term that scampers across the mediascape with all the exuberance and appeal of a young puppy. It is found across other makeover shows (*What Not to Wear, Ten Years Younger,* for example); advertising; corporate mission statements; corporate philanthropy (e.g. Avon's Empowerment jewellery, L'Oreal's Empowerment Programme for Women In Need); the popular press; public health and political campaigns; and a raft of self-help. As crude (and unscholarly) hint of its pervasiveness, 'empowerment' is rewarded with over 40,000 hits on *Amazon* (UK) book search and some 12,400,000 in a basic *Google* search at the time of writing. This ubiquity takes its toll on its conceptual clarity. Within lifestyle media, 'empowerment' can refer simultaneously to the ability to make informed consumer lifestyle choices; the release of one's inner personal power ('inside every woman there's mystery and magic, power and passion, spirit and substance' – Gillette Venus Razors) or can refer to exerting control ('Take control of your skin everyday – because we're worth it' – L'Oreal New Age Perfect Serum). However, no matter what meaning is deployed, 'empowerment' primarily accompanies media representations of women and femininity, and functions as an unabashed celebration of women's agency.

The currency of empowerment owes much to a feminist politics emerging from the 1960s; a period of feminist history loosely referred to as Second Wave feminism. Second Wave feminism broadly conceptually aligned empowerment with resistance. Although, these terms were far from stable, 'empowerment' was imagined as resulting from the exposure and then opposition of male power and oppressive gender relations and identities. The actions of exposing and opposing were imagined as empowering women to develop and practice self-determined femininities. That empowerment broadly meant *power to* is evident across feminist literature with women's empowerment being related to, amongst other things, the space to develop self-esteem, self-expression and self-determination (Freysinger and Flannery, 1992); the acquisition of specific skills (Wheaton and Tomlinson, 1998); increased physicality and physical confidence (Brace-Govan, 2004); access to, and confidence in, decision-making processes (Harrington et al., 1992); a discourse of female sexual agency (Ryan, 2001); the organisation of 'own' time (Currie, 2004; Gillespie et al., 2002); and the pleasure of defying gendered expectations about appropriate behaviours and activities (Auster, 2001). In short, empowerment was an integral aspect of resistance, being both an *outcome* of resistance (women are empowered through their agency) and part of the process of resisting (women are empowered through the acquisition of skills, knowledge and vision that enable them to resist). The result was that empowerment referred to freedom, confidence and independence won from political struggle (Shaw, 2001).

Freedom, confidence and independence still define empowerment in the current mediascape, but there's a discernable emptying out of its political passions and aspirations. The 'emptying out' is a product of gains in certain rights and liberties for women; the confidence of (some) women to negotiate their own lives in the makeover culture;

the aggressive spread of neoliberal (market) rationality in the cultural imagination and the presumptions of meritocracy it drags in its wake; and an active media degradation and mis-representation of feminism. Skeggs (1997, p. 157), picking up on this last point, argues that 'contradictory and confusing discourse transmitted through popular culture' provides women with 'discursive strategies for dismissal' leading to what she called women's active *dis-identification* with feminism. This may be best evidenced in the oft-heard way of *speaking* feminism while simultaneously *distancing* oneself from it in the opening gambit, 'I not a feminist, but...'. As a result, feminism is framed in ways that render it irrelevant for contemporary women's lives and is represented so that it's language of misogyny, patriarchy and insistence on oppressive gender relations are cast as suspicious, discomforting and, at times, elitist. As such, feminism has undergone a *reverse makeover* in the cultural imagination – and even within academic writings as Stevi Jackson (1999b) and Angela McRobbie (2008) testify – to become an 'invented social memory' as something 'inevitably shrill, bellicose and parsimonious' (Tasker and Negra, 2007, p. 3) that speaks to 'feminist struggles no longer needed' (McRobbie, 2008, p. 523).

However, as Diane Negra (2009) argues, it might be a mistake to regard the 'emptying out' as a straightforward backlash against the prescriptions of an older, demanding feminism. 'Empowerment' still manifests through a language of women's rights, needs, worth and pleasures (Meagan Tyler, 2008). Rather than a rejection of feminism, it's possible to discern certain incorporations, appropriations, distortions and what Angela McRobbie calls an 'instrumentalization of a specific modality of "feminism"' (2008, p. 531) within neoliberal culture. This cultural repacking of feminism helps the construction and the appeal of a specifically empowered self – a representation of women as 'feisty, sassy and sexual agentic' (Gill, 2008a, p. 438). A representation which we see animated in technicolour vivacity in Gok Wan's naked ladies at the point of the reveal.

That this 'emptying out' and repackaging of feminism should *matter* speaks to a growing concern that we are losing critical purchase on women's lives, gender relations and subjectivities in this specific cultural and historic juncture – and we are losing a critical opposition or position to critique the phenomenon of neoliberal rationality; what Axel Honneth (2004, p. 475) has described as 'the creeping metamorphosis of the whole society into a market'. The emptying out encourages some contemporary theorisations and conceptualisation of selfhood to rely on uncritical notions of freedom, choice and independence: the blank slate thinking discussed in Chapter 1. As a result, the conditions, contexts and consequences of the frames, discussed in the previous part of this book, are effaced or treated as a matter of indifference. It is not surprising then that scholars, such as Ros Gill, Bev Skeggs and Angela McRobbie, each militate against what they describe as 'complicit' theorisations – those theorisations that endorse and reproduce neoliberal ideals and values.

In fairness, this 'complicit' work may have been well intended. A concern to start research from the epistemological standpoint of women's lived experiences expressed in their own way, to share epistemic authority and the political need to adopt a more reflexive stance towards the role of the researcher/academic in re-presenting those lives and voices have revolutionised how research is done and added an important sensitivity to our theorisations (Ramazanoglu and Holland, 2000). Yet, it has also paved *some* of the way for a worryingly apolitical and asocial celebration of those lives and voices, which pays scant critical attention to the cultural habitats, symbolic repertories and hegemonic narratives through which *all* life-stories and personal accounts must necessarily draw to be intelligible, recognisable and *possible* (Bruner, 2004; Butler, 2005). Ros Gill is concerned then with what she sees as the erosion of critical thinking, which serves, she argues, to harmonise with, not challenge, the culturally insistent construction of selves as enterprising, self-responsible, consumer-citizens:

> Just as neoliberalism requires individuals to narrate their life story as if it were the outcome of deliberate choices so too does some contemporary writing depict young women as unconstrained and freely choosing.
>
> (Gill, 2008a, p. 436)

Gill (2007) has termed this instrumentalisation of feminism a *postfeminist sensibility*, and it's to that we now turn to best make sense of what shaping of the self is occurring through these 'new', strident, lively discourses of empowerment. In common with the term 'empowerment', postfeminism is something of a sliding signifier, cropping up in different texts to chaperon or champion a host of different arguments and theoretical stances. It is helpful then to start by simply saying that by arguing that postfeminism is a *sensibility*, Gill (2007) removes postfeminism from the status of a political or theoretical analytic tool, and approaches it as a cultural phenomenon. As such, it demands critical scrutiny in its own right. Through her analysis of the so-called 'chick-lit' drama (e.g. *Sex in the City* and *Desperate Housewives*) and a portfolio of adverts, Gill identifies several identifying characteristics of postfeminist sensibility as it shapes cultural representations of women.

Postfeminist sensibility and those feminine wiles

Gill's (2007) postfeminist sensibility speaks to a range of discourses (bundles of vocabularies, practices, dispositions, imaginations and attitudes) that circulate through popular culture. These may be regarded as anti-feminist discourses but as we've discussed above are a curious mingling of anti-feminist sentiment and purpose with a feminist-inspired tone of rights, desires and assertiveness (Ringrose and Walkerdine, 2008). I want to illustrate Gill's 'sensibility' by referring to the following extract from Marie Forelo's (2008) *Make Every Man Want You Or Make Yours Want You More: How to be So Irresistible You'll Barely Keep From Dating Yourself*:

> We are all so desperate to attain what we imagine will make us equal and happy (a successful career, marriage, family, 2.2 kids) that we forget who we really are: brilliant, sexy, and magical beings like no other. We've forgotten that our power lies in not competing or trying to be like men but in embracing our natural and womanly strengths of compassion, enchantment and tenderness [...] our sexuality and feminine wiles inspire, enliven and empower.
>
> (p. 3)

The first discourse Gill identifies in the postfeminist sensibility works to locate femininity in the body, more specifically in women's bodily *sexiness*. Indeed sexiness is recast as a feminine inner power ('magical', 'enchantment') the expression of which is imagined as the key to confidence and self-esteem. As Forelo states, this power could be lost when a woman gets her man, her family and career or when she, misguidedly, tries to compete or be like a man. Because it can be lost and forgotten, sexual power demands vigilance, management and enhancement (why else would we need to buy books urging us to reveal and revel in our irresistibility?). As sexiness rests in the body, the body too demands constant surveillance, monitoring and discipline. This is related, Gill argues, to the second discourse: the assertion of women as 'active, desiring subjects' (p. 151) who flex and flaunt their sexual power in an increasingly sexualised society. Forelo urges all women to 'claim your irresistibility' (p. 5) and use it to 'inspire, enliven and empower' and to get what *you* want. The third discourse is that of individualisation, involving 'notions of choice', of 'being oneself' and 'pleasing myself' (Gill, 2007, p. 153). Being oneself is a core injunction in the postfeminist sensibility. For Forelo 'who we really are' indicates a true self with its own rights and demands: the real self has the right and power to attract the man it wants – or indeed, there's a suggestion in the title (*How to be So Irresistible You'll Barely Keep From Dating Yourself*) that the real self is so attractive that it offers fascination for itself, placing others, men included, secondary.

The final discourse reasserts sexual difference; encouraging the notion that there is a natural difference between men and women which plays out in 'battle of the sexes' rhetoric in self-help. This has been very lucrative for Australian writing duo Allan and Barbara Pease who have developed a global business on the back of their books explaining and reproducing gender differences; '*Why Men Don't Listen and Women Can't Read Maps* (2001); *Why Men Can Only Do One Thing At A Time and Women Never Stop Talking*' (2003); and *Why Men Don't Have a Clue and Women Always Need New Shoes* (2006). Ros Gill notes that a cultural belief in biologically underwritten sexual differences indicated in such books is lent further legitimacy through the growing influence of evolutionary psychology and genetic science (p. 158). There is a necessary logic here encouraged by self-help authors like Marie Forelo, for it is only by reserving sexiness as a natural and unique property of *women* that she can make a claim for their unique sexual power and desire. And it's here we can see that while sexual power can be fun and exciting, it also has more emotional depth – Forelo speaks of the 'natural and womanly strengths of compassion, enchantment and tenderness' further invoking essentialised (fictive) traits of femininity.

What's apparent in the postfeminist sensibility is a celebration and encouragement of women's uniqueness and of their agency. There is a positive endorsement here to live life to the full, pursue desires and to shrug off any inhibitions, imagined as keeping past generations of women tied to a life of self-sacrifice and duty. The neoliberal terrain is imagined then as opening up unparalleled opportunities for women and girls, suggesting that now they are 'untethered by gender constraints' and are now entitled to 'have it all' (Baker, 2010, p. 187). Women are invited to follow the rhythms of their choices and desires to create life in the image of their inner self. Indeed, so instinctive is this that women are encouraged to avoid any infection caused by the 'epidemic of over-thinking' and just go for it (Nolen-Hocksemo's (2004) *Women Who Think Too Much*). The postfeminist sensibility constructs a young (or youth-aspiring) heterosexual woman who exudes confidence, sexual desire and power. There is too, notes Gill, a certain ironic playfulness and sexual knowingness of this figure that is expressed through freedom and abundant choice-making. The upbeat, preppy, cheerleading tone of postfeminist sensibility is itself buoyant, uplifting and palatable to wider neoliberal rationalities with which it shares a palpable affinity (Gill, 2008a). What we are witnessing here, argues Gill, is the construction of a new gendered subjectivity (Gill, 2007).

Empowered het-sex?

To move into a discussion of is occurring within the postfeminist formation of self, I want to briefly return to Gok Wan's *How to Look Good Naked*. Although all the shows end on an emotional high (Frith et al., 2010) one of the most moving involved his transformation of 29-year-old identical twins, Suzy and Jeanie (season 4). Jeanie was married with a small young family but pregnancy and breast feeding had left her body saggy and scarred with stretch marks. Her disgust at what her body had become was palpable as, with shame-flushed cheeks, she punctuated her story of body-hatred and erosion of confidence, with prods and heavy handling of her 'problem areas'. What was interesting was the way she framed her story in terms of loss. For not only did she lose the body still enjoyed by her childless twin, she spoke of the loss of certain *vitality* and *visibility*. She said, 'before I had my children I know I was more confident. I was proud of my body.

I knew I turned heads. I used to be really confident; I knew I turned heads'. The relationship here between confidence and her ability to successfully pass the appraising/sexually appreciative looks of men ('to turn heads') offers an immediate example of the stress on sexual power circulated by the postfeminist sensibility.

Yet, here we can see more clearly how it operates to create and also *diminish* a sense of self and how it takes hold as a narrative though which the body is known, understood and *experienced*. Without her power to turn heads, Jeanie feels invisible and worthless; she cannot enjoy her life and all aspects of it are tainted by her loss and grieving. Gok of course turns this around. The reveal is spectacular – the twins adorned with all the trappings of 1930s sexual nostalgia (semi-pornographic) are paraded down a cat walk before discretely baring all. With camouflage make-up, special underwear (Gok has his own line) and other clothes that draw the eye to her 'fabulous breasts', Gok declares that Jeanie is 'finally flaunting' her sexy body. She asserts that she is now 'a real woman' and proudly declares her stretch-marks 'lady-lines' and thus part of her empowered femininity.

What are we to make of this? Jeanie, in common with the rest of Gok's 'babes', declares her real womanhood when clad only in designer underwear and is heavily made-up and 'pampered' to such a degree that she is barely recognisable to herself ('I can believe it's me', she says in breathless excitement). She is also physically situated on one of the most iconic settings for objectified and commercialised femininity – the cat walk. Further, Jeanie feels she can only be 'someone' if she is recognised as a woman – and to be recognised as such involves fitting, squeezing, moulding and sculpting into frames saturated with very particular registers of heteronormative desire. Her re-translation into these frames is marked by a successful passing of a form of erotic scrutiny that combines sexual objectification and appraisal. Her 'real' womanhood is anchored in her ability to once again turn heads, and she draws her confidence and zest for life from it. In terms of the consumer culture (Bauman, 2007) discussed in Chapter 2, we can understand Jeanie's transformation as her conversion into a commodity, which now has a restored value in a heterosexual economy: Jeanie, with Gok's help, has 're-branded' and she can once again trade in the appraising scopic economy.

For some scholars, Jeanie's tale is telling of the ways lifestyle media creates opportunities for women to practice 'style politics': 'to use the ritual of consumption in dress, cosmetics, hairstyle and gesture to bend the norms socially prescribed by the market and to challenge family and other authority' (Hall Gallagher and Pecot-Hébert, 2007, p. 62). The makeover is thus just a playful engagement in escapism, fantasy and reinvention – perhaps edged with a slight political intent. However, there is a wider chorus of concern around the very tight parameters in which women are persuaded to 'do' their new subjectivities and play their ironic, knowing games. There are warnings, points of critique and criticism provided through Gill's 'reveal' of the postfeminist sensibility, which challenge the celebratory tone surrounding women's empowerment. Via Gill, what we see in Jeanie's story is the generation and fulfilment of selfhood based on very rigid definitions of heterosexual desire. Gill (2008a) argues that what is at stake here is a 'rewriting of femininity so that it seems to reside in sexiness' (p. 440). Similarly, Diane Negra (2009) argues that 'discourses on the heroism of the relentlessly self-disciplined, fit, female body tend to camouflage the centrality of that body in the reinforcement of traditional heterosexual desirability' (p. 127). Both suspect that a more aggressive form of exploitation is at work here, where women's agency and power are enabled and celebrated if *only* it is harnessed to the construction of a self that subscribes to and inflames heterosexual male fantasy and heteronormative fictions of appropriate gender performances. There is, then, a powerful re-sexualisation of women's bodies and *agency* enfolded in giddy notions of empowerment. This may be illustrated in the title of Ian Kerner's 2008 self-help book. *Passionista: The Empowered Woman's Guide to Pleasing a Man.*

Of course, there's a risk here of sounding prudish and 'anti-sex' and Gill takes us back to the wider social context in which women and men negotiate their lives – a context which houses the intelligibility of domestic violence, and a cultural imagination that makes sexual double-standards, trafficking, prostitution, sexual abuse and rape *possible*. We need only to return to the Christopher Williams (2008) bleak observation, in the previous chapter, that 'where our interpersonal realities are defined by difference and dissimilarity, the promise of injustice is amplified' (p. 7), to be concerned at how women's difference is being so overdrawn and so *targeted*. Further, as the sexy body becomes the key site for identity, other resources of identity construction are marginalised (education, employment) – privileging the young, sexy body, or rather its public appearance, as means for viable selfhood. As Diane Negra (2009) states, this reduces women's 'lives, interests and talents' (p. 4) to sites culturally marked 'feminine', which, as Ros Gill argues, fills women with an endless anxiety to hold on to the little power they are afforded. Gill's discussion of popular magazines that aggressively scan and ridicule even the best of bodies for sweat stains, veins, visible panty lines, wrinkles and the ultimate transgression – cellulite – serves, she argues, to condemn all women to negotiate their 'choices' with the towering expectation that all women need to constantly manage, monitor and mould their bodies. There are two points we can draw from this. The first is that Jeanie's choices and jubilant empowerment operate within regulated parameters. The second is that the movement of the makeover culture is not driven by narcissism, or even consumption, but by *survival* – a life-long struggle for viability: 'it is this constant quest for change in becoming a "better you" that speaks to women performing under the norms of heterosexuality' (Hall Gallagher and Pecot-Hébert, 2007, p. 76).

The volitional imperative

It's timely at this point to reiterate that these cultural representations *matter* and cannot be dismissed by demeaning popular culture, such as 'chick-lit' or lifestyle TV makeover shows for their 'trivial' nature and content (Skeggs, 2009). Joffe and Christian Staerklé (2007) have argued in these pages that cultural representations influence commonsense everyday imagination and knowledge. To underscore this point in terms of gender, I'd like to add the argument made by Jane Ussher:

> Representations of 'woman' are of central importance in the construction of female subjectivity. We learn how to *do* 'woman' through negotiating the warring images and stories about what 'woman' is (or who she should be), among the most influential being those scripts of femininity that pervade the mass media.
>
> (Ussher, 1997, p. 13, original emphasis)

We thus return to the *pedagogical function* of lifestyle media that the book is concerned with so far. Although reading, viewing and general engagement with popular cultural forms are complex and uneven enough to make any claims of propagandist ideology highly suspect, nonetheless, popular culture resources reflect the cultural imaginary and help resource the ways we make sense of our lives and the (generative) stories that we tell of ourselves as Ussher argues above. By way of example; Joanne Baker's (2010) interviews with 55 women, in Australia, aged between 18 and 25 years, led her to identify what she calls a 'volitional imperative' in the women's accounts. By this she refers to the ways the postfeminist stress on individualism in combination with the 'can-do' mentality of neoliberalism, encouraged women to present their lives as if they were produced through choices and determination. Baker's participants all spoke their lives through postfeminist markers of personal success, individual responsibility and enterprise (p. 198). This framing meant an avoidance of any talk of vulnerability, discrimination or disadvantage; any 'problems' were divorced from any structural/cultural explanation and instead recast as medical or psychological issues, which it was one's duty to repair. Indeed, Baker suggests that problems of discrimination or disadvantage were cast as obstacles *to be overcome* – it was in facing and managing them that selfhood was done.

The wider social implications of these interviews lies in ways the 'volitional imperative' shapes (mis)-recognition of Others. Baker notes that as vulnerability and dependence were shunned from the self they were projected onto Others to form a causal and essential trait:

> Volitional talk facilitated a disinclination to regards other as 'legitimately disadvantaged'. There were consistent example of negative comments about Indigenous Australians, asylum seekers, unemployed people, women experiencing violence and young sole mothers [...] it was most common for reduced empathy to be articulated in relation to such group's receipt of welfare support and criticism consistently cohered around a perceived lack of personal effort and initiative.
>
> (Baker, 2010, p. 199)

Baker warns that this reduced and contingent compassion for the socially disadvantaged is attributable to 'the fetishizing of a heightened personal responsibility' (p. 200). We could add here that this fetish smoothes the way for more right-wing, conservative policies and lends credibility to its rhetoric. For example, it hardly needs stating that the recent launch by the new UK's coalition government to end 'sick note culture' (and get a million people off benefits and back to work) is fuelled by the assumption that the sick and vulnerable are malingering/corrupt or lack a personal responsibility that will now be forced upon them.

We end this section then with a contradiction on which the makeover culture thrives – the get-going agency of women who can, and should have it all, 'are powerfully re-inscribed as sexual objects' (Gill, 2008a, p. 442). The tensions and anxieties born of this contradiction are the very motors for makeover culture: Not getting it right? Over or under sexed? Need romance – need to reclaim your self? Lifestyle media has the cure! What we can draw from this section is the argument that feminist notions of empowerment have been effectively transmuted in support of a wider apoliticising, individualising social and political climate. This works to 'fit' women and their bodies into registers of increasing self-surveillance and the lifestyle consumption choices through which they *have* to develop and maintain a viable self. Postfeminist sensibility, then, preens and plumps women to position them in specific relations to neoliberal rationality – so much so that Gill ponders whether the sexy woman *is* neoliberal's ideal citizen.

Seductive affective appeals

Why is compulsive, conservative, heteronormative consumption so appealing? As Ros Gill (2008a) has noted, despite the sophisticated vocabularies and methodological innovations at the hands of social scientists there is still little known about how 'culture relates to subjectivity', how 'culture "gets inside" and transforms and reshapes our relationships to ourselves and others' (p. 433). For her something is amiss because cultural representations and their parade of ideal lives, authentic selves, clutter-free homes and sexiness are 'internalised and made our own, that is, really, truly, deeply our own, felt not as external impositions but as authentically ours' (p. 436). To explain this, she launches from the work of Stuart Hall, to argue that connections and attachments to 'old' subject positions are severed and then cajoled towards degrees of identification with the 'new'. These de- and re-attachments involve material, discursive relations and, she adds, those of *affect*. In support, she notes just how overblown Others are in the cultural imaginary. As we have seen in this book, stereo-typical caricatures produce hyperbolic monstrous, dangerous Others who are constructed through fictive truths that attach onto the bod-ies and dispositions of Others to reside there as essential traits; with, as Skeggs (2004, 2009) notes, dire material consequence for those so 'fixed'. It is the fear and rejection of the Other that orientates the self (where possible) to seek more positive, fulfilling identifications in other subject positions.

A useful example of the affective dimension of Othering is pro-vided by the respective work of Steph Lawler (2005a) and Imogen Tyler (2008). They each draw upon William Miller's (1997) defini-tion of disgust, who states that while disgust shares some common ground with 'distaste' and 'contempt' for a lowly 'other' it can be dis-tinguishable because it is 'bound to metaphors of sensation' needing 'images of bad taste, foul smells, creepy touchings, ugly sights, bod-ily secretions and excretions' (1997, p. 218). What's interesting here is the *visceral* nature of disgust – it is felt in the body as a lurch in the stomach, and as an 'instinctive' recoil and shudder (Raisborough and Adams, 2008). Disgust as *felt* offers certain reassurances of the 'natural' and rightful status of one's own tastes (Bourdieu, 1984) – for Lawler and Tyler, disgust lends a legitimacy to middle-class tastes and ways of living and supports the rejection and expulsion of working-class tastes, bodies and habitats. As it feels like moral proof, disgust justifies the recoil from its source and helps re-orientate the self towards new subject positions. The slummy mummy and the zom-bie fat body are then rendered disgusting to help, through a bodily felt recoil, to orientate the self towards more acceptable, culturally becoming subject positions, and then, through their very existence, to police and regulate those positions through their relational haunt-ings. As I have argued via Samantha Murray's (2008) analysis of the fat, female body, the ways of reading and fixing bodies are not just unsavoury and hurtful descriptions but are constitutive and gener-ative – they constitute the bodies which they purport to describe and thus set and govern subject positions taken up in relation to them.

However, the affective does not just speak to fearful rejection. Vikki Bell (1999) drags our attention to the affective dimension of 'belong-ing'. Starting from Elspeth Probyn's (1996) acute observation that belonging combines 'be-ing' with a 'yearning' and 'longing' (cited in Bell, 1999, p. 1), identity is not regarded as a pre-given but rather an achievement of specific cultural labours, emotional attachments and investments. Anne Phoenix (2005) argues these investments and attachments are informed and directed by the social recognition and approval of others, returning us to the necessarily dialectical nature of recognition. As this book has argued, social recognition and self-hood are repeatedly read on the body in the form of cultural and medical literacy (discussed in Chapter 4), which, as they construct and then denigrate the zombie body, heap social rewards and rights upon a self that *works itself* into its frames of cultural knowingness. Harrington (2002) adds, through Judith Butler's notion of the psychic life of power, that there is an empowered pleasure in 'living out an authoritatively recognised identity. It is the pleasure of being somebody and escaping not-being' (p. 110). In Jeanie's case – sexual viability is a willing price to pay to escape shameful invisibility. The current shape and narrative of empowerment thus demands sharp critical attention.

Men: recalibrating masculinity

> They [men] never fondle their own bodies narcissistically, display themselves purely as sights, or gaze at themselves in the mirror... men have been portrayed as utterly oblivious to their beauty.... The ability to move heavy things around, tame wild creatures – that's manly business. Fretting about your love handles, your dry skin your sagging eyelids? That's for girls.
>
> (Bordo, 1999, p. 197)

Of course, 'gender' is not restricted to women. There are good justifications for a bias towards women so far in this chapter; women are overrepresented in lifestyle TV, and are the assumed audience of much popular self-help literature (Heller, 2007; McGee, 2005). Further, their bodies are under more intense (erotic) scrutiny than men's, as their increased sexualisation and beautification is argued to be a key to the construction and maintenance of heteropolar gender identities (Jeffreys, 2005). Furthermore, as we have seen above, feminine selfhood is increasingly produced and experienced through the occupation of a sexy body. However, there is a risk in such bias, of weakening critical purchase on gender relations and also their heteronormative orchestrations.

Although there has been serious historical neglect of masculinity in the social sciences, a feminist political concern with gender helped to create a critical interest in men as a gendered social category. Subsequent work, pursuing the socially constructed nature of gender, has argued against masculinity as a monolithic category and has explored a number of 'masculinities' from the starting point of men's embodied experiences of 'being' men and performing manhood. R.W Connell's (1995) identification of 'hegemonic masculinity', although extensively critiqued, has been key to the development of this work. Hegemonic masculinity refers to the power relations and processes that help produce normalising cultural ideals of what men are and should be. As a critical extension of this work, Michael Atkinson's (2008) ethnographic study of Canadian men argues that men's bodies are coming under intense scrutiny and as a means of 'doing' accepted citizenship are forced to parade their moral selfhood on its appearance and look of the body. He argues that this is partly a result of a numerous social changes, the economic, social, political changes described here in Chapter 1, and the challenge posed by more 'empowered' women and their discourses of entitlement. Atkinson argues that these changes have unsettled masculinity resulting in 'gender doubt' and 'anxiety' (p. 73). Within the context of consumer-culture, which privileges the visible body, men have sought some security by turning *towards* the body and seeking restored viability in its presence and presentation. Atkinson argues, with reference to cosmetic surgery, that the management of appearance is 'a tool for "re-establishing" a sense of empowered masculine identity' (p. 73). He concludes

> The surgically tucked, sharpened, minimized or masculinised body provides men with a restored or re-established sense of social control – especially when other forms of institutional control and knowledge production are fragmented.
>
> (2008, p. 83)

Self-care and accompanying body-appraisal are not, then, 'just for girls'. There has been a steadily growing interest in men for cosmetics (mainly skin-care, anti-ageing, hair removal) and plastic surgery. The latter more focused on 'nose jobs', hair-implants, implants to improve muscle definition and liposuction (Frederick et al., 2007; Quinn, 2005).

This interest is reflected and encouraged in lifestyle media; for example, in the makeover shows like *Ten Years Younger, Queer Eye for a Straight Guy* and *Extreme Makeover* as well as in the buoyant market of lifestyle magazine's for men (*Men's Health, FHM*). That said, men are underrepresented on makeover TV shows, they are, as Judith Franco (2008) observes, more of an 'exception rather than a rule' (p. 477). We could suggest that the prevailing discourse of natural sexual difference, identified by Gill above, and the historic association of 'pampering' as 'feminine' create social and psychological obstacles for some men. Franco notes how this concerns the producers of *Extreme Makeover* who work hard to entice male participants and they hope a wider male audience. While the *Extreme* team are understandably widening their audience demographics and their appeal for advertisers and sponsors, Franco suggests too that the observable gender bias unsettles the US sensibilities of 'egalitarian democracy and equal opportunity for all' (Franco, 2008, p. 477). In an attempt to lure men in, Franco argues that men are presented on *Extreme* as 'men's men'. They are often heroic men in traditionally masculine occupations – army veterans, police officers, fire-fighters and so on – and their rationale for a 'makeover' is to recover a 'functioning' body – one best able to reap the rewards of a society that favours youth, and self-responsibility written on the bodies. Throughout the show there is a sharp distancing of bodily enhancement as vain (and thus 'feminine') or narcissistic; indeed, the makeover is presented as a way of *doing* masculinity *better.*

This point is flayed open by Lisa Blackman's analysis. Her exploration of the ways men and women are positioned to makeover culture and their emergence from the journey of transformation reveals an entrenchment of heteronormative gender identities and roles. She observes how men tend to transform through what she calls 'practices of self-mastery' (2004, p. 227) by which she means that men acquire better *working knowledge* of what women want and expect. She argues, this is not about men's psychological reinvention or self-transformation but the 'intellectual mastery of the other' (p. 227). For example, she draws on the use of neurolinguistic programming in men's magazine to argue that this is 'about' enabling a man to better 'manipulate what is constructed as a woman's more complex sexuality' (p. 227). Indeed, dealing with the technical aspect of women's more problematic sexuality forms a raft of self-help books from the seriously minded *Lifetime of Sex: Ultimate Manual On Sex, Women and Relationships For Every Stage in a Man's Life* (Men's Health Books, 1999), to *Rock Her World: The Sex Guide for the Modern Man* written by Adam Glassner (2008) aka the porn star Seymore Butts, who draws on his experience of having sex with over 600 women to reveal just how women's sexuality *works*. The makeover is then a skill-set that neatly complements a (madeover) women's empowered sassiness. Men are provided with the (consumer) skills to deal with the demanding, yet mysterious and problematic sexuality of women. And more help is on hand in the form of the gay man who is afforded media space as the straight men's guide to feminine wiles. It's to the gay man that this chapter moves to next.

Gay men in the lifestyle mediascape

> Across the Anglophonic west there is growing mainstream interest in gay men's domestic sensibilities. This is apparent in the increasing presence of gay men as designers and participants on lifestyle television.
>
> (Gorman-Murry, 2006, p. 227)

If *Extreme* tries appealing to men through standard heterosexual markers and self-help books are supporting men's heterosexual working knowledge, what does this mean for gay men in lifestyle TV? Scholars have noted with interest the increased visibility of gay men in the wider media, and the appearance of gay men as Lifestyle TV expert-presenters (e.g. Gok Wan, the 'boys' of *Queer Eye for the Straight Man*, the late Kristian Digby and the interior designer couple Colin and Justin) and as contestants and participants on shows such as *Location, Location, Location*. This visibility *generally* marks a shift from the explicitly pathological images of the past to less vilified and even normalised characterisations of the present. However, a healthy scepticism infuses critical responses to this shift. Battles and Hilton-Morrow (2004), for example, urge some restraint in assuming that 'greater visibility equals greater social acceptance' (p. 89). I want to offer a brief outline of the social and wider context around gay visibility before closing this book with a discussion of gay men and lifestyle TV shows.

This scepticism speaks from wary observation of the wider socio-political climate which in terms of its 'tolerance' of homosexuality is generously described as 'differentiated' by Mitchell (2005). She maps out the contradictory status of attitudes towards homosexuality within the United States. She argues that, on one hand, there exists an overt homophobia seemingly entrenched in many US institutions, and on the other hand, the existence of sensitive portrayals of homosexuality in mainstream media and Hollywood, and a crop of successful 'out' gay stars who hold the affection of their viewing public. This contradictory state is produced by the growing strength of the Lesbian, Gay, Bisexual and Transgendered Movement (LGBT) which has done much to publicise the harm and irrationality of homophobic, heterosexist attitudes while campaigning for the recognition of the humanhood of LGBT people. Additionally, to return once more to the bundle of social changes mentioned throughout this book; detraditionalisation has unsettled traditional notions of family, relationships and love to allow more space for the intelligibility of homosexuality beyond pathology. But this has co-existed with an increased and incensed defence of the family, marriage and child-rearing. Mitchell is keen to avoid any reductive modelling here which pitches gay activism against straight conservatives, for contradictions exist in both 'sides'. She argues that it's best to view the 'state' of gay acceptance as a 'site of social negotiation' (Mitchell, 2005, p. 1051) – and it's this negotiation we see played out in the production and consumption of popular culture.

However, to this we need to add the economic drivers of TV. Gay visibility started in the late 1990s, according to Becker (2004), because of the need for networks to expand audience share: 'the audience is crucial to the business of television' (p. 389) hence the use of ratings and marketing to identify audience and consumer bases. Network TV especially 'has always been driven by selling viewers to sponsors' (Becker, 2004, p. 390). A TV show, then, has to be sold, earn advertising revenue and pull in high audience figures. To do so, it has to 'conform to social conceptions of acceptability, thereby remaining inoffensive' (Mitchell, 2005, p. 1053), but in ways that do not isolate or marginalise a potentially lucrative market: 'to secure the largest market audience possible, gays need to feel represented, straights must feel included' (Mitchell, 2005, p. 1053), Yet, Becker stresses that, sometimes, controversial, 'edgy' shows are the most successful. He argues that attracting Christian Right condemnation might be just the thing! Indeed, such condemnation appeals to the more liberal sensibilities of the US demographic Becker names 'Slumpies' (socially liberal, urban minded professionals). The Slumpie is not only comfortable with gay material but attracted to that content as a means of exercising and performing their liberalism.

So as we move more specifically to address lifestyle TV shows, we can argue that gay visibility on shows like *Queer* provide space for gay men to be represented in refreshing and positive ways other than as AIDS-victims or as hapless 'side kicks' providing comedy value (Ramsey and Santiago, 2004, p. 353) and may widen the appeal of the show in non-offensive ways. However, we are attendant to what else is occurring in these otherwise 'positive' representations. Samantha Murray's (2008) notion of 'cultural knowingness' could explain how stereotypical traits of femininity are attached to the gay male body. This attachment serves to limit gay men to certain spheres of cultural expertise and specific media-genres. As Gorman-Murry (2006) notes in the quote opening this section, the lifestyle programme, particularly those focusing on design, seems to happily fit with a stereotype of gay men 'as arbiters of good taste, with inherent concern and flair for domestic styling' (p. 228) and 'as the vanguard of gentrification and imbued with instinctive domestic sensibilities' (p. 232). Gorman-Murry calls this 'gay domesticity' which warns of the perhaps desexualised and heteronormative construction of gay men in lifestyle TV.

By way of explanation, Ramsey and Santiago (2004) argue that *Queer Eye* actively *neutralises* the sexuality of its hosts, even as those hosts are presented as gay and presented under the banner 'queer'. They are neutralised through the stark contrast between their 'feminine' pursuits and the conventional masculinity of the straight participants, whom Franco described as 'men's men' above, and the traditionally masculine-coded jobs that they do (e.g. Firefighters). The contrast between the gay host and the masculine straight participant is also built into the entire premise of the show: gay men are so removed from straight masculinity they can share, or at least access, the view point and mindset of women. Only the gay man knows just what a woman wants in her man. There is, then, as Avila-Savvedra (2009) notes, 'nothing queer' in *Queer* (p. 5) citing Shugart's (2003) observation that gay men are 'defined through their privileged access to women' often in the guise of the gay best friend, 'but as impotent in their homosexuality' (p. 6). This impotence has been identified across the mediascape by representations of gay men as divorced from gay culture and politics, or other gay men, with few portrayal of sexual affection/expression. There is a considerable amount of cultural labour here which forges a distance between normative and gay masculinities by underscoring the traditional masculinity of straight men and insistently aligning gay masculinity to the feminine. This work situates gay men in the heteropolar gender identities required by heteronormativity. This serves to reduce any threat to that order by directing a specifically shaped expression of 'tolerance' for the gay man, who, similar to the 'empowered' woman above, can excel in the tightly reduced symbolic space afforded to them.

Indeed, what is notable about the gay men on lifestyle TV is their *ordinariness*. Dean (2007) argues that gay men are presented as isolated 'normal' and ordinary individuals' (p. 381). Indeed, once we move away from the gay hosts in *Queer* there is often little to distinguish the 'straight' from the 'gay'. The gay male participant and many lifestyle TV experts present as gender conforming, as defending long-term relationships (in fact, work hard to save them), but most importantly endorse and embody individual enterprise and consumer culture. The consequence is that Becker's Slumpies can exercise their 'tolerance' upon known individuals without confronting homosexual politics and culture. As normal citizens who are seeking homeownership in *Location, Location, Location* or who are 'becoming better' in the makeover show, impotent gay men are incorporated into lifestyle media to do some of the symbolic work that upholds the status, institutions and practices of heterosexuality. Becker concurs:

> instead of images of nelly queens or motorcycle dykes, we are presented with images of white, affluent, trend setting, Perrier-drinking, frequent-flier using, Ph,D-holding, consumer citizens.
>
> (Becker, 2004, p. 397)

What is telling about this reductionist and sanitised representation is the way that a 'positive' image depends on the cultural alignment of a mediated homosexuality with the prevailing ethos of neoliberal rationality. Certain patterns of what passes as 'normal' swirl into the conditions of gay men's inclusion in the mediascape: 'this association also provides a way to regulate and sanitize a dissident sexuality' Gorman-Murry (2006, p. 233).

This book has ended on the joy of the 'after'. In particular, we have the empowered woman, the newly skilled straight man, and an abundance of positive representations of gay men. On the face of it there is much to 'feel-good' about when the reveal of the makeover reveals citizens who can happily exercise their selfhood through confident consumer choices. However, a certain sculpting, undoing and squeezing are needed to get to that point. As the previous chapter argued, the self has to be pressed into a specific narrative that simultaneously forces a denouncement of structural forces upon life and demands a personal responsibility for them. Lifestyle media becomes a site then of *casting off* – of 'poor' attitudes, 'faulty' will, slack bodies, softened self-esteem, of shameful, lame excuses. And it is a site of *taking on* – new shiny, joyous opportunities that are positive, viable and empowered. However, these actions are, as Butler has it, mediated through frames 'politically saturated' with strategic blend of conservatism and neoliberal rationality. In this chapter these have worked to preserve a traditional heteronormative order even through representations of individual 'get-going' empowerment. The question here is what is lost in these framings? What different ways of 'being' and 'becoming' our gendered selves are also cast off?

Conclusion

> When people use the term 'self' they often think it is a neutral concept, but, as with all concepts, there is no neutrality.
> (Skeggs, 2004, p. 134)

This book has sought to dismantle the heady assumptions that attach to 'freedom', 'choice' and a self-authored self, by locating lifestyle media within its neoliberal contexts. The self has been shown to be far from 'neutral' but rather only manifest through specific frames saturated with the injunction of a makeover culture (Butler, 2009; Jones, 2008). It started by asking what selves are possible, and it concludes that viable selves are only those who work themselves into specific relations of recognition. Further, following Meredith Jones, it has shown that this viability is precious and fragile, it only exists in a forward momentum of *becoming*. There are then casualties; those who must be fixed as abject zombies to steer and prompt the 'rightful' labours of others and those who find little discursive space to articulate structural harms other than in the pathologised register of self-lack. Lifestyle media may look trivial, 'eye-candy', and it may only form the part of the cultural background noise of our everyday lives, but it enters the cultural imagination to help a dislocation of compassion and political passion from the self, a degradation of those most vulnerable in our societies and a renewed shaping of the cultural fiction of gender and gender differences. It's pedagogical function? To tell us that this symbolic harm and psychic injury is OK.

Notes

Being Scrooge-Like: An introduction to *Lifestyle Media and the Formation of the Self*

1. See Bratich (2007, p. 9).
2. The tendency of TV to manifest as the solver of ordinary problems is not in itself new. Lifestyle TV has strong antecedents in consumer-advice programming and instructional 'how to' shows in activities such as DIY and gardening (Lewis, 2008), and has developed through these didactic formats to a programming concerned more with entertainment; info-tainment may best describe contemporary lifestyle shows (Brunsdon, 2003).

1 When Life is not Enough: Making More of the Self

1. Please see Adams (2007) for a more detailed account
2. For example, 27 August 2009 – the last television was rolled off the production line at Toshiba's Plymouth factory marking the end of mass production of TV sets in the United Kingdom.
3. Interestingly many photos do not include the child. 'Yummy' seems to speak to a mother's ability to maintain herself, body and lifestyle.

2 Makeover Culture: Becoming a Better Self

1. Of course check-lists can be completed in cursory ways and scores can be met with derision. This book does not speak of how readers relate to and regard them, or indeed whether that relation or regard is consistent and even. Self-help books may be picked up, flicked though and set down, just as lifestyle TV may be 'on' but not watched. Yet, it's the assumptions, the opportunities and the labours of lifestyle media that form part of a wider injunction to become better as defined by prevailing social norms and neoliberal economic rationality that is of interest here.

3 Living Autopsies: Visualising Responsibility

1. The UK government's white paper *Choosing Health: Making Healthy Choices Easier* is an example (Department of Health, 2004).

4   Headless Zombies: Framing the Fat Body

1. In one of its first uses, the BMI was deployed in a correlation of under-weight and tuberculosis in Norway (Evans and Colls, 2009).
2. Just as useful space has been opened up by distinguishing between homo-phobia and heterosexism (see Tamsin Wilton's (2000) excellent descrip-tion) there is some advantage in teasing out phobic responses to the fat body from that general and powerful expectation that all bodies will be 'normally' sized (whatever that can mean). I opt then for terms like weight-ism, because they locate the problem and problematisation of fat into wider structures and cultural imaginations that operate upon all bodies, and avoid reducing the problem of fat-prejudice to individual 'phobics'.

References

Adams, M. (2007) *Self and Social Change* (London, Thousand Oaks, CA, New Delhi: Sage).

Adams, M. and Raisborough, J. (2010) 'Making a Difference: Ethical Consumption and the Everyday', *British Journal of Sociology*, 61, 2, 256–274.

Adkins, L. (2000) 'Objects of Innovation: Post-Occupational Reflexivity and Re-Traditionalisation of Gender', in S. Ahmed, J. Kilby, C. Lury, M. McNeil, and B. Skeggs (eds.) *Transformations: Thinking Through Feminism* (pp. 259–272) (London: Routledge).

Allen, R.E. (1990) *The Concise Oxford Dictionary of Current English* (Oxford: Clarendon Press).

Allen, T., Bell, A., Graham, R., Hardy, B. and Swaffer, F. (2004) *Working Without Walls: An Insight into the Transforming of Government Workplace* (London: Office of Government Commerce).

Alter, C. (2009) *Up for Renewal* (New York: Simon and Schuster).

Aslama, M. and Pantti, M. (2006) 'Talking Alone: Reality TV, Emotions and Authenticity', *European Journal of Cultural Studies*, 9, 2, 167–184.

Atkinson, M. (2008) 'Exploring Male Femininty in the "Crisis": Men and Cosmetic Surgery', *Body and Society*, 14, 67–87.

Auster, C.J. (2001) 'Transcending Potential Antecedent Leisure Constraints: The Case of Women Motorcycle Operators', *Journal of Leisure Research*, 33, 272–298.

Avila-Savvedra, G. (2009) 'Nothing Queer about Queer Television: Televized Construction of Gay Masculinities', *Media, Culture and Society*, 31, 1, 5–21.

Baker, J. (2010) 'Claiming Violation and Evading Victimhoo: Post-Feminist Obligations for Young Women', *Feminism and Psychology*, 20, 186–204.

Barash, S.S. (2009) *Toxic Friends: The Antidote for Women Stuck in Complicated Friendships* (Bedford, New York: St Martin's Press).

Battles, K. and Hilton-Morrow, W. (2004) 'Gay Characters in Conventional Spaces: *Will & Grace* and the Situation Comedy Genre', *Critical Studies in Media Communication*, 19, 1, 87–105.

Bauman, Z. (1998) *Work, Consumerism and the New Poor* (Buckingham: Open University Press).

Bauman, Z. (2007) *Consuming Life* (Cambridge: Polity Press).

BBC News Online (2008) 'Obesity in Statistics'. http://news.bbc.co.uk/mpapps/pagetools/print/news.bbc.co.uk/1/hi/health/715181.stm. Accessed 8 March 2010.

Beck, U. (1996) *The Reinvention of Politics: Rethinking Modernity in the Global Social Order* (Cambridge: Polity Press).

Beck, U. and Beck-Gernsheim, E. (1995) *The Normal Chaos of Love* (Cambridge: Polity Press).

Beck, U. and Wilms, J. (2004) *Conversations with Ulrich Beck* (Cambridge: Polity Press).

Becker, R. (2004) 'Primetime Television in the Gay Nineties', R.C. Allen and A. Hill (eds.) *The Television Studies Reader* (pp. 389–400) (London, New York: Routledge).

Belk, R.W., Yong Seo, J. and Li, E. (2007) 'Dirty Little Secrets: Home Chaos and Professional Organisation', *Consumption, Markets and Culture*, 10, 2, 133–140.

Bell, V. (ed.) (1999) *Performativity and Belonging* (London, Thousand Oaks, CA, New Delhi: Sage).

Bell, D. and Hollows, J. (eds.) (2005) *Ordinary Lifestyles: Popular Media, Consumption and Taste* (Milton Keynes: Open University Press).

Benford, R. and Gough, B. (2006) 'Defining and Defending "Unhealthy" Practices: A Discourse Analysis of Chocolate "Addicts" Accounts', *Journal of Health Psychology*, 11, 427–440.

Benford, R.D. and Snow, D.A. (2000) 'Framing Processes and Social Movements: An Overview and Assessment', *Annual Review of Sociology*, 26, 611–639.

Berridge, V. and Edwards, G. (1981) *Opium and the People: Opiate Use in Nineteenth Century England* (London: Allen Lane).

Billig, M. (1999) 'Commodity Fetishism and Repression: Reflections on Marx, Freud and the Psychology of Consumer Capitalism', *Theory & Psychology*, 9, 3, 313–329.

Binkley, S. (2004) 'Everybody's Life is Like a Spiral: Narrating Post-Fordism in the Lifestyle Movement of the 1970s', *Cultural Studies <=> Critical Methodologies*, 4, 71–96.

Blackman, L. (2004) 'Self-Help, Media Cultures and the Production of Female Psychopathology', *European Journal of Cultural Studies*, 7, 2, 219–236.

Blaine, B. (2007) *Understanding the Psychology of Diversity* (London, Thousand Oaks, CA, New Delhi: Sage).

Blum, L.M. and Stracuzzi, N.F. (2004) 'Gender in the Prozac Nation: Popular Discourse and Productive Femininity', *Gender and Society*, 18, 3, 269–286.

Bonner, F. (2003) *Ordinary Television: Analysing Popular TV* (London, Thousand Oaks, CA, New Delhi: Sage).

Bordo, S. (1993) *Unbearable Weight: Feminism, Western Culture, and the Body* (Berkeley, CA: University of California Press).

Bordo, S. (1999) *The Male Body: A New Look at Men in Public and Private* (New York: Farrar, Straus and Giroux).

Bourdieu, P. (1984) *Distinction: A Social Critique of the Judgement of Taste* (London, New York: Routledge).

Brannen, J. and Nilsen, A. (2005) 'Individualisation, Choice and Structure: A Discussion of Current Trends on Sociological Analysis', *The Sociological Review*, 53, 3, 412–428.

Bratich, J. (2006) 'Nothing is Left Alone for Too Long': Reality Programming and Control Society Subjects', *Journal of Communication Inquiry*, 30, 65–83.

Bratich, J. (2007) 'Programming Reality: Control Societies, New Subjects and the Powers of Transformation', in Heller, D. (ed.) *Makeover Television: Realities Remodelled* (pp. 6–22) (London: I.B. Tauris).

Brace-Govan, J. (2004) 'Weighty Matters: Control of Women's Access to Physical Strength', *The Sociological Review,* 52, 503–532.

Brown, S. (2005) 'The Worst Things in the World: Life Events Checklists in Popular Stress Management Texts', in Bell, D. and Hollows, J. (eds.) *Ordinary Lifestyles; Popular Media, Consumption and Taste* (pp. 231–242) (Maidenhead: Open University Press).

Brown, L.K. and Brown, M.L. (2001) *How to be a Friend: A Guide to Making Friends and Keeping Them* (New York: Little Brown Company).

Brownlie, J. (2004) 'Tasting the Witches' Brew: Foucault and Therapeutic Practice', *Sociology,* 38, 3, 515–532.

Bruner, J.S. (2004) 'Life as Narrative', *Social Research,* 71, 3, 691–710.

Brunsdon, C. (2003) 'Lifestyling Britain: The 8–9 slot on British Television', *International Journal of Cultural Studies,* 6, 1, 5–23.

Burkitt, I. (2008) *Social Selves: Theories of Self and Society,* 2nd edn (London, Thousand Oaks, CA, New Delhi: Sage).

Butler, J. (1990) *Gender Trouble: Feminism and the Subversion of Identity* (London, New York: Routledge).

Butler, J. (1993) *Bodies that Matter* (London: Routledge).

Butler, J. (1997) *The Psychic Life of Power: Theories in Subjection* (Palo Alto, CA: Stanford University Press).

Butler, J. (2004) *Undoing Gender* (London, New York: Routledge).

Butler, J. (2005) *Giving an Account of Oneself* (New York: Fordham University Press).

Butler, J. (2009) *Frames of War: When Life is Grievable?* (London, New York: Verso).

Callahan, S., Nolen, A. and Schuman, K. (2008) *Mothers Need Time Outs, Too: It's Good to be a Little Selfish – It Actually Makes You a Better Mother* (New York: McGraw-Hill).

Callero, P. (2003) 'The Sociology of the Self', *Annual Review of Sociology,* 29, 115–133.

Campo, S. and Mastin, T. (2007) 'Placing the Burden on the Individual: Overweight and Obesity in African American and Mainstream Women's Magazines', *Health Communication,* 22, 3, 229–240.

Campos, P., Saguy, A., Ernsberger, P., Oliver, E. and Gaesser, G. (2006) 'The Epidemiology of Overweight and Obesity: Public Health Crisis or Moral Panic?' *International Journal of Epidemiology,* 35, 55–60.

Carnegie, D. (2007) *How to Win Friends and Influence People,* 7th edn (New York: Vermillion).

Carr, D. and Friedman, M. (2005) 'Is Obesity Stigmatizing? Body Weight, Perceived Discrimination and Psychological Well-Being in the United States', *Journal of Health and Social Behaviour,* 46, 3, 244–259.

Cassiman, S.A. (2008) 'Resisting Neo-Liberal Poverty Discourse: On Constructing Deadbeat Dads and Welfare Queens', *Sociology Compass,* 2, 1690–1700.

Castillo, B. (2006) *If I'm So Smart, Why Can't I Just Lose Weight? Tools To Get it Done* (New York: Booksurge Publishing).

CBS News (2010) 'TV Show Hoarders Fights Urge to Clutter', January 11. http://www.cbc.ca/health/story/2010/01/11/hoarders-tv.html. Accessed 13 January 2010.

Clarke, J. and Newman, J. (2007) 'What's in a Name? New Labour's Citizen-Consumers and the Remaking of Public Services', *Cultural Studies*, 21, 738–757.

Commodity Online (2009) 'A Self-Help Book is Amazon Bestseller in an Hour!', 26 March. http://www.commodityonline.com/globalmarkets/A-self-help-book-is-Amazon-bestseller-in-an-hour!-16383-3-1.html. Accessed 2 August 2009.

Connell, R.W. (1995) *Masculinities* (Berkeley, CA: University of California Press).

Cooper, C. (1998) *Fat and Proud: The Politics of Size* (London: The Women's Press).

Covey, S.R. (1989) *The Seven Habits of Highly Effective People* (London: Simon and Schuster).

Crawford, R. (1980) 'Healthism and the Medicalisation of the Everyday', *International Journal of Health Services*, 10, 3, 365–388.

Cruikshank, B. (1993) 'Revolutions Within: Self-government and Self-esteem', *Economy and Society*, 22, 3, 327–344.

Currie, J. (2004) 'Motherhood, Stress and the Exercise Experience: Freedom or Constraint?', *Leisure Studies*, 23, 225–242.

Daily Mail (2009) 'New Mum Sarah Michelle Geller Slips Skinny Jeans Just Weeks Giving Birth', 18 October. http://www.dailymail.co.uk/tvshowbiz/article-1221071/New-mum-Sarah-Michelle-Gellar-slips-skinny-jeans-just-weeks-giving-birth.html#ixzz0UJ0IScQS. Accessed 15 December 2009.

Daniels, C.R. (1997) 'Between Fathers and Fetuses: The Social Construction of Male Reproduction and Politics of Fetal Harm', *Signs*, 22, 3, 579–616.

Dean, J.J. (2007) 'Gays and Queers: From the Centring to the Decentring of Homosexuality in American Films', *Sexualities*, 10, 3, 363–386.

Dean, M. (1999) *Governmentality: Power and Rule in Modern Society* (London, Thousand Oaks, CA, New Delhi: Sage).

Department of Health (2003) *On The State of the Public Health: Annual Report of the Chief Medical Office 2002* (London: HMSO).

Department of Health (2004) *Choosing Health: Making Healthy Choices Easier* (London: HMSO).

Dixon, W.W. (2008) 'Hyperconsumption in Reality Television: The Transformation of the Self Thorough Televisual Consumerism', *Quarterly Review of Film and Video*, 25, 52–63.

Douglas, M. (1966) *Purity and Danger: An Analysis of the Concepts of Pollution and Taboo* (London: Routlege, Kegan Paul).

Drewnowski, A. (2009) 'Obesity, Diets, and Social Inequalities', *Nutritional Review Supplement*, 67, 1, 36–37.

Dubrofsky, R.E. (2007) 'Therapeutics of the Self', *Television and New Media*, 8, 4, 263–284.

Dworkin, S.L. and Wachs, F.L. (2004) ' "Getting Your Body Back": Post-industrial Fit Motherhood in *Shape Fit Pregnancy* Magazine', *Gender and Society*, 18, 5, 610–624.

Elliott, A. (2001) *Concepts of Self* (Cambridge: Polity Press).

Epstein, D., Johnson, R. and Steinberg, D.L. (2000) 'Twice Told Tales: Transformation, Recuperation and Emergence in the Age of Consent Debates 1998', *Sexualities*, 3, 1, 5–30.

Epstein, D. and Steinberg, D.L. (1998) 'American Dreamin': Discoursing Liberally on the *Oprah Winfrey Show*', *Women's Studies International Forum*, 21, 77–94.

Evans, B. and Colls, R. (2009) 'Measuring Fatness, Governing Bodies: The Spatialities of the Body Mass Index (BMI) in Anti-obesity Politics'. *Antipode* 41, 5, 1051–1083.

Featherstone, M. (1991) *Consumer Culture and Postmodernism* (London, Thousand Oaks, CA, New Delhi: Sage).

Ferris, J.E. (2003) 'Parallel Discourses and "Appropriate" Bodies: Media Constructions of Anorexia and Obesity in the Cases of Tracey Gold and Carnie Wilson', *Journal of Communication Inquiry* 27, 3, 256–273.

Field, L. (2004) *Weekend Life Coach. How to Get the Life You Want in 48 Hours* (London: Vermillon).

Fife, K. (2009) 'Exceeding Roles: Negotiating the Fat Subject in Contemporary Society', Conference Paper. *Cosmetic Cultures: Beauty, Globalization, Politics, Practices.* 24–26 June. University of Leeds, Leeds, UK.

Fitzpatrick, M. (2000) *The Tyranny of Health: Doctors and the Regulation of Lifestyle* (London, New York: Routledge).

Forelo, M. (2008) *Make Every Man Want You or Make Yours Want You More: How to be so Irresistible You'll Barely Keep from Dating Yourself* (New York: McGraw-Hill Contemporary Books).

Foucault, M. (1977) *Discipline and Punish: The Birth of the Prison* (trans. A. Sheridan) (London: Allen Lane).

Foucault, M. (1982) 'The Subject and Power', *Critical Inquiry*, 8, 4, 777–795.

Foucault, M. (1988) 'The Ethic of Care for the Self as a Practice of Freedom', in J. Bernauer and D. Rasmussen (eds.) *The Final Foucault* (pp. 1–20) (Boston, MA: MIT Press).

Foucault, M. (1993) 'About the Beginnings of the Hermeneutics of the Self (Transcription of Dartmouth Lectures in Nov 17th and 18th 1980) by Mark Blasius', *Political Theory*, 21, 2, 198–227.

Fox, N. and Ward, K.J. (2008) 'Pharma in the Bedroom ... and the Kitchen. The Pharmaceaticalization of Daily Life', *Sociology of Health and Illness*, 30, 6, 856–868.

Fraj, E. and Martinez, E. (2007) 'Ecological Consumer Behaviour: An Empirical Analysis', *International Journal of Consumer Studies*, 31, 26–33.

Franco, J. (2008) 'Extreme Makeover: The Politics of Gender, Class, and Cultural Identity, *Television and New Media*, 9, 6, 471–486.

Frankenberg, R. (1993) *White Woman, Race Matters: The Social Construction of Whiteness* (London: Routledge).

Fraser, K. (2007) 'Now I am Ready to Tell How Bodies are Changed Into Different Bodies ...' Ovid, The Metamorhoses', in Heller, D. (ed.) *Makeover Television: Realities Remodelled* (pp. 177–192) (London: I.B. Tauris).

Fraser, N. (1995) 'From Redistribution to Recognition? Dilemmas of Justice in a "Post-Socialist" Age', *New Left Review*, 212, 68–94.

Fraser, N. (2000) 'Rethinking Recognition', *New Left Review*, 3, 107–120.

Frederick, D.A., Lever, J. and Peplou, A. (2007) 'Interest in Cosmetic Surgery and Body Image: Men and Women Across the Lifespan', *Plastic and Reconstructive Surgery*, 120, 1407–1415.

Freysinger, V. and Flannery, D. (1992) 'Women's Leisure: Affiliation, Self-determination, Empowerment and Resistance?', *Loisir et Societe*, 15, 303–321.

Frith, H., Raisborough, J. and Klein, O. (2010) 'C'mon Girlfriend: Sisterhood, Sexuality and the Space of the Benign in Makeover TV', *International Journal of Cultural Studies*, 13, 1–19.

Furedi, F. (2004) *Therapy Culture: Cultivating Vulnerability in an Uncertain Age* (London, New York: Routledge).

Galvin, R. (2002) 'Disturbing Notions of Chronic Illness and Individual Responsibility: Towards a Genealogy of Morals', *Health*, 6, 2, 107–137.

Gauntlett, D. (2008) *Media, Gender and Identity: An Introduction*, 2nd edn (London, New York: Routledge).

Gard, M. and Wright, J. (2005) *The Obesity Epidemic* (London, New York: Routledge).

Gartman, D. (2004) 'The Three Ages of the Automobile: The Cultural Logics of the Car', *Theory, Culture and Society*, 21, 169–195.

Gavey, N., McPhillips, K. and Doherty, M. (2001) 'If It's Not On, It's Not On – Or Is It? Discursive Constraints on Women's Condom Use', *Gender and Society*, 15, 6, 917–934.

Ghoshal, R. (2009) 'Argument Forms, Frames, and Value Conflict: Persuasion in the Case of Same-Sex Marriage', *Cultural Sociology*, 3, 1, 76–101.

Giddens, A. (1991) *Modernity and Self-Identity: Self and Society in the Late Modern Age* (Cambridge: Polity Press).

Gill, R. (2007) 'Postfeminist Media Culture: Elements of Sensibility', *European Journal of Cultural Studies*, 10, 2, 147–166.

Gill, R. (2008a) 'Culture and Subjectivity in Neoliberal and Postfeminist Times', *Subjectivities*, 25, 432–445.

Gill, R. (2008b) 'Empowerment/Sexism: Figuring Female Sexual Agency', *Feminism and Psychology*, 18, 1, 35–60.

Gillespie, D.L., Leffler, A. and Lerner, E. (2002) 'If it Weren't for My Hobby, I'd Have a Life: Dog Sports, Serious Leisure, and Boundary Negotiations', *Leisure Studies*, 21, 285–304.

Gilman, S.L. (2008) *Fat: A Cultural History* (Cambridge: Polity Press).

Glassner, A. (2008) *Rock Her World* (London: Vermillion).

Glenn, E.N. (1999) 'The Social Construction and Institutionalisation of Gender and Race', in M.M. Ferree, J. Lorder and B.B. Hess (eds.) *Revisioning Gender* (pp. 3–43) (London, Thousand Oaks, CA, New Delhi: Sage).

Goffman, E. (1974) *Frame Analysis: An Essay on the Organisation of Experience* (New York: Harper Colophon).

Gordon, T., Holland, J., Lahelma, E. and Thomson, R. (2005) 'Imagining a Gendered Adulthood; Anxiety, Ambivalence, Avoidance and Anticipation', *European Journal of Women's Studies*, 12, 1, 83–104.

Gorman-Murray, A. (2006) 'Queering Home or Domesticating Deviance? Interrogating Gay Domesticity through Lifestyle Television', *International Journal of Cultural Studies*, 9, 2, 227–247.

Gray, A. (2003) 'Enterprising Femininity: New Models of Work and Subjectivity', *Cultural Studies*, 6, 4, 489–506.

Greco, M. (1993) 'Psychosomatic Subjects and the 'Duty to be Well': Personal Agency Within Medical Rationality', *Economy and Society*, 22, 3, 357–372.

Grosz, E. (1994) *Volatile Bodies: Toward a Corporeal Feminism* (Indianapolis, IN: Indiana University Press).

Gunn, J. and Treat, S. (2005) 'Zombie Trouble: A Propaedeutic on Ideological Subjectification and the Unconscious', *Quarterly Journal of Speech*, 91, 2, 144–174.

Guthman, J. (2009) 'Teaching the Politics of Obesity: Insights into Neoliberal Embodiment and Contemporary Biopolitics', *Antipode*, 41, 5, 1110–1133.

Hall Gallagher, A. and Pecot-Hébert, L. (2007) 'You Need a Makeover! The Social Construction of the Female Body in A Makeover Story, What Not to Wear and Extreme Makeover', *Popular Communication*, 5, 1, 57–79.

Hann, A. and Peckham, S. (2010) 'Cholesterol Screening and the Gold Effect', *Health, Risk and Society*, 12, 1, 33–50.

Hardy, B., Graham, R., Stansall, P., White, A., Harrison, A., Bell, A. and Hutton, L. (2008) *Working Beyond Walls: The Government Workplace as an Agent of Change* (London: Office of Government Commerce).

Harrington, C. (2002) 'Agency and Social Identity: Resistance among Pakeha New Zealand Mothers', *Women's Studies International Forum*, 25, 1, 109–126.

Harrington, M., Dawson, D. and Bolla, P. (1992) 'Objective and Subjective Constraints on Women's Enjoyment of Leisure', *Loisir et Societe*, 15, 203–222.

Hay, J. (2000) 'Unaided Virtues: The (neo-) Liberalization of the Domestic Sphere', *Television and New Media*, 1, 1, 53–73.

Haylett, C. (2001) 'Illegitimate Subjects?: Abject Whites, Neoliberal Modernisation, and Middle-class Multiculturalism', *Environment and Planning D: Society and Space*, 19, 351–370.

Hayward, K. and Yar, M. (2006) 'The "Chav" Phenomenon: Consumption, Media and the Construction of a New Underclass', *Crime Media Culture*, 2, 9–28.

Haywood, K. (2004) *City Limits: Crime, Consumer Culture and the Urban Experience* (London: Glasshouse Press).

Hazelden, R. (2003) 'Love Yourself: The Relationship of the Self with Itself in Popular Self-help Texts', *Journal of Sociology*, 39, 413–428.

He, S. and Wu, F. (2009) 'China's Emerging Neoliberal Urbanism: Perspectives from Urban Development', *Antipode*, 41, 2, 282–304.

Heller, D. (ed.) (2007) *Makeover Television: Realities Remodelled* (London, New York: I.B. Tauris).

Heyes, C.J. (2007a) *Self-Transformations: Foucault, Ethics, and Normalised Bodies* (Oxford: Oxford University Press).

Heyes, C.J. (2007b) 'Cosmetic Surgery and the Televisual Makeover', *Feminist Media Studies*, 7, 17–32.

Herrick, C. (2009) 'Shifting Blame/Selling Health: Corporate Social Responsibility in the Age of Obesity', *Sociology of Health and Illness*, 31, 1, 51–65.

Hill Collins, P. (1990) *Black Feminist Thought* (London: Unwin/Hyman).

Hodgetts, D., Bolam, B. and Stephens, C. (2005) 'Mediation and the Construction of Contemporary Understandings of Health and Lifestyle', *Journal of Health Psychology*, 10, 1, 123–146.

Holmes, S. and Jermyn, D. (eds.) (2004) *Understanding Reality Television* (London, New York: Routledge).

Holt, M. and Griffin, C. (2005) 'Students Versus Locals: Young Adults' Constructions of the Working Class Other', *British Journal of Social Psychology*, 44, 241–267.

Hook, D. (2003) 'Analogues of Power: Reading Psychotherapy Through the Sovereignty–Discipline–Government Complex', *Theory Psychology*, 13, 5, 605–628.

Honneth, A. (2004) 'Organized Self-Realization', *European Journal of Social Theory*, 7, 463–478.

Howell, K. (2003) *Weight Loss: Brain Wave Subliminal Audio CD* (New York: Brain Sync Corp).

Howson, A. (1999) 'Cervical Screening, Compliance and Moral Obligation', *Sociology of Health and Illness*, 21, 4, 401–425.

Hurrell, W. (2009) 'BBC Channels to Launch in South Korea', *Broadcast*, 30 June 2009. http://www.broadcastnow.co.uk/news/international/bbc-channels-to-launch-in-south-korea/5002978.article. Accessed 2 August 2009.

Illouz, E. (2008) *Saving the Modern Soul: Therapy, Emotions and the Culture of Self-Help* (Berkeley, CA: University of California Press).

Illouz, E. and Wilf, W. (2008) 'Oprah Winfrey and the Co-production of Market and Morality', *Women and Performance*, 18, 1, 1–7.

Inthorn, S. and Boyce, T. (2010) ' "It's Disgusting How Much Salt You Eat!" Television Discourses of Obesity, Health and Morality', *International Journal of Cultural Studies*, 13, 1, 83–100.

Isaacs, F. (1999) *Toxic Friends/True Friends* (New York: William Morrow).

Jackson, S. (1999a) *Heterosexuality in Question* (London, Thousand Oaks, CA, New Delhi: Sage).

Jackson, S. (1999b) 'Feminist Sociology and Sociological Feminisms: Recovering the Social in Feminist Thought', *Sociological Research Online*, 4, 3. http://www.socresonline.org.uk/socresonline/4/3/Jackson.html.

Jeffreys, S. (1990) *Anticlimax* (London: The Women's Press).

Jeffreys, S. (2005) *Beauty and Misogyny: Harmful Cultural Practices in the West* (London, New York: Routledge).

Joffe, H. (2007) 'Identity, Self-Control and Risk', in G. Moloney and I. Walker (eds.) *Social Representations and Identity* (pp. 197–213) (Basingstoke, New York: Palgrave MacMillan).

Joffe, H. and Staerklé, C. (2007) 'The Centrality of the Self-control Ethos in Western Aspersions Regarding Outgroups: A Social Representational Approach to Stereotype Content', *Culture & Psychology*, 13, 395–418.

Jones, A. (1993) 'Becoming a Girl: Post-structuralist Suggestions for Educational Research', *Gender and Education* 5, 2, 157–166.

Jones, M. (2008) *Skintight: An Anatomy of Cosmetic Surgery* (Oxford: Berg).

Keane, H. (2000) 'Setting Yourself Free: Techniques of Recovery' *Health*, 4, 3, 324–346.

Kelly, M. (2002) *Becoming the Best Version of Yourself (CD)* (Boston, MA: Beacon Publishing).

Kent, L. (2001) 'Fighting Abjection: Representing Fat Women', in J.E. Braziel and K. LeBesco (eds.) *Bodies Out of Bounds: Fatness and Transgression* (pp. 130–150) (Los Angeles: University of California Press).

Kerner, I. (2008) *Passionista: The Empowered Woman's Guide to Pleasing a Man* (London: Harper Collins).

Khatib, L. (2004) 'The Politics of Space: The Spatial Manifestations of Representing Middle Eastern Politics', *Visual Politics*, 3, 1, 69–90.

Kleinman, A. and Kleinman, J. (1997) 'The Appeal of Experience, The Dismay of Images: Cultural Appropriations of Suffering in Our Times', in A. Kleinman, V. Das and M. Lock (eds.) *Social Suffering* (pp. 1–23) (Berkeley, CA: University of California Press).

Kline, K.M. (2009) 'The Discursive Characteristics of a Prosocial Self-help: Re-Visioning the Potential of Self-Help for Empowerment', *Southern Communication Journal*, 74, 2, 191–200.

Kosofsky Sedgwick, E. (1993) *Tendencies* (Durham, NC: Duke University Press).

Laermans, R. (1993) 'Learning to Consume: Early Department Stores and the Shaping of the Modern Consumer Culture (1860–1914)', *Theory, Culture & Society*, 10, 79–102.

Lawler, S. (2005a) 'Disgusted Subjects: The Making of Middle-Class Identities', *Sociological Review*, 53, 3, 429–446.

Lawler, S. (2005b) 'Rules of Engagement: Habitus, Power and Resistance', in L. Adkins and B. Skeggs (eds.) *Feminism after Bourdieu* (pp. 110–128) (Oxford, Malden, MA: Blackwell Publishing).

Lemke, T. (2000) 'Foucault, Governmentality and Critique', *Rethinking Marxism Conference*. 21–24 September. University of Amherst, Amherst, MA.

Lewis, T. (2008) 'Transforming Citizens? Green Politics and Ethical Consumption on Lifestyle Television', *Continuum: Journal of Media and Cultural Studies*, 22, 2, 227–240.

Lindenfield, G. (2000) *Self Esteem: Simple Steps to Develop Self-Worth and Heal Emotional Wounds* (Berwick on Tweed: ElementBooks).

Lloyd, M. (1995) 'Does She Boil Eggs? Towards a Feminist Model of Disability', in M. Blair and J. Holland (eds.) *Identity and Diversity: Gender and the Experience of Education* (pp. 211–224) (Maidenhead: Open University Press).

Lovejoy, M. (2000) 'Disturbances in the Social Body: Differences in Body Image and Eating Problems among African American and White Women', *Gender and Society,* 15, 2, 239–261.

Lunt, P. and Lewis, T. (2008) 'Oprah. Com: Lifestyle Expertise and the Politics of Recognition', *Women and Performance,* 18, 1, 9–24.

Marshall, C. and Pienaar, K. (2008) ' "You are Not Alone": The Discursive Construction of the "Suffering Victim" Identity on the Oprah Winfrey Show', *Southern African Linguistics and Applied Language Studies,* 26, 4, 525–546.

Martin, C.E. (2007) *Perfect Girls, Starving Daughters: The Frightening New Normality of Hating Your Body* (London: Piatkus).

Massey, D. and Jess, P. (eds.) (1995) *A Place in the World? Places, Culture and Globalisation* (Milton Keynes: Oxford University Press, The Open University).

Maycroft, N. (2004) 'Cultural Consumption and the Myth of Life-style', *Capital and Class,* 84, 61–75.

McDowell, L. (2006) 'Reconfigurations of Gender and Class Relations: Class Differences, Class Condescension and the Changing Place of Class Relations', *Antipode,* 38, 4, 825–850.

McEntee, J. and Agyman, J. (2010) 'Towards the Development of GIS Method for Identifying Rural Food Deserts', *Applied Geography,* 30, 1, 165–176.

McGee, M. (2005) *Self-Help Inc: Makeover Culture in American Life* (Oxford: Oxford University Press).

McGregor, S. (2001) 'Neoliberalism and Health Care', *International Journal of Consumer Studies,* 25, 2, 82–89.

McKenna, P. and Willbourn, H. (2005) *Motivational Power* (London: Gut Vision Limited).

McLaren, L. and Godley, J. (2009) 'Social Class and BMI among Canadian Adults: A Focus on Occupational Prestige', *Journal of Environmental and Public Health,* 17, 2, 290–297.

McMurria, J. (2008) 'Desperate Citizens and Good Samaritans: Neoliberalism and Makeover Reality TV', *Television and New Media,* 9, 4, 305–332.

McNay, L. (1994) *Foucault: A Critical Introduction* (Cambridge: Polity Press).

McNay, L. (2000) *Gender and Agency. Reconfiguring the Subject in Feminist and Social Theory* (Cambridge: Polity Press).

McPherson, K., Marsh, T. and Brown, M. (2007) *Tackling Obesities: Future Choices – Modelling Future Trends in Obesity & Their Impact on Health* (London: Foresight: Department of innovation Universities and Skills).

McRobbie, A. (2004) 'Notes on "What not to wear" and Post-Feminist Symbolic Violence', *Sociological Review,* 52, 2, 99–109.

McRobbie, A. (2008) 'Young Women and Consumer Culture: An Intervention', *Cultural Studies,* 22, 5, 531–550.

Men's Health Books (1999) *Lifetime of Sex: Ultimate Manual for Sex, Women and Relationships for Every Stage in a Man's Life* (Emmaus, PA: Rodale Press).

Mendible, M. (2004) 'Humiliation, Subjectivity, and Reality TV', *Feminist Media Studies,* 4, 3, 335–338.

Merritt, S. (2008) 'Escape from Self-Help Hell', *The Observer,* Sunday 31 August 2008.

Miller, P. and Rose, N. (2008) *Governing the Present* (Cambridge: Polity Press).

Miller, T. (2007) *Cultural Citizenship: Cosmopolitanism, Consumerism and Television in a Neoliberal Age* (Philadelphia, PA: Temple University Press).

Miller, W.I. (1997) *The Anatomy of Disgust* (London: Harvard University Press).

Mirza, H.S. (ed.) (1997) *Black British Feminism: A Reader* (London, New York: Routledge).

Mitchell, D. (2005) 'Producing Containment: The Rhetorical Construction of Difference in *Will & Grace*', *The Journal of Popular Culture*, 38, 1050–1068.

Monaghan, L. (2007) 'Body Mass Index, Masculinities and Moral Worth: Men's Critical Understanding of "Appropriate" Weight-for-height', *Sociology of Health and Illness*, 29, 4, 584–609.

Morganstein, G. (2008) ' "To Look Good Naked" Becomes Most-Watched Reality Series Premiere in Lifetime *Thomsen Reuters*'. http://www.reuters.com/article/pressRelease/idUS188929+07-Jan-2008+PRN20080107. Accessed 2 March 2009.

Morreale, J. (2007) 'Faking It and the Transformation of Identity', in D. Heller (ed.) *Makeover Television: Realities Remodelled* (pp. 95–106) (London: I.B. Tauris).

Morrison Thomson, D. (2009) 'Big Food and the Body Politics of Personal Responsibility', *Southern Communication Journal*, 74, 1, 2–17.

Moss, J. (ed.) (1998) *The Later Foucault* (London, Thousand Oaks, CA, New Delhi: Sage).

Murray, S. (2008) *The 'Fat' Female Body* (London, New York: Palgrave Macmillan).

Murray, S. and Ouellette, L. (eds.) (2009) *Reality TV; Remaking Television Culture*, 2nd edn (New York, London. New York University Press).

Mwaniki, C. (2009) *Becoming the Better You* (London: Authorhouse).

Navratilova, M. (2006) *Shape Your Self: An Inspirational Guide to Achieving Your Personal Best* (London: Time Warner Books).

Negra, D. (2009) *What a Girl Wants? Fantasing the Reclamation of Self in Postfeminism* (London, New York: Routlegge).

Nettleton, S. (1997) 'Governing the Risky Self: How to Become Healthy, Wealthy and Wise', in A. Petersen and R. Bunton (eds.) *Foucault: Health and Medicine* (pp. 207–222) (London, New York: Routledge).

Newman, J., Barnes, M., Sullivan, H. and Knops, A. (2004) 'Public Participation and Collaborative Governance', *Journal of Social Policy*, 33, 2, 203–232.

Nolen-Hocksemo, S. (2004) *Women Who Think Too Much* (London: Piatkus Books).

Oliver, J.E. (2006) *Fat Politics: The Real Story Behind America's Obesity Epidemic* (Oxford: Oxford University Press).

Ouellette, L. (2009) 'Take Responsibility for Yourself; Jude Judy and the Neoliberal Citizen', in S. Murray and L. Ouellette (eds.) *Reality TV: Remaking Television Culture*, 2nd edn (pp. 223–242) (London: New York University Press).

Ouellette, L. and Hay, J. (2008) *Better Living Through Reality TV* (Oxford: Blackwell).

Palmer, B. (2009) *Clutter Busting: Letting Go of What's Holding You Back* (Novato, CA: New World Library).

Palmer, G. (2004) ' "The New You" Class and Transformation in Lifestyle Television', in S. Holmes and D. Jermyn (eds.) *Understanding Reality Television* (pp. 173–190) (London, New York: Routledge).

Papacharissi, Z. and Fernback, J. (2008) 'The Aesthetic Power of the Fab 5: Discursive Themes of Homonormativity in Queer Eye for a Straight Guy', *Journal of Communication Inquiry*, 32, 4, 348–367.

Parker, R. (2009) 'Bebo Orders Twenty Twenty Fashion Show', *Broadcast*, 18 August. http://www.broadcastnow.co.uk/news/multi-platform/bebo-orders-twenty-twenty-fashion-show/5004605.article. Accessed 19 August 2009.

Paterson, M. (2006) *Consumption and Everyday Life* (London, New York: Routledge).

Pease, A. and Pease, B. (2001) *Why Men Don't Listen and Women Can't Read Maps* (London: Orion).

Pease, A. and Pease, B. (2003) *Why Men Can Only Do One Thing At A Time and Women Never Stop Talking* (London: Orion).

Pease, A. and Pease, B. (2006) *Why Men Don't Have a Clue and Women Always Need New Shoes* (London: Orion).

Peck, J. and Tickell, A. (2002) 'Neoliberalizing Space', *Antipode*, 34, 3, 380–404.

Phillips, D. (2005) 'Transformation Scenes: Television Interior Makeover', *International Journal of Cultural Studies*, 8, 2, 213–229.

Phoenix, A. (2005) 'Remembered Racialization: Young People and Positioning in Differential Understanding', in K. Murji and J. Solomos (eds.) *Racialization: Studies in Theory and Practice* (pp. 103–122) (Oxford, UK: Oxford University Press).

Pizzaro, D. (2000) 'Nothing More Than Feelings? The Role of Emotions in Moral Judgement', *Journal for the Theory of Social Behaviour*, 30, 355–375.

Plumridge, L. and Thomson, R. (2003) 'Longitudinal Qualitative Studies and the Reflexive Self', *International Journal of Social Research Methodology*, 6, 3, 213–222.

Powell, H. and Prasad, S. (2007) 'Life Swap: Celebrity Expert as Lifestyle Advisor', in D. Heller (ed.) *Makeover Television: Realities Remodelled* (pp. 56–66) (London: I.B. Tauris).

Probyn, E. (2008) 'IV: Silences Behind the Mantra: Critiquing Feminist Fat', *Feminism and Psychology*, 18, 3, 401–404.

Prokhovnik, R. (1999) *Rational Woman: A Feminist Critique of Dichotomies* (London and New York: Routledge).

Quinn, J. (2005) 'Drawing a line under men's wrinkles', *BBC News Magazine*. http://news.bbc.co.uk/1/hi/magazine/4433343.stm

Raisborough, J. and Adams, M. (2008) 'Mockery and Morality: Popular Cultural Representations of the White, Working Class', *Sociological Research Online*, 13, 6. http://www.socresonline.org.uk/13/6/2.html.

Raisborough, J. and Bhatti, M. (2007) 'Women's Leisure and Auto/Biography: Empowerment and Resistance in the Garden', *Journal of Leisure Research*, 39, 3, 459–476.

Ramazanoglu, C. and Holland, J. (2000) 'Still Telling It Like It Is? Problems of Feminist Truth Claims', in S. Ahmed, L. Kilby, C. Lury, M. McNeil and B. Skeggs (eds.) *Transformations: Thinking Through Feminism* (pp. 207–220) (London, New York: Routledge).

Ramsey, E.M. and Santiago, G. (2004) 'The Conflation of Male Homosexuality and Femininity in *Queer Eye for a Straight Guy*', *Feminist Media Studies* 4, 3, 353–355.

Reavey, P. and Gough, B. (2000) 'Dis/Locating Blame: Survivor's Stories of Self and Sexual Abuse', *Sexualities*, 3, 3, 325–346.

Rice, C. (2007) 'Becoming the "Fat Girl": Acquisition of an Unfit Identity', *Women's Studies International Forum*, 30, 158–174.

Rich, E. and Evans, J. (2005) 'Fat Ethics: The Obesity Discourse and Body Politics', *Social Theory and Health*, 3, 341–358.

Richardson, D. and May, H. (1999) 'Deserving Victims?: Sexual Status and the Social Construction of Violence', *Sociological Review*, 47, 2, 308–331.

Rimke, H.M. (2000) 'Governing Citizens Through Self-Help Literature', *Cultural Studies*, 14, 1, 61–78.

Ringrose, J. and Walkerdine, V. (2008) 'Regulating the Abject: The TV Make-Over as Site of Neo-liberal Reinvention Toward Bourgeois Femininity', *Feminist Media Studies*, 8, 3, 227–246.

Roberts, K., Clark, S.C. and Wallace, C. (1994) 'Flexibility and Individualisation: A Comparison of Transitions into Employment in England and Germany', *Sociology*, 28, 1, 31–54.

Roberts, M. (2007) 'The Fashion Police: Governing the Self in "What Not to Wear"', in Y. Tasker and D. Negra (eds.) *Interrogating Postfeminism: Gender and the Politics of Culture* (pp. 227–248) (Durham, NC: Duke University Press).

Room, R. (2003) 'The Cultural Framing of Addiction', *Janus Head*, 6, 2, 221–234.

Rose, N. (1996) 'Identity, Genealogy, History', in S. Hall and P. Du Gay (eds.) *Questions of Cultural Identity* (pp. 128–150) (London, Thousand Oaks, CA, New Delhi: Sage).

Rose, N. (1999a) *Governing the Soul: The Shaping of the Self,* 2nd edn (London: Free Association Books).

Rose, N. (1999b) *Powers of Freedom* (Cambridge: Cambrige University Press).

Rose, N. (2001) 'The Politics of Life Itself', *Theory, Culture & Society*, 18, 1–30.

Roy, S. (2008) ' "Taking Care of Your Health": Discourses of Responsibility in English-Canadian Women's Magazines', *Sociology of Health and Illness*, 30, 3, 463–477.

Ryan, A. (2001) 'Feminism and Sexual Freedom in an Age of AIDS', *Sexualities*, 4, 1, 91–108.

Salonen, M.K., Kajantie, E., Osmond, C., Forsén, T., Ylihärsilä, H., Paile-Hyvärinen, M., Barker, D.J.P. and Eriksson, J.G. (2009) 'Role of Socioeconomic Indicators on Development of Obesity from a Life Course Perspective', *Journal of Environmental and Public Health*, 1, 1–7.

Savage, M. (2003) 'Review Essay: A New Class Paradigm', *British Journal of Sociology of Education*, 24, 4, 535–541.

Sayer, A. (2005) *The Moral Significance of Class* (Cambridge: Cambridge University Press).

Seale, K. (2006) 'Location, Location: Situating Bondi's 'Rubbish House', *M/C Journal*, 9, 5. http://journal.media-culture.org.au/0610/07-seale.php.

Seid, R.P. (1989) *Never Too Thin* (New York: Prentice Hall Press).

Sellers, J. (2009) 'Teens to Be Privy to "The Secret"', *Publishers Weekly*, June. http://www.publishersweekly.com/pw/by-topic/childrens/childrens-book-news/article/12037-teens-to-be-privy-to-e2-80-98the-secret-e2-80-99.html. Accessed 8 June 2009.

Sender, K. and Sullivan, M. (2008) 'Epidemics of Will, Failures of Self-Esteem: Responding to Fat Bodies in *The Biggest Loser* and *What Not To Wear*', *Continuum Journal of Media and Cultural Studies*, 22, 4, 573–584.

Sennett, R. (2006) *The Culture of New Capitalism* (New Haven, CT: Yale University Press).

Shaw, S.M. (2001) 'Conceptualising Resistance: Women's Leisure as Political Practice', *Journal of Leisure Research*, 33, 186–201.

Shildrick, M. (2002) *Embodying the Monster: Encounters with the Vulnerable Self* (London, Thousand Oaks, CA, New Delhi: Sage).

Skeggs, B. (1997) *Formations of Class and Gender* (London, Thousand Oaks, CA, New Delhi: Sage).

Skeggs, B. (2004) *Class, Self, Culture* (London, New York: Routledge).

Skeggs, B. (2005) 'The Making of Class and Gender through Visualising Moral Subject Formation', *Sociology*, 39, 5, 965–982.

Skeggs, B. (2009) 'The Moral Economy of Person Production: The Class Relations of Self-Performance on "Reality" Television', *Sociological Review*, 57, 4, 627–644.

Skeggs, B. and Wood, H. (2008) 'The Labour of Transformation and Circuits of Value "Around" Reality Television', *Continuum: Journal of Media and Cultural Studies*, 22, 4, 559–572.

Silva, E.B. and Wright, D. (2009) 'Displaying Desire and Distinction in Housing', *Cultural Sociology*, 3, 1, 31–50.

Silverstone, R. (2007) *Media and Morality: On the Rise of the Mediapolis* (Cambridge: Polity Press).

Singer, B. (2009) *Little Voice Masterly: How to Win the War Between Your Ears in 30 Seconds or Less and Have an Extraordinary Life* (Leesburg, VA: XCEL Press).

Smith Maguire, J. (2008) 'The Personal is Professional Personal trainers as a Case Study of Cultural Intermediaries', *International journal of Cultural Studies*, 11, 2, 211–229.

Smith Maguire, J. and Stanway, K. (2008) 'Looking Good: Consumption and the Problems of Self-Production', *European Journal of Cultural Studies*, 11, 1, 63–81.

The Sunday Express (2009) 'I Won't be a Slummy Mummy'. http://www.express.co.uk/posts/view/140595/I-won-t-be-a-slummy-mummy. Accessed 2 December 2009.

Tako, B. (2010) *Clutter Clearing Choices: Clean Clutter, Organize Your Home and Reclaim Your Life* (New York: O Books).

Talking Heads (1984) *Once in a Lifetime*. EMI Music.

Tasker, Y. and Negra, D. (eds.) (2007) *Interrogating Post-Feminism: Gender and the Politics of Popular Culture* (Durham, NC: Duke University Press).

Thompson, B. (1996) 'Multiracial Feminist Theorizing about Eating Problems: Refusing to Rank Oppressions', *Eating Disorders*, 4, 3, 104–116.

Thompson, R. (1999) *Be the Best You Can Be: A Guide to Etiquette and Self-improvement for Children and Teens* (Baltimore, MD: Robin Thompson Charm School).

Throsby, K. (2008) 'Happy Re-Birthday: Weight-Loss Surgery and the New "Me" ', *Body and Society*, 14, 117–133.

Tischner, I. and Malson, H. (2008) 'Exploring the Politics of Women's In/Visible "Large" Bodies', *Feminism and Psychology*, 18, 2, 260–267.

Tomlinson, J. (1999) *Globalisation and Culture* (Cambridge: Polity Press).

Turner, B. (1982) 'The Discourse of Diet', *Theory, Culture, Society*, 1, 23–32.

Tyler, I. (2008) 'Chav Mum, Chav Scum': Class Disgust in Contemporary Britain', *Feminist Media Studies*, 8, 1, 17–34.

Tyler, M. (2008) 'Sex Self-help Books: Hot Secrets for Great Sex or Prompting the Sex of Prostitution? *Women's Studies International Forum*, 31, 363–372.

UK Trade and Investment (2008) 'Television (TV) Industry Overview'. http://www.ukti.gov.uk/export/sectors/creativemedia/screen.html. Accessed 3 August 2009.

Ussher, J.M. (1997) *Fantasies of Femininity: Reframing the Boundaries of Sex* (Piscataway, NJ: Rutgers University Press).

Vidmar-Horvat, K. (2010) 'Consuming European Identity: The Inconspicuous Side of Consumerism in the EU', *International Journal of Cultural Studies*, 13, 1, 25–41.

Vitellone, N. (2002) 'Condoms and the Making of Sexual Difference in Aids Heterosexual Culture', *Body and Society*, 8, 3, 71–94.

Wagner, H. (2009) *Happiness on $10 a Day: A Recession-Proof Guide* (London: Harper Paperbacks).

Waisbord, S. (2004) 'McTV: Understanding the Global Popularity of Television Formats', *Television and New Media*, 5, 4, 359–383.

Walkerdine, V. (2003) 'Reclassifying Upward Mobility: Femininity and the Neo-liberal Subject', *Gender and Education*, 15, 3, 237–248.

Warde, A. (2004) 'Consumption, Identity-formation and Uncertainty', *Sociology*, 28, 4, 877–898.

Warin, M., Turner, K., Moore, V. and Davies, M. (2008) 'Bodies, Mothers and Identities: Rethinking Obesity and the BMI', *Sociology of Health and Illness*, 30, 1, 97–111.

Watts, A. (2009) 'Melancholy, Merit, and Merchandise; The Postwar Audience Participation Show', in S. Murray and L. Ouellette (eds.) *Reality TV; Remaking Television Culture*, 2nd edn (pp. 301–320) (New York, London: New York University Press).x

Way, J. (2009) 'Inner Self'. http://www.innerself.com.au. Accessed 2 April 2010.

Wee, L. and Brooks, A. (2010) 'Personal Branding and the Commodification of Reflexivity', *Cultural Sociology*, 4, 1, 45–62.

Williams, C.R. (2008) 'Compassion, Suffering and the Self: A Moral Psychology of Social Justice', *Current Sociology*, 56, 5–24.

Wilton, T. (2000) *Sexualities in Health and Social Care: A Text Book* (Buckingham: Open University Press).

Wiseman, R. (2009) *59 Seconds: Think a Little, Change a Lot* (London, New York: Macmillan).

Wheaton, B. and Tomlinson, A. (1998) 'The Changing Gender Order in Sport? The Case of Windsurfing Subculture', *Journal of Sport and Social Issues*, 22, 252–274.

Wray, S. (2004) 'What Constitutes Agency and Empowerment for Women in Later Life?', *The Sociological Review*, 52, 22–38.

Wright, E. (2004) *Shaun of the Dead* (Universal Pictures).

Wright, C. and Madrid, G. (2007) 'Contesting Ethical Trade in Colombi's Cut-Flower Industry: A Case of Cultural and Economic Injustice', *Cultural Sociology*, 1, 12, 255–275.

Xu, J.H. (2007) 'Brand-New Lifestyles: Consumer Orientated Programmes on Chinese Television', *Media, Culture and Society*, 29, 3, 363–376.

Index